# PROMISED
*by*
# HEAVEN

# PROMISED

## *by*

# HEAVEN

A Doctor's Return from the Afterlife
to a Destiny of Love and Healing

## DR. MARY HELEN HENSLEY

**ATRIA** PAPERBACK

*New York   London   Toronto   Sydney   New Delhi*

**ATRIA** PAPERBACK
An Imprint of Simon & Schuster, Inc.
1230 Avenue of the Americas
New York, NY 10020

First Atria Paperback edition September 2015

**ATRIA** PAPERBACK and colophon are trademarks of Simon & Schuster, Inc.

For information about special discounts for bulk purchases,
please contact Simon & Schuster Special Sales at 1-866-506-1949
or business@simonandschuster.com.

The Simon & Schuster Speakers Bureau can bring authors to your live event. For more
information, or to book an event, contact the Simon & Schuster Speakers Bureau at
1-866-248-3049 or visit our website at www.simonspeakers.com.

Interior design by Kyoko Watanabe

Manufactured in the United States of America

10 9 8 7 6 5 4 3 2 1

Library of Congress Cataloging-in-Publication Data

Hensley, Mary Helen, date.
 Promised by heaven / Dr. Mary Helen Hensley.—First Atria paperback edition.
  pages cm
 1. Hensley, Mary Helen, date—Psychology. 2. Clairvoyants—United States—
Biography. 3. Traffic accident victims—United States—Biography. I. Title.
 BF1283.H375A3 2015
 133.9092—dc23
 [B]                    2014043644

ISBN 978-1-4767-8620-9
ISBN 978-1-4767-8621-6 (ebook)

*For My Mother, Helen*

*You, with your quiet strength, glorious humor, and tenacious spirit, not only gave me life, but the tools with which I could make the most of it.*


*For My Father, Dick*

*I sought my Source, just as you taught me, and indeed, was delivered from all of my fears.*

To one who has faith,
No explanation is necessary.
To one without faith,
No explanation is possible.

—*St. Thomas Aquinas (1225–1274)*

Imagine two unborn babies in their mother's womb. One is a believer that life lies ahead. The other, a disbeliever, feels that only death awaits. They are arguing together in the mother's womb.

The believer says, "Nature has been at work on us for nine months and nature isn't crazy. It means something . . . something is coming of this. We're not just going to die."

"What are you talking about?" says the disbeliever. "There's no such thing as living outside the matrix of this womb. We'll be cut off from all nutrition. Of course we're going to die!"

"No!" says the believer. "Things have been going on here for the last nine months that have prophetic meaning. I believe in the wisdom of nature."

"Well," continues the disbeliever, "describe to me exactly what you think is going to happen." And with that, the believing baby is stuck. He can't imagine anything like sunshine, breathing or eating, running, jumping, or playing. So the argument ends with the disbeliever seeming to have won.

—*Unknown*

# PART I

*Promised*

# Chapter 1

"YOU'RE ONE lucky little lady." The voice seemed to float in from beside me with a deep, soothing Southern drawl. "Are you feeling strong enough to tell me what happened?" My nose burned with the smell of disinfectant, and every square inch of my body ached as if I had been trampled by a herd of wild elephants. I opened my eyes and tried to focus on the man standing next to me. As my sight adjusted to the harshly lit room, I realized that I was in a hospital. The man who was speaking to me was not a doctor but a policeman. There were nurses walking in and out from behind a curtain, constantly checking monitors, smiling, but saying nothing. I could hear a woman's voice requesting assistance in the ER over a loudspeaker.

I looked over at the officer, careful not to make any sudden movements, because it felt as if my head would split in two if I did. In a raspy voice, sounding as if I hadn't had a drop of water in days, I said, "Hey, I know you. You were at the accident."

"That's right," he replied, with a slightly puzzled look on his face. "Can you remember any details that might help me figure out how all of this happened?"

I swallowed and grimaced with pain, unaware that I had fractured a bone in my neck and that the rest of my spine was now shaped like a backward letter C. I thought back to earlier in the afternoon, when I had set out on a short drive to town, and suddenly blurted out, "You should talk to my friend from college. She was only a few cars behind me when it happened and saw the whole thing! Did you find the piece of paper on the front seat of the car? A lady put it there, and it had her name and number on it, but then she ran away. There was a guy in some kind of uniform who turned the engine off. Surely he saw something!"

The officer became visibly uncomfortable and confused. "Young lady," he queried, "how do you know about the lady who put her phone number in the car?"

"I saw her, of course."

"And just how did you know that your friend was at the scene of the accident?"

"I saw her, too," I replied, starting to get a little agitated.

With a tone much less confident than when our conversation had begun, he wrestled with his words. "Miss, there is *no way* you could have seen any of that happen! Your friend . . . the lady with the phone number . . . the man in uniform. All of those things were going on while you were still unconscious and pinned in the car."

It was at that moment the penny dropped.

I struggled to pull myself up so that I could look my inquisitor in the eye. What I was about to share was going to change me in ways that I could scarcely imagine. I immediately became emotional as I proceeded to tell him what had *really* happened that afternoon. He listened carefully as I described exactly how the accident had taken place and the unusual circumstances that surrounded it. He stared at me with his mouth partially open, his brow furrowed as he listened on in amazement and confusion. It all seemed *so* clear to me, but he was obviously very disturbed by the uncanny way in which I was able to describe the incident. When I had finished speaking, he asked no more questions. In fact, he didn't say another word and quietly left the room.

As I sat on the hospital bed, I looked around at my sterile surroundings and reflected on what I had told the policeman but more so, things I *hadn't* told him. The day had started out like any other, but what had transpired that evening was nothing short of miraculous, and until now, *no one has ever heard it in its entirety.*

*

An elderly man dressed in dirty overalls and worn-out work boots got into his car to run a few errands in the afternoon. He drove down Highway 17, one of Charleston, South Carolina's, busiest motorways, and proceeded toward his destination. No one will ever know if he simply didn't see the red light, or if he sped up in an attempt to make it through the intersection before the oncoming traffic entered. His speed would indicate the latter, and his collision with a young couple earlier in the year suggested his deteriorating driving skills and slow reaction time should have taken him off the road permanently. We never met face-to-face, but this man's life was now forever entangled with mine. He shot through the red light, smashing into me, broadsiding my car, and hurtling me into oncoming traffic. The violent impact literally knocked me out of my body.

My first memory of death was that no matter how we die—in an accident, a murder, or even from an illness—we can exit the body just prior to its actual demise, if we choose to do so. *Time means nothing during the transition from this form to the next.*

The day had been unusually warm, even for the South. It was December 14, 1991. I was on my way to a Christmas party and just two months shy of turning twenty-two. Dressed in a Santa Claus T-shirt and bright-red Bermuda shorts, I had just left my apartment and reached the major intersection at the end of my road. Little did I know I was about to become the newest member of the old statistic that states: "Most accidents occur within two miles of home." Waiting for my light to turn green, I had no idea that the crossroads before me was to be the metaphorical *and* metaphysical crossroads of my life. When the light finally changed, I moved slowly through the intersection, safely making it past the first few lanes of cars that had stopped at the light. Just as I was passing by the last lane before turning toward town, I looked left, immediately realizing I was about to die.

Time ground to a halt as I felt my body brace for the collision. *Then a funny thing happened.* I became consciously aware that not only was this accident *waiting* to happen, it was waiting for me to make a *decision* as to *how* it would take place. I was consumed with a clarity that I am still unable to adequately describe. I had the distinct choice of remaining in my body, experiencing the horrific impact with all senses intact, or I could simply exit, allowing the remainder of the scene to unfold without feeling the sensation of having my body crushed.

It all seemed very natural, and it felt as if I had all the time in the world to make this decision. Its deceptive illusion is so obvious when faced with death. I was so overwhelmed with a certainty that I had "been there and done that" so many times before, I sensed I had nothing to gain from experiencing this impact *inside* my body this time. This time. . . . It was this choice that has shaped the rest of my life, because this time, unlike the countless times before, *I remembered dying.* Call it evolution of the spirit or an old soul finally figuring it all out again. At that moment, I became engulfed by the peace that passes all understanding. I was comfortable with the familiarity of it all as I recognized that I was not about to become a helpless victim of death, but an active contributor in my own passing.

Time resumed at an explosive rate as I catapulted upward and out of my body, moving instantly from participant to spectator. I watched the driver make no attempt to swerve as he slammed his car into mine, like an old sea captain, purposely steering his ship of fate into the waters of my destiny. I could hear the festive jingle-bell necklace I wore around my neck banging out an eerie tune at the instant I saw my head smash into the driver's side window. The sound of bending steel echoed as I watched the seat fold in half beneath my body, crumpling like piece of paper. I looked on with peculiar and detached interest as blood began to soak through my clothes. The glass had shattered and flown up my shorts, cutting my most personal areas and embedding into my bare legs. The safety belt had pinned me to the back of my seat, as if my battered frame was hanging in suspended animation. As the momentum slowed, the car finally came to rest in the middle of the highway, stopping six lanes of traffic in its tracks.

Now out of my body, I noticed that a friend from college had been only a few cars behind me at the same stoplight. I simply observed her horror as she recognized the mangled body that was trapped inside the now-crushed Toyota Corolla. It was then it occurred to me as strange—I had just *witnessed* this accident. A shocked state of awareness set in as I took note that I was effortlessly floating, looking down at the body that had taken me through twenty-one years of life, and it did not faze me that I was no longer inside it. I quickly adjusted to the absolute freedom of being unencumbered by a physical form and watched as the rest of the scene continued below.

A lady, who was either in a rush to be somewhere else, or too afraid to get involved at the time, ran over to the car, placing her name and phone number on the front seat of the passenger side. A man in uniform reached in, turned the ignition off, and frantically looked to see if he could pull me out. He soon realized that the entire left side of my body was pinned between what was left of the seat and the bashed-in driver's side door. He tried to keep onlookers from getting in the way. People were rapidly beginning to congregate, some attempting to offer a helping hand, but most just trying to catch a glimpse of the wreckage and the unfortunate soul it belonged to.

As I began to gather my wits, I comprehended that I was transitioning from life into death. Immediately, one of my greatest childhood fears was instantaneously dissolved. I had always had a terrible dread that when we die, we cease to exist. Poof! Gone! No memory or identity, just nothing. It was a ridiculous fear, in my case, as I had been exposed to numerous extraordinary paranormal experiences. In fact, the first two decades of my life had not been without their share of visions, visitations, and prophetic dreams. Nonetheless, there was still a deep-rooted anxiety that periodically gripped me in my youth, no matter how many times I had seen proof of life after death. At the time, like so many in their formative years, I was young and confused and didn't fully understand my dreams and visions.

I was overjoyed to remember that I knew exactly who I was, with all of this lifetime's memories intact, but with a complete lack of concern for my body and the end of the life I had actually been living only moments before.

I know people have described near-death experiences with the "tunnel of light." I did see the light, but the trip through the tunnel must have been so fast that I actually missed it. I will, however, never forget the *sound* that accompanied me on this journey. It was the most bizarre buzzing noise, unlike any hum I had ever heard. It was present as I watched what happened on the ground; however, a most beautiful drone, the otherworldly tones of the Music of the Spheres, replaced it as I landed in a magnificent bright light. How could one ever adequately describe the symphony of the heavens? One second I was hovering above my car, watching the spectacle that was my own accident, then, in a flash, I was somewhere else. Somewhere so miraculous that my human mind and limited vo-cabulary could never articulate its awe-inspiring beauty.

Without delay, I became conscious of two "Beings," illuminated by the most stunning backdrop of fluid light. The colors weren't from our world, as I have never seen such translucence in a rain-bow or vibrant shades in any work of art. I was surrounded by a mixture of a distant relative of magenta with a shimmering, pearly sheen. The atmosphere seemed to breathe this unusual hue with the palpable texture; I could feel it all around me, in me. . . . These two Beings appeared to be a part of these colors, yet seemed to step from the palette, taking on a solid and recognizable human form. They were wearing what resembled flowing gowns, but the brushed caramel material from which the gowns were made looked to be a part of them, as opposed to separate pieces of clothing.

They greeted me with a love and joy so pure; it was as if I could feel myself melt right into them. For a moment, I became *one* with them. I had temporarily become that extraordinary wash of light, feeling it course through my soul, cleansing me and welcoming me home. It was perfectly clear that the spirits before me were not friends or family from the life I had just abandoned. They were guardians who had spanned millennia with me, watching and guiding lovingly from this place that was becoming more familiar as each second passed.

The stories of Divine Beings who lovingly watch over us were true! These were *my* guides, *my* spiritual watchdogs. *They really did exist!* They were there to assist me in my transition from incarnation in the physical to life on the spiritual plane. I was now becoming fully aware of how I had known these Beings, sharing in the excitement of this reunion. We were not speaking in the manner I had been accustomed to in my earthly existence. We were sharing from our hearts, soul to soul, in a universal language that knew no bounds or limitations. There were no words spoken, only thoughts and feelings that filled my spirit with lucidity that far surpassed that of any dialogue I had ever partaken in on Earth.

\*

As I felt the presence of these Guides, these watchdogs, I was flooded with the memories of how it all began: an odyssey of adventures as my lifetimes unfurled before me. The backdrop of colors that greeted me on my arrival was now like a grand cinema screen, surrounding me 360 degrees and in multiple dimensions.

In a single instant, it all became crystal clear. I was ready to examine the story of my life. With the interest of an actress critiquing her own performance, it was as if I was watching a film with my best friends. My spiritual cheerleaders enveloped me in their love, proceeding to guide me, step by step, through twenty-one years on Earth as Mary Helen Hensley: the marvelous, the mediocre, and the dreadfully disappointing bits of my intriguing young life.

How startling it was to see how tiny gestures had snowballed into life-changing moments for those who had witnessed them, and how heartbreaking it was to see the same effect with thoughtless acts and unkind words. Still, I watched, taking mental notes as to where I had been excellent at taking on soul-inspiring lessons about the importance of kindness and compassion in *all* situations. I also became painfully aware of how, in the course of history, the phrase "judge not lest ye be judged" had been invariably altered, losing its most vital point—that no one great deity judges us in the end. It is *we* who must judge our own performances. This is truly a daunting prospect when watching your life play out in front of you: aware of the contents of each scene, unable to change them, yet *knowing* what's coming next.

*In that all-loving space, I understood that it was me, myself, to whom I must be accountable.*

Far from the stories I had grown up with in the Bible Belt of America, there was no fire and brimstone, no wrath of a vengeful God. Only the hushed solitude of a place so beautiful it hurts to remember.

While looking back at my life, I was experiencing humankind's most difficult challenge—to sit with oneself. The experience was despairing as well as euphoric, but ultimately it was love revealed in its highest form, which no person should fear. Remaining ever mindful that every second really does count, in the midst of all the chaos, joy, and pain, we are never disconnected or more than a "passing" away from home.

To adequately and fully describe all that went on during that journey back to the Source of Life would take volumes. To be honest, some but not all details as to the inner workings of life's greatest secrets were hidden behind a veil of forgetfulness that those in Spirit must have felt was necessary to conceal, so that I could return and experience a productive life. To pine away for the splendor and love of that extraordinary place would be to throw away the precious, short time we have in this world. I didn't fully understand at the time that I would now walk between the two worlds for the remainder of my days.

One of the benefits and burdens of remembering your death is a feeling of tremendous responsibility to always strive to do the right thing. To treat people with anything less than kindness, fairness, and respect carries a heavy price tag when you are able to remember who you really are. The intensity of emotion while witnessing my life story is one that I will never be able to translate appropriately. Remembering beyond the veil carries an indescribable sense of *knowing* that isn't always that easy to live up to when dealing with others, especially those who don't remember what lies ahead. It gives new meaning to rising to the occasion, turning the other cheek, doing unto others, and all of the other clichés to which we have become so numb. I think of the quote: "A hero is someone who is excellent when *no one* is looking." But guess what, heroes: Someone *is* looking and that someone is *you*.

Of the many things that I can remember, there is one that I feel compelled to convey with certainty—I think it is important to state that reincarnation is a *fact*. It's not too often that I emphatically state anything without following up with "in my perception" or "in my opinion." In this case, I simply can't do lip service. I hang my hat firmly on the fact that continuous life is not some dream fantasy those who are afraid to die soothe themselves with in order to quell their fears or lessen their apprehension. I will emphatically profess, without any reservation, *we have lived before*. We have lived here, and in many other places, just as we will continue to do so until such time as the great unknown becomes fully revealed. Earth is one of many options for growth and expansion, and just like going to school, we come here and reincarnate here, until we are finished here. We don't jump in and out of "Earth school"—we work our way through until we feel that we have exhausted all that is offered and can move on. I'd had experiences of this knowledge as a child, and now I stood face-to-face with the reality that life really does go on. This was a red-letter day for the preacher's daughter. Imagine, for a moment, the enormity of coming face-to-face with the memory of reincarnation, when prior to that day, the concept had never existed in my belief system or been mentioned in my upbringing. Returning to a battered body would pale in comparison to the challenges I would face reinventing my entire perception of existence prior to birth and following death.

It was the relaxed and very familiar way in which the Guardians guided me through the journey of my life that made this all so evident. While watching the stories of my life, I was building on the knowledge and information gathered from previous lifetimes. It all became obvious during this process, which also made it easy to disengage from any feelings of blame, resentment, or anger toward missed opportunities of accomplishment in the life I had just left. The prospect of moving up and onward in a different body, with a different set of circumstances, was patiently waiting around the corner.

I discovered that we are like actors in a guild who tend to incarnate together, taking on various roles in different lifetimes. In this life, I am playing the part of daughter to my mother and father, the sibling of my two brothers and one sister, and currently, I have the role of the mother of two beautiful little girls. I have played the girlfriend, the wife, divorcee, and now, single mother. I have been the student as well as the teacher, doctor turned metaphysician and author. In my next life, any of these people may appear as a parent, a partner, a good friend, or even an aggravator. This is why all of us have had the experience where we felt as if we knew someone we had never met before, or taken an instant liking or disliking to another person for seemingly no reason at all. As for soul mates, I discovered that we have many.

What we need to remember, as we get caught up in the romantic notions of finding our one true soul mate, is that we may have decided long ago to experience life with several of our soul mates, as friends, family, or lovers. We play our roles in one another's lives, loosely following a script, allowing the freedom of improvisation at each actor's discretion. This is the stuff that being human is made of. It's what makes life so worth living. While you might be following your lines word for word, your costars may choose to deviate from the script, throwing you completely off track and into a situation that creates even more opportunities for growth and expansion of the soul.

The term "soul group" has been used to describe these players and is an appropriate description for how it all works. Members of a soul group incarnate together at various times and in appropriate lifetimes, teaching or learning a similar set of lessons in conjunction with the other members of the group. They support one another through many journeys, and certain themes have a tendency to appear consistently, as each member strives to reach a new level of spiritual awareness. It is a most amazing approach to living and one that will never allow the human race to grow tired of itself.

For example, a soul yearning to learn compassion may return to this world as a dastardly character, ruthless and without conscience. He may find a soul mate in his child, a cherished and long-awaited heir, who is then taken away, killed by cruel and tragic circumstances. The soul who died knew prior to incarnation that its time on Earth was limited. Its mission was to provide an arena for its companion soul to experience tremendous feelings of grief and loss, possibly resulting in a better understanding of compassion.

Another soul wishing to learn lessons in devotion may find itself married to the most disloyal of spouses, not because this soul is inherently unfaithful, but because it is playing the part of the infidel, so that the soul on the receiving end of this painful relationship might embrace the value of commitment.

The combinations are endless, and members of the same soul group have a *complete understanding* of the roles they will play before the curtain even opens. All roles, whether we understand or embrace their value, are equally important, and by the same token, divine in the eyes of our Creator. It changes one's entire perspective and begs the question *Is it actually possible for another person to harm us?*

For those who have lost loved ones to violence or acts of malice, it is nearly impossible to comprehend. But in the grand scheme, each and every spirit is fully aware of who they are to become—aware that perceptions may be that they are anything *but* an all-loving spiritual being. But no matter what appearances may seem, each life and every lifetime is a crucial component in the expansion of the heart of humanity, while furthering its own personal evolution as it moves back toward The One.

I remembered exactly why I had chosen to incarnate into my family. Its specific value system and any idiosyncrasies were all custom-ordered for my personal development and any advancement my spirit had set out to achieve. My father's dedication to spiritual and physical discipline, paired with my mother's overwhelming capacity to see the good in everything, were a combination that I requested in order to obtain the background necessary to accomplish my work in adulthood. The respect that I had for my brothers and sister without sharing a deep emotional closeness was also part of the plan. I had chosen to become a member of a family unit that had allowed me to grow and develop with an independence that was never overshadowed by any one sibling's influence. My brother Jonathan, and my sister, Beth, provided complete stability and "normality," if there is such a thing. My older brother, David, inspired a sense of adventure and mystery. They were equally important pieces of the puzzle of my life. We had been born so far apart; David, seventeen years my senior, Beth, ten years ahead, and Jonathan almost five years older, meant that I spent the vast majority of my time on my own, developing my personality traits and building close friendships outside the family.

My siblings were meant to be an easy source of love and friend-ship in my youth, rather than a battleground for life lessons this time around. I had chosen a different curriculum this lifetime that had primarily to do with my parents' belief system, the teachings of Christianity in its present form and a comparative study as to how it had been altered from its origins, and integrating that influence into my own personal convictions—the ones that had been formed from my individual experiences. It all made sense now: why I had spent so much time on my own with my parents as a preteen and young adult. I had more to gain from what I was to discover when being weaned from my mother and father than I did by waging war or developing extremely close relationships with my brothers and sister. My Guardians had rekindled my understanding of just how vital the choosing of one's family is to laying the foundation of who we are to become in the future. They also reminded me that what was to be now, might not be the same down the line.

The most fascinating aspect of the reincarnation cycle for me was learning how a thread of lifetimes works. The thread is a simple expression used to describe how a soul will incarnate into a theme or situation over and over, approaching the lesson from every pos-sible angle. The kind soul to the homeless man on the street, the disinterested passerby who never even glances at the man with the cup of loose change, the homeless person himself, the teen who taunts and jeers, the sensitive child who cries for his troubles. It's the opportunity to walk in the shoes, be the one who picks out the shoes, the one who pays for the shoes, the one who makes fun of the shoes, the one who discards the shoes, and the one who eventually outgrows the shoes. . . .

I was overcome with a new zest for living and a tremendous feeling of recommitment to my life on Earth. My spiritual teachers, the Guardians, knew before I breathed this thought. . . . I was choosing to go back. I recognized that I just wasn't finished yet. We do have that choice, and as I learned that day, there are many opportunities to leave this life, *if we choose to take them*. These are what I call *portals of exit*. They are the near misses—we've all had them—close calls that could have been *the big one*, the lucky break, the miraculous recovery by the grace of God, the time when "someone was definitely looking out for me." I learned that our higher selves are well aware of these portals; it is our own souls who determine how, when, or if we use them. I had just squeezed through a portal to study my performance rather than letting it pass me by. I was now preparing to shove myself back through it, with a new vision from a place I now remembered as home.

The Spirits impressed upon me that there is not one life set in stone, with a concrete beginning and an unchangeable end. That would be incongruent with the way the rest of the universe operates. Free will, it's been called in the past, but it's more like *Thy* will be done . . . on Earth, as it is in Heaven.

I had always thought that *thy* meant God's will, when in actuality, it means our own free will and what we chose to do with it. Portals of exit give us the chance to be the authors of our own stories, not puppets on a string, doing the bidding of an unwavering or disinterested master. We can write and rewrite the script as we go along, with the guidance of our spiritual companions and departed loved ones. It is the most amazing part of the grand plan. We have been given the tools to experience ourselves in life for as long or as short as we choose, with as much happiness and health, or as much pain and suffering as we see fit in order to learn the lessons of growth and development that this earthly school has to offer.

Thankfully, I retained that memory; it is the keystone on which I forged the new foundation of my life, postaccident.

I had been given a wonderful gift. The chance to live on, make changes, and begin a new direction in life, complete with fresh memories of where I had come from—*the place from where all of us have come*. I had also been given specific impressions of how my life would change when I returned. *Things would definitely not be the same*. I would go back into my body, with access to different gifts and abilities that I had not been privy to before the accident. The bar had been raised, and so much more was going to be expected of me, if I chose to follow this path. I knew that this course of action was not going to be easy. However, with this endowment also came a promise: constant guidance and support, if only I would open my heart and allow myself to receive.

With no tearful good-byes—in fact with no farewells at all—I heard a deafening, whooshing noise; it sounded so harsh compared to the unearthly Music of the Spheres. Pain and terror were the next things I felt as I was sucked back into my body, which was now out of the wreckage and lying on the road. I have no memory of how I got there. I know I had regained consciousness before the ambulance arrived. I had demanded to show that I was okay and had convinced somebody to let me stand on my own. I vaguely recall speaking to and then seeing my boyfriend's sister, first by phone, then when she arrived at the scene just before I left for the hospital. There were brief moments of lucidity, as if I had only been in a minor "fender bender" in the car. However I got there, I was now in shock, crumpled in a heap on the hard pavement before being strapped to a board, neck and back immobilized, then placed in an ambulance.

A lady was leaning over me and stroking my hair, attempting to soothe me as I sobbed, trying to piece together what in the world had just happened. She kept saying over and over that there was no way they were going to let me die, most likely because I kept crying and talking about dying. She thought that I was fearful that I might actually be passing away, when little did she know, I was babbling about the fact that I had *already* died. I *knew* that I was going to make it, but at that stage, I couldn't have told her or anyone else *why*. My encounter with that beautiful place, those sounds, my Guardians, now seemed like a distant dream as I faded in and out of consciousness, on the way to the emergency room. And the fate of the elderly man who crashed into me? His massive, uninsured four-door vehicle had allowed him to simply walk away.

Unbelievably, I was released from the hospital just a short time later, never scanned or X-rayed, riddled with a host of unidentified and very serious injuries. It used to boggle my mind as to how this could have happened. My car was hit at an estimated 75 mph, yet somehow I slipped through the cracks, only to discover how badly I had been injured weeks, months, and years later. I have since developed a greater understanding as to why this was all part of the plan. Each wound and subsequent complication brought me closer to the new path laid out before me. Divine timing was most certainly at work. As far as the medics in the hospital were concerned, they had patched me up as best as they could, and it was time for me to face up to the emotional trauma of this crash on my own. My boyfriend, Ben, took me home when I was released, where I spent the night in shock and bewilderment. Most of all I remember the horrific pain of my physical body, which now felt like a two-ton weight, compared to the spiritual body that had just taken me to another world and back again.

For the first time in my colorful medical history, I downplayed my story when I called my parents. No gut-wrenching tales of twisted steel and smashed glass, no stories of blood and broken ribs, hearing loss, or head injuries. Not a word was mentioned about where I had actually been, whom I had met there, or the fact that I had been so lovingly reminded of the reason I came into this life in the first place. I simply told them that I had been in a little accident. No big deal. They were so far away, it was nighttime, and the news that I had died and come back was a little much for anyone to stomach just before bed.

It was a long time before I told them what really happened, and I never really gave the full story to my boyfriend or his family. I just didn't think they were ready. As I now look back, it was me who wasn't able to share. I played the scene over and over in my mind, trying to figure out if this all could have been the product of smashing my head through the driver's side window. Easy enough to explain my life review and the "Beings of Light" as hallucinations, but I would have imagined that my "delusions" and all of the information I was exposed to would have been in some way congruent with my current beliefs, or at the very least, in line with the way in which I had been raised to believe things were. I also simply couldn't explain away the fact that I had seen the collision take place, as well as the people who came to my aid, all with a bird's-eye view of my unconscious body. I would discover soon enough that this most certainly had not been due to any sort of delirium.

Ready or not, Pandora's box had burst at the seams. The young girl who had always experienced the peculiar dreams and visions— she who communed freely with spirits as a child—was now about to understand why her entire life had been leading to this day, this serendipitous "accident," this glimpse of another world, and most of all, the incredible new course that life was about to take.

# Chapter 2

ON FEBRUARY 23, 1969, I slid comfortably into my place as the youngest of four in the Hensley clan. By all accounts, the day was unforgettable. I was born in a heavy snowstorm in the Shenandoah Valley of Virginia. My parents didn't have snow tires on their car, so they had to solicit the help of a friend with the necessary equipment to plow through the storm to get Mom to the hospital in time. The rest, as they say, is history. It was exactly ten years to the day after my sister, Beth, had made the journey. I always thought it was so cool that we had chosen the same special day to arrive on the planet; however, through the eyes of a ten-year-old, I'm sure she felt differently about sharing the limelight with her new baby sister. I made it safely with all parts intact, despite the grim prognosis my folks had been subjected to over the previous nine months.

My mother had been diagnosed with rubella in her first trimester of pregnancy, something no mother-to-be wants to hear, as it can be seriously damaging to a growing baby's health. Along with fears of possible blindness or hearing or limb loss, Mom was also slightly older than the average mother at the time. This was a point that I would so graciously bring up whenever I got into trouble as a child, blaming any poor behavior on the fact that I was probably never right in the head because she was *so old* when she had me. While I'm sure opinions as to my being "normal" have varied over the years, I was as normal as any other healthy child and suffered no known side effects from my mom's illness, other than a peculiar gleam in my eye and a slightly twisted sense of humor.

For as long as I can remember, my dad has told me that I was *promised*. Sometime during my mother's pregnancy he received an otherworldly visit from a Celestial Being assuring him that not only would I be born without complications from the German measles, but that I was destined to live a very "special," unusual, and lengthy life. He had been told that I would always be assisted by a Divine spiritual guidance in my endeavors. And there would be gifts . . . unique abilities to assist me in the work I would do throughout my life. Dad described the feeling as overwhelming, and he knew with certainty that this promise that had been made was one that would be kept. I know that all parents have these wishes for their children, but there was something different, emphatic even, about the way he expressed this knowledge. He had faith in what this Heavenly Being had shared, believed it to be so . . . and so it was.

I was always made to feel like a gift. I was forever being reminded that this sacred promise had been made and that nothing or no one could ever change this fact. Dad was also quick to remind me that I was the only one who could stand in the way of my own destiny.

*

Growing up in the hills of Virginia for as long as I can remember, I was deeply spiritual. I didn't really understand, as a child, that I had a gift but I always knew I was a little bit different. I was raised a Baptist and the church played a very integral part in my upbringing. We belonged to First Baptist Church of Martinsville, and in addition to his full-time positions as assistant principal and head football coach at Martinsville High School, my father was a lay speaker at numerous churches in the region. Throughout my entire childhood and until I graduated from high school he spoke each Sunday at a small, nondenominational church about twenty miles from our home. His sermons were more motivational and inspirational, not solely scripture-based, and Dad regularly used anecdotes from Friday night's football game to drive a point home. He never focused on the scary stuff. I always remember his sermons and eulogies, accentuating the human potential, exemplified by the life of Christ.

The congregation consisted of simple country folk who loved to sing and deeply revered my father as a speaker. Sunday and Wednesday nights were spent at First Baptist, where I sang in the choir, played handbells, and was extremely active with the youth group. I remember the church being very social and welcoming to the community with ice cream socials, Christmas programs, singing in nursing homes, and reaching out to those in need. But my education within the church and my own increasing spiritual abilities did not necessarily go hand in hand.

When I try to pinpoint how and when my abilities began, the first thing that comes to mind is my sleep patterns. I have never been a great sleeper. From the cradle onward, two hours here, a catnap there, have always been standard fare for me. My mind seems to rev up rather than wind down at night. The hours of darkness have always been a strange, exciting time, full of anticipation as well as a bit of a foreboding feeling. From the moment I go horizontal, my body begins to vibrate as if I am plugged into some unseen energy source. I can't remember a time when this internal pulsation wasn't present. I have always awakened in the morning with vivid memories of the previous night's dreams/memories, which seem to "stick" with me throughout my day.

From early childhood on, I regularly experienced the distinct feeling of leaving my sleeping body and taking flight, sometimes around my home or out into the neighborhood. I also recall "visiting" people I knew, as well as those I had never met in this incarnation, absorbing their feeling, and seeing their dreams and thoughts. Often I would awaken with a clear picture of events that were about to take place. When I told my mom about these experiences, she said that she, too, had also remembered "flying" on many occasions while she slept. She would vividly describe a sensation of leaving the body, having to "work" to stay afloat until suddenly she was soaring and able to see everything below her. She likened the sensation to swimming up to the surface from the bottom of a pool and then floating with great ease. Standard dream material, some would say, but these sojourns into the night were not the average, for either of us. I was well aware from an early age that *something unusual was going on.*

I seemed to be experiencing a parallel existence. Daytime wasn't all that unusual, but nighttime, on the other hand, was full of experiences that were unique. I spent night after night outside my body, soaring above the neighborhood, visiting familiar faces and sometimes not-so-familiar places. This had become a regular ritual.

Sleep was always such a strange thing for me; most of the time I avoided it for fear of, perhaps, missing something. In actuality, my greatest adventures unfolded while my body rested. While there have been thousands of theories as to what happens when we dream, I don't think science will ever be able to produce a definite answer. Objective science struggles to answer that which is subjective, and while they may be able to pinpoint what happens to the physical body during sleep, no one will ever be able to validate, or discredit, the individual experiences had by our *energetic bodies.*

Exiting my body was as common to me as dreaming "normal" dreams; however, I was well able to distinguish between the two, as each possessed very distinct and individual characteristics. Dreaming, in a way with which most people are familiar, creates stories that could be based on fact or fantasy. Some say it is the subconscious mind processing the vast amount of information that we are bombarded with every day. Dreams are often thought to be some type of built-in mechanism to sort through and dissipate massive amounts of daily stimuli. Whatever they are, they are part of who we are, and our feeble attempts to decipher them may never come to fruition.

Separation from the body while sleeping is a totally different kettle of fish. In my experience, out-of-body travel during sleep never resembled what others have described as a typical dream state. There were no stories, only real scenarios in which I observed this side of life and spoke to other beings living in extraordinary places that I had yet to experience when awake. The realms that I reached while out of body are difficult to explain, especially here, on the page.

There was a man who would appear both in my dreams and while I was awake, most nights from as early as I can remember. He would tell me stories, showing me incredible visuals while I slept or he would appear at the foot of my bed. From the time I was able to scratch out my first letters, I used to love to put these stories on paper and then perform them as plays. I was always interested in topics that seemed a little too grown-up for the average kid. I was in my element when I was put into the classroom of my second-grade teacher, Miss Smith. I called her on a Saturday morning (this is what she told my mother years later), heralding the news of the upcoming performance of a new play I had just written. It was about a doctor involved in the first expeditions to the North Pole—loosely based on fact—with the details having been filled in by my dreamtime companion. My controlling tendencies were already beginning to show, as I arrived in school on Monday and performed the one-girl show, playing all characters, bar the dying patient, who had no lines. The beautiful, wonderful Miss Smith, as I always referred to her, not only allowed but encouraged this un-usual behavior. No one ever knew where I really got these stories, but this dreamtime companion, *my grandfather*, never let me down.

There is only one photo of Dr. Garland Clark: holding his three-month-old granddaughter, less than a year before his death in 1970. It was Easter, and the picture made it very clear that his ailing body was exhausted and unable to house his life force for much longer. I never thought much about not knowing him in life, because he seemed to always be with me, especially at night. The fact that I slept so lightly and woke so often is what allowed me to become skilled at recalling what went on during those hours. I definitely attribute my interests in health and medicine to the "special appearances" he made throughout my childhood. I cherished the stories he would tell me, particularly those about my mother when she was a little girl. In between the wonderful adventures he would share about people from this world, he would stop to remind me that I wasn't like most other children. He said that I could see beyond this dream and I would eventually come to live between the worlds. He always assured me that he would be there and that even if no one else understood, he did. I never had to look for him. He was simply always there. Early on, he was well aware of the fact that the prophetic nature of my abilities would present a frightening element—that I would have the ability to know when people were going to die, including myself. This was a daunting prospect to anyone, not to mention a young child. It was for this reason that my grandfather showed me, while I was a child, the times and circumstances of my parents' deaths, as well as my own. Some people might find this an awful bit of information to live with, but for me, it put my mind at ease, allowing me to live free from the fear of envisioning the passing of the two people I held most dear. Knowing that I would later be riddled with a host of bizarre injuries and ailments, the information of the time and means of my own death has always been a comfort. The influence that my grandfather ("Judge," as he was called by my family) was to have on me would take another twenty-something years to fully accept. It would become a landmark discovery in my life.

In addition to my visits from Judge, my young mind possessed an unusual series of mental images that would occur on a regular basis anytime my family would take a vacation. Whenever we went to the beach, I got a very distinct visual of driving down a road and seeing sand dunes ahead of us. I could envision driving onto the beach and seeing a number of small tents placed randomly around the sand, with people in old-fashioned bathing costumes emerging from these makeshift dressing rooms and playing on the beach. I could also see ships in the water that looked old and out of place.

At the time, I never understood that these "waking dreams" were somehow triggered by physically being in the location. I now know that these visions were glimpses into the past—some kind of collective universal memory. I knew that they weren't my own memories, but they certainly belonged to someone. They were like energetic impressions in my mind of what the area had actually looked like in years gone by. I often experienced this sensation, not only near the beach, but when visiting any new destination. It was like having a "mind movie" of the past and it always made me appreciate the places we visited, especially because both of my parents were history buffs. They were forever taking us to battlefields, colonial townships, war memorials, battleships, and graveyards, all which held the energy of amazing historical events. It never seemed odd to me that oftentimes there were residual impressions of people, long gone, lingering in these spaces. I had never seen the world around me in any other way.

One summer in particular, my parents, my brother Jonathan, and I took a trip to the beach. As was customary for our travels, no reservations had been made, and we always took a chance, hoping for the best when searching for somewhere to stay. Our destination was Virginia Beach, and the region had recently been plagued with a severely eroding coastline. We had tried several spots before finally coming to rest at a hotel that was located directly in front of the ocean. On the shore side of the hotel, there was a massive undertaking to pump sand onto the dwindling beach, and I was fascinated by the whole operation. I was a precocious five-year-old, and therefore had been duly warned not to go near the pipes that were blasting sand in front of the hotel and farther up the beach. It was very late and we had spent most of the evening looking for somewhere to stay. As my parents unloaded the car, curiosity got the best of me despite numerous words of caution. I wandered down to the beach to see what was going on.

Unknown to my parents, who were still trying to get our things into the hotel, I was gone in a flash! I had followed the water's edge and was now perfectly lost, as children are so adept at doing. As soon as my folks discovered I was missing, my father embarked on a frantic journey that he proclaimed aged him twenty years.

I continued to walk, eventually coming upon two men who could only be described as hippies. It *was* the early seventies, and with their Doobie Brothers hairstyles and beach-bum motifs, it looked as if I had landed in the middle of a really bad seventies sitcom. They were sitting around a small fire, with sleeping bags and a makeshift stove, talking and laughing. I remember a funny smell coming from the skinny little cigarettes they were smoking. I walked straight up to them and, in my innocence, asked if they knew where my mom and dad were. They were very kind and asked me what hotel we were in. I instantly offered up the name of one of the many hotels we had tried—of course, it was one that had no vacancy. Hand in hand, these two men walked me down the beach to the hotel I had told them, only to find that my parents were not there. Luckily, the night clerk remembered recommending a few other places to stay to a man and his family. She thought if we checked them out, we might find my mom and dad.

My hippies and I turned the other way and walked back up the beach, trying everywhere that had been suggested. Several hours had now passed and I was having the time of my life! My parents, of course, were distracted with worry. We entered yet another hotel from the beachside entrance and I remember my mother's face as she saw me cross the threshold with my newfound friends. As there were no mobile phones at that time (they were as futuristic as compact discs or cable TV), there was no way to notify my father until he returned on his own. I was absolutely petrified of how angry he was going to be.

I had no regard in my young mind as to the drama I had caused over the last few hours. My only concern was that I had disobeyed orders and would most certainly be punished. When he eventually returned, I saw my dad in tears for the first time in my life. He was livid, but mostly relieved as he lectured me about the danger I had put myself in. The reason this story is so significant in my history is that my father went into great detail as to *how I could have drowned* that night.

As a great little swimmer, a Pisces by nature, I never had a fear of the water, only a deep respect for it, and I took great pleasure from all it had to offer. As my father lectured me that night, his voice was reduced to a murmur and seemed to fade into the background as I spontaneously recalled a very alarming memory, so distinct and yet so strange, of having drowned before.

I was standing outside of a temple of some sort, in a modestly embellished, full-length purple gown, watching fiery objects sail through the sky. I appeared to be in my early thirties. I distinctly recall looking across a field at the beautiful seaside village where I had grown up and which now was home to my own children. This village looked far more futuristic than antiquated, oddly enough. Its buildings were glimmering, crystalline structures, yet they blended into their surroundings, symbiotic with the land. I had been frantically working inside the temple in some sort of preparation for the imminent devastation. There were symbols: multidimensional holograms containing a vast history of the world to date and they were in my care. It appeared that I was working feverishly to somehow imprint the information in my own mind. The iconographs had been sent off with my father and my eldest son, months prior to the impending disaster. My father and his grandson were Keepers of the Light. They had been chosen to survive.

A global catastrophe had sparked off a massive tidal wave that quickly took me, and a multitude of others to our deaths. As I went under the colossal wall of water, I felt the fear and sadness of going through this alone, without being able to hold my husband and two younger children as they faced their looming demise. I knew it was the way and I also knew that we would all return; however, my human form and emotions could not help but grieve the passing from this particular life. The splendor and solace of that world would never be created again . . . and I knew it.

I was lost in this unexpected flashback, the first of many to come, when Dad snapped me back to the present.

"Do you understand me, young lady?" was the next thing I heard.

Dad was still lecturing, not aware that I had just experienced my very first recall of death in a former life. I was wise enough, even at the age of five, to know that losing me for the night had been a little too traumatic to share this new insight with my parents. The events of the night were to be filed away and not spoken about until many years later, a habit that I had already begun to master.

I revisited the memory of drowning from a different perspective when I was in the fifth grade. It was a Wednesday afternoon. I know this, because I was at church, where I spent every Wednesday afternoon and evening of my childhood. Handbell practice, then Family Night dinner followed by choir practice was the normal routine from about age four until I graduated from high school. I remember this particular evening so well because I had spent the whole of the day waiting in fear for the clock to strike five. The talk around school had been that on *this* day, the planets were supposed to align in such a way that Earth was to see her last moment before exploding at around five that evening. There had been something mentioned in the papers and some reference on the news that had led us to believe that this Wednesday was to be our last, as our planet was ripped apart due to this unique stellar alignment. Real or not, the fear it conjured up in me was absolutely staggering.

I asked one of my teachers from school, who was also a member of our church, if this was truly the fate we were to meet. With complete calmness, Ms. Debbie Simpson held my hand as she attempted to convince me that she genuinely didn't think so. She then said that if it was going to happen, hadn't we been so lucky to have lived the time that we had? I will never forget that moment, because so often adults dismiss children and their fears as folly. Ms. Simpson had given me her undivided attention, along with her true feelings about a situation that had me in the most panicked state that I had ever experienced. Her single act of interest and honesty was one that has inspired me to always listen to the concerns of young people, no matter how silly they may sound. I felt respected, and most of all heard, not brushed off because my worries were childish or stupid.

Needless to say, five o'clock came and went, but I remained on high alert for the rest of the night, just in case somebody had gotten the time wrong. The overwhelming terror I was feeling was heightened by flashbacks of that woman in the beautiful purple gown looking up into the sky as flaming asteroids, meteors, and pieces of another planet streaked by, just before the giant wall of water took her to her death. I had not thought of this since I had been lost at Virginia Beach several years earlier. These feelings of sadness and fear were just so familiar to me. My parents had not yet arrived at the church for dinner, and I thought that I might die again without my family by my side.

To this day, I have a disproportionate reaction to anything dealing with outer space, asteroids, comets, shooting stars, etc. I will not watch movies with this theme and if I happen to glance at a tabloid heading with anything to do with the subject, I immediately get a bit panicky. Spiritual development and a bit of maturity have allowed me to put these fears into perspective, but nonetheless, my heart still pounds a little harder when I see or hear about these celestial events. I do not believe that past lives necessarily dictate the persons that we become, but I do know that who we have been can lend itself to creating tendencies in our present, regardless of what our rational minds tell us to accept as truth.

I probably could have shared my past life memory of the lady in the purple gown, the temple, the holographic symbols, the wall of water with my parents on that day, but I didn't. While my parents attempted to integrate the numerous accounts of the paranormal experiences I was having up to that point, there was something about this memory that was too sacred, too meaningful to my current life story for me to share just yet. I was still completely unaware of the major role it would play in my future. Mom and Dad did the best they could to honor the significance of the stories and dreams I had shared over the years, unable to discount them as childish fantasy. But their main priority was my safety and well-being, and while stories of visits from my mother's father were naturally exciting for her, my father kept a close watch and strongly encouraged me not to share these events with anyone other than them. Always referring back to the visit where he had been told I was "promised," he never discounted the God-given nature of my gifts, but he would express his concerns of future exploitation by saying, "Even Jesus didn't heal everyone, sugar." As the story goes, I continued to pick and choose very carefully, just how much, *and what*, I thought they could handle.

# Chapter 3

THE HUMAN body has always fascinated me. I was absolutely thrilled when I got my first doctor's kit as a child. The little black bag contained a plastic stethoscope, a thermometer complete with elevated temperature reading, and a blood pressure cuff that registered dangerously high numbers on its red paper dial. Every night, I would check Mom and Dad for any ailments that might have cropped up during the day. Dad always required a bandage around his head, and he would sit patiently allowing me to wrap him up like a mummy. *I always wrapped him that way.* It was at this same time that my Dad had a book on John Wilkes Booth that contained photos of his mummified body that absolutely intrigued me. Strange as it sounds, there was something terribly familiar about the way his body had been preserved. Many years and several not so glamorous memories of a particular lifetime in Egypt as an embalmer would pass before I realized just why I was so fascinated with the process.

I quickly discovered that the longer I stayed in "surgery," the later I got to stay up. I spent most nights massaging backs, pounding calves, and performing minor surgery on bumps, lumps, cysts, and pimples. I would routinely prepare Dad for his ops by shaving his face with lotion and a butter knife. I often cupped my hands around my mother's knee and imagined filling it with "good energy." She had destroyed that knee while helping me climb out of a swimming pool when I was two, and I felt so sorry for her each time I worked on the big surgical scar across her leg.

Along with my love of doctoring my folks came an obsession with my own infirmities. If I didn't mention it before, my best friend, my grandfather in spirit, had been a *surgeon* in life. I was constantly talking about illnesses, real or imagined, that bordered on hypochondria. If the truth be known, I loved being sick. I loved going to the doctor; I couldn't wait to hear the explanation of what was happening to my body, and I was utterly disgusted when I would get some average ailment like a sinus infection or the flu. I was delighted with each and every diagnosis of the standard childhood diseases. I proudly boasted when I received my *second* bout of mumps (each side of my face had been infected individually) and considered myself very lucky to have contracted the dreaded fifth disease, a distant relative of the measles. I was only too thrilled to back my brother Jon into a corner, waving my rash-covered arms in his horrified face!

I quickly grasped the concept that *sickness equated leverage and power*, an unfortunate preview of how I would manifest real illnesses to escape any number of stressful situations in the years to come.

One New Year's Eve, I was playing football with the children in our neighborhood. I was seven going on seventeen when I ran deep to make a spectacular catch from my neighbor, Steve, the quarterback. I caught the pass but slipped on the grass and fell to the ground, smashing my chin into the ball. The only thing that kept my teeth from smacking together was my tongue. I bit straight through it and severed it in two. It required a number of stitches to reattach. Most important, it was good for almost a month's worth of sympathy, as well as a new pair of Hush Puppies shoes, my reward for being so brave. It was totally worth it because I had been begging for those shoes for ages and only something as serious as biting off my tongue gave good enough reason for Mom to cave in and make the purchase! It has made for a lifetime of great stories, complete with an amazing scar for visual effect.

My love of ailments was a running joke in our family. Mom and Dad always went on a date every Saturday night, without fail. A phone number was always left in case of emergency. I don't think a single Saturday night was free from a phone call to the restaurant, in which I preceded my news with:

"Now don't you worry, but . . ."

One time I was sure my teeth were growing *up* through the roof of my mouth instead of down. Another time I was certain that my appendix was ready to burst. You can be sure that it was always something very serious, as well as very unique.

My sicknesses always seemed to worsen during the school year. It wasn't that I didn't like school, because I did. There was something at the time that meant much more to me than the world of academia. I was a tremendous fan of old movies. These were the kind my parents would have seen in the theaters as they were growing up. I knew each and every star from Virginia Mayo and Maureen O'Hara to the Marx Brothers and the Three Stooges. I would dance around with Ginger Rogers and Fred Astaire, go West with "The Duke," and travel on hilarious adventures with Bob Hope and Danny Kaye. I was mesmerized by Bing Crosby's voice and could watch Gene Kelly glide on air all day long. It was remarkable how my temperature would drop and I would suddenly feel better at one o'clock, just in time for the feature film. There were even times when I started my day at school but deteriorated just in time to be home for the afternoon lineup. It didn't happen often, as my folks wouldn't allow it—and there *really* were days that I wasn't well, but I cherished the moments when I was lucky enough to spend the afternoon with my Hollywood heroes.

If I had to sum up the greatest qualities given to me by my parents in two words, those words would be *attitude* and *gratitude*. My father was a top-notch disciplinarian. I mean this in the most positive sense of the word. I have yet to meet an individual as dedicated to a personal regimen of health and fitness as my father. Standing at six feet one inch, his once-blond hair had turned into a thick shock of silver by the time I came along. His face was handsome and distinguished, his physique was chiseled, and his arms reminded me of Popeye. His attitude toward the care and upkeep of both his mental faculties and physical body made no room for laziness or excuses. His approach toward his relationships with his wife and children saw him strive to balance work and time with his family, even when things were a little tight. Dad once wrote to me:

> You should recognize that your ability to fuse work and play in everything that you do is something that nobody can take from you, unless you thoughtlessly give it away. The beauty of a holistic attitude towards work and play will turn out to be that the more that you learn how to play at your work, the better the products of your work will naturally be, without having to worry about your work at all.

It is because of this attitude that I have always loved to work. Even when I was young, work was not something to dread; it was yet another arena to learn, to grow, and to express myself through my own unique talents. Dad's attitude toward *accountability* is one that I probably appreciate most. As children, we were bound to make mistakes, as all children do; it's a natural part of the process of growing up. The difference is that when we made mistakes, excuses were not tolerated; only a willingness to accept responsibility and come up with solutions to our challenges was suitable. His approach wasn't always sensitive or perfect, but his desire to teach us to better ourselves was always in earnest.

Mom, on the other hand, is the perfect ying to Dad's yang. Her capacity to find the silver lining in *any* dark cloud is remarkable. Not only was she Hollywood beautiful in her youth, with shoulder-length auburn hair and a figure to die for, Father Time has been most kind to her in the aging process. Looking years younger than her actual age, Mom is still smiling, always support-ive, but unlike Dad, her physical discipline seems to come and go like the ocean tide. She hides candy bars in the freezer on occasion to eat in secret after a healthy meal of tuna fish and cottage cheese salad. She exercises . . . sometimes. She watches her diet . . . some-times, and her optimism toward starting a new lifestyle regime *every* Monday morning is endearing. She was, and still is, just one of those people that you love to be around.

In her imperfection toward health and fitness is found her per-fection at accepting everyone as they are. When I went through my chubby phase as a preteen, she was always right there with a safety pin or needle and thread if my shirt button looked as if it were going to pop. There was never any criticism about my weight, just reassurance that all was as it should be and that I was beautiful *just like I was.* She is the kind of mom who acted as if she had just won the lottery whenever I gave her a handmade card.

In regard to my scholastic achievements, my father always wanted me to do my best. If my grades were not what they should be, he wanted to know if I had given my best effort. If not, I was to work harder next time. When it came to my grades, I tended to be overly optimistic, and I attribute that quality to my mother. I remember coming home once in grade school after a very tough test, having to face my parents with the results. When asked how I had done, I responded cheerfully, "I got the third highest F in the class!"

Mom went into fits of laughter and said that I had just named the title of my first book, as Dad looked on with "the face"—*you all know the one.* Mom's gracious nature and her attitude of gratitude played such a huge role in the person that I have strived to become, and the balance and stability that she and my father created in our household were their greatest gifts as parents. Even though Dad was a devout student of the Bible, ministering every Sunday, en-suring that our lives were deeply involved in the church, Mom and Dad both held a firm belief that the pinnacle of the Baptist faith, the acceptance of Jesus as Lord and Savior, was a highly personal decision. They never pushed in regard to baptism. In fact, they never mentioned it at all, as I recall.

When I was eleven, I decided that even though I didn't really "get" the whole Christianity thing, I was sick of being the only one in my group at church who wasn't baptized. In the Baptist faith, it is up to the individual to decide when he or she accepts the Lord as personal savior. I simply could not get my head around the idea that the *only* people who got to go to heaven were the ones who be-lieved in Jesus Christ. This was so different than what I knew in my heart to be true. I allowed peer pressure to get the best of me and decided to take the plunge (actually, the dip, in our church). When I came forward to make my proclamation, I was "introduced" to the church (they'd known me all of my life) and asked a few ques-tions. One of these questions happened to be about my hobbies. I immediately responded with WWF Wrestling—the cheesy wres-tling program on Saturday night TV—*and* that I aspired to be the first female quarterback for the Dallas Cowboys. How cute; they all laughed, but the reality was that I didn't have a clue why I was up there. It just didn't make sense to me that they all believed that making this proclamation of faith, followed by the symbolic dunk in the water, was the *only* ticket to heaven.

At eleven, I was trying to save my soul from a place I didn't even believe in, but hey, when in Rome. . . . Despite my apathy, there was one deciding factor that caused me to take the walk of faith that day. A girl in the church who was the same age as me had been taking communion for nearly a year. I couldn't bear it every Sunday when she got to have the wafers and the grape juice like all of the grown-ups. It had nothing to do with the body or blood of Christ; this girl got snacks right in the middle of church and yours truly *did not*! I was certain that she had no more of a clue than I did as to why she was receiving communion. This hostility reared its ugly head on the night that little Annie Whelan made her own walk of faith. The minister had just finished the sermon and as the last hymn was played, he asked anyone who was ready to take the Lord Jesus Christ as Savior to come forward. Well, up shot Annie Whelan, and I was absolutely mortified! In the last words that I was to speak for a while, I shouted out from the back pew of a packed church, "She's doing it for the juice and the bread!"

I never got spanked much as a child—*never*, according to my siblings—but boy, did I get it that night! The preacher's daughter was already building quite the little reputation for herself.

In no way do I wish to make a mockery of the religion in which my parents brought us up. While a lot of things didn't seem to click with my own personal experiences, the power of group bonding and community did. I learned all about living a life of service and the importance of giving. My love for music has been one of the greatest gifts that going to church provided for me, as I had the opportunity to learn to read music, play instruments, and perform in public with Mr. Bob Chapman, one of the most outstanding musicians I have ever known. I was a testament to the fact that learning through osmosis is possible. I spent a lot of time in the hallway listening to the music through the door because I talked incessantly during choir practice and had to be put out on a regular basis. Still, I adored him and was delighted when he eventually married the beautiful piano player who used to giggle at my antics from behind the sheet music. I also learned about the importance of stewardship from a dedicated youth minister named Nancy. I discovered that being a churchgoing teenager could still be cool from David, a very hip young minister who brought fresh new ideas about making worship fun.

I came to understand that the church, in and of itself, was not a complete structure, only a foundation on which to build. It was also where I really learned that *all* people are fallible, regardless of faith. The confines of a church or organized religion can bring out the very best and the very worst in human beings. It is often blamed on the religion itself, but no matter what the conviction, people are simply going to make mistakes.

While I no longer subscribe to any particular organized religion, it saddens me to see people throw the baby out with the bathwater when they think that their chosen faith has let them down. On the contrary, the mistakes and misjudgments made by the church throughout history have provided more opportunity for personal growth than most realize. It is in the understanding of these short-comings that we can gain the most spiritual enlightenment.

The awe-inspiring power behind the statement "when two or more are gathered in his name" became obvious to me. The true potential, the real power of a church congregation, is held in its ability to pray together. The chance to gather as a collective unit, warts and all, sending love, energy, and hope into the cosmos, is a miraculous ability that is often misunderstood, even by those who practice it.

I can't speak for the other members of my family, but for me, I think that while my parents wanted to expose me to the joy and security that they found from their faith and relationship with the church, they knew the importance of allowing us to find our own feet in terms of a relationship with God. In my case, they were both painfully aware that the spiritual dilemmas that I faced came from the fact that my personal experiences had presented challenges that the average child did not have to deal with. At that time, not only was I regularly conversing with those who had passed on, and having dreams that would inevitably come to fruition, I was secretly harboring the memory of a lifetime that involved the de-mise of an entire civilization.

# Chapter 4

AS WELL as being a minister and assistant principal, my dad was also the head football coach of our local high school team. The mascot for Martinsville High was the mighty bulldog. School spirit was abundant in those days, and my greatest ambition as a youngster was to own my very own bulldog. When my parents felt that I was old enough for the responsibility, I became the proud mother of Otto Von Bismarck, the beautiful fawn-colored pedigree of royal lineage. I loved this dog—though, to tell the truth, I left most of the burden of parenting this pet to my poor folks. He represented my school pride, my first real responsibility in life, and all of my dreams come true.

During Otto's first summer with us, I went away to camp for a week with my church youth group. We left on a Sunday, and on the Wednesday that followed, I awakened in the night with a jolt, jumped down from the top bunk, and ran out of my cabin. I hadn't a care for disturbing the twenty other campers who were asleep at the time. My camp counselors awakened and came running into the rain after me. I was headed up the hill, to the main building, insisting on using the phone to call my parents. The girls managed to calm me down long enough to find out what was so upsetting. I proceeded to tell them of a horrible "dream." My precious dog, Otto, had been wheeled into an animal hospital with all four legs up in the air. People in gowns and masks were frantically working over him, when all of a sudden his legs went limp and he fell over. I sobbed as I told these strangers that my best friend was dead! The counselors tried to console me, saying that it was just a bad dream. It *was* the middle of the night, and they weren't going to let me phone home unless it was an absolute emergency. They promised that if I was still upset in the morning, they would let me speak to my parents.

First thing the following morning, I rang home, only to be told that Otto was fine. Mom and Dad said they loved me, advising me to enjoy the rest of camp. They would pick me up on Saturday. Those next three days dragged on forever as I couldn't wait to get home. Even at that age, I knew that my dreams were out of the ordinary and that something was seriously wrong. Mom and Dad picked me up that Saturday morning with hugs and smiles and no mention of Otto. Every time I asked about him on the short drive home, they changed the subject.

To this day, I will never forget arriving to the house, looking everywhere for my dog, before being sat down on the edge of my parents' bed, and told that my sweet little Otto had contracted a "doggy disease" that had damaged his brain. It was then they told me that, in fact, he *had* died during the week, but they chose not to ruin camp by telling me over the phone. I was devastated, my young mind and grieving soul unable to accept the compassionate deception.

*I have never doubted the accuracy of my dreams since.*

For the first time, I wasn't looking forward to football season in the fall. I had been so excited at the prospect of walking my genuine, bona fide bulldog around at the games while my dad was coaching. Martinsville High School football games in the seventies were like something out of a Hollywood film. The marching band with their plumed hats and shiny instruments, the cheerleaders in their saddle oxfords and ponytails waving pom-poms, posters of support all over the place, and a jam-packed stadium ready to cheer the Dawgs to victory was the standard scene, every Friday night. Ever since I had lost Otto, my enthusiasm waned and I really didn't care if I got to go to the game or not. I was truly grieving the loss of my little friend.

One Friday afternoon that same season, Mom told me I was not going to the game because I had to get a booster vaccination and would be too tired afterward. I didn't object to missing the game but was definitely not wild about the reason why. The doctor told my mother the usual: "She may feel feverish, sore, and tired. Just give her some aspirin and she'll be fine."

Mom left me at the home of some family friends while she went to the game. I remember the man carrying me into the house because I felt so unwell. Mom genuinely thought I was just sluggish from the shot, and went on to the game, not realizing what was about to take place. This couple did all sorts of things to try to entertain me and "liven" me up. They even folded a hat out of a newspaper for me to wear.

I was stretched across the couch, paper hat perched on my head, when all of a sudden, I looked down, and I was looking at me. I appeared to be asleep at the time, but I could see all of me, head to toe. This was an unusual sight when you were only accustomed to seeing parts of yourself through your own eyes, or your reflection in the mirror. I remember having a bit of a look around the house, then outside. The experience was similar to leaving my body while asleep, but still, this felt different. This time, I was aware that something wasn't right. Unlike my spirit leaving my body on midnight adventures, I seemed to be fixated on the fact that I was looking at my own body and that something was seriously wrong with it. After what felt like an eternity, I landed back with a thud.

Next thing I knew, my mother was standing next to the couch, gently shaking my arm. I tried to explain what happened, but they all laughed. I felt a bit like Dorothy trying to describe "the land of Oz" to her family after the tornado. They said that I must have been dreaming. Were they kidding? Whom did they think they were dealing with, here?

I knew that I had experienced some sort of reaction to the vaccine, and it had temporarily kicked me out of my body. I wasn't afraid because the sensation was so familiar and I eventually figured out what was different; it was the first time I had recalled *looking back* at my body after exiting. I often wonder how many others have experienced these things but have brushed them off as dreams, delirium, or flights of fancy.

Chapter 5

AS FAR as traumas go, compared to what so many children in the world have faced, I sailed through childhood with no major challenges. My family was solid, we were always provided for, and most of all, we were loved. In my own experience, only a couple of things stand out as significant. One of these was when my father retired from coaching. I loved football, I loved the Martinsville Bulldogs, but most of all, I loved being the coach's daughter. At the time, I valued it as my actual identity. The other momentous emotional upset was when my father decided to leave the public school system in order to become headmaster of a dwindling private school.

For our family, it was a fantastic move. Dad had the chance to use his remarkable motivational skills to rebuild a struggling school and turn it into a thriving institution. For my ego, it was a nasty blow. I had grown up with the same kids from kindergarten straight through to the tenth grade. I had forged lasting friendships and loved them all. Although I was given the choice, I was *strongly* encouraged to finish my last two years of high school with a new bunch of teens in the private school. I was fifteen at the time, a little overweight, and well established with my position among my life-long pals as class clown. I was extremely conscious of what it would mean to redefine my role, attempting to fit in with a different group of peers. To me, private school equated families with lots of money and kids with clothes and cars that my parents couldn't afford. It also meant being in class with everyone who had paid to be there, knowing that the only reason I was there was because my dad was headmaster.

I wallowed in self-inflicted misery for a while, until reason kicked in and I began to see this as an opportunity. I had the chance to be in smaller classes, play different types of sports than I had in public school, and since there was no cheerleading squad, I could start one *and* be its captain. It's funny how I perceived their world as so shallow, when it was actually I who was lacking substance. While I missed the atmosphere that can only be found in a big high school—the pep rallies, the marching bands, and the huge crowds at all sporting events—I found myself surrounded by new ideas and diverse ways of learning. While the transition was a little bumpy, I worked my way into this different world and carved a nice little niche for myself.

I was in the process of deciding the future of my next level of education. I really wanted to follow in my sister's footsteps, attending James Madison University. JMU was in Harrisonburg, Virginia, and my sister, Beth, had studied graphic design there ten years earlier. I also wanted to study graphic design, and I think familiarity with the school was dictating my decision, not to mention its great reputation for being a massive party school.

One day I was hanging out in the senior lounge during my final months as a high school student, when I was called to my father's office. Earlier that day, Dad had heard a familiar voice outside of his office door, and when he looked out, he was greeted by an old friend with whom he had coached football many years earlier. This man was now the president of a small, private college in South Carolina, and was on a visit to recruit new students for his school. When I went into Dad's office, I was introduced to his friend as a prospective candidate. I was a little shocked; I had more or less made up my mind to go to James Madison, and my dad knew it.

I suppose he wanted me to consider the possibility, as this was a prestigious school, and the president was offering a partial academic scholarship as incentive to attend. There was a weekend coming up to show students around the college, so my father and I decided that I would attend. I figured I would have a look, just to please my folks, but in my mind, I was JMU-bound.

In exchange for entertaining the possibility of attending this college, my one stipulation was that my parents let me attend this weekend *on my own*. I wanted to have a proper look, without their influence. As an eighteen-year-old who had never strayed from my parent's protection, I was determined to give the college scene a good go. I arrived at Coker College on a Friday afternoon to attend the welcome dinner party that evening. Much to my surprise, I was the *only* prospective student who had not been accompanied by their parents. We met some of the Coker students that night and the usual college rituals of drinking and partying commenced. I had never been around anything like it. The next day was full of activities designed to entice us into choosing this small but very lively school. In reality, all of us were eagerly waiting for the nighttime shenanigans to begin.

Each prospective had been paired up with a buddy for the weekend: a student living on campus. My buddy was responsible for "looking after me," sharing her room, as well as introducing me to the college experience. Just imagine the excitement I felt, first time away from the nest, with guys and girls living in the same dorms and alcohol everywhere I turned!

I was not an experienced drinker at all. I came from a household where alcohol never crossed our threshold, not even on special occasions. This wasn't for religious reasons; both Mom and Dad had simply chosen to be total abstainers before they even met, therefore making it a quality that each found incredibly appealing about the other in their very long list of similar values. I had never really indulged, so even a little bit was way too much. That night, I found myself in a situation that would change the direction of my entire life.

There were students gathered all through the hallways, drinking and smoking, with music blaring. A guy who had been flirting with me all night took me by the hand, led me down the hall, and said he wanted to show me something. No, *really*, that's what he said and yes, I *really* did go. Sheer stupidity was now dictating my every move.

I was well intoxicated at this stage, letting this guy lead me into a darkened room, where suddenly, I became aware that we were not alone. I could just make out the face of another person from the light of the bathroom next door. Before I knew what was happening, I was being stripped by two pairs of hands and pushed to the floor. I screamed for help, but no one could hear me over the loud music and laughter. The next few minutes were a terrifying blur, as I realized that every parent's worst nightmare was happening to me, and there was absolutely *nothing* I could do to stop it.

Somehow, sometime later, I made it back to my buddy's room, and passed out. I awakened the next morning with a very sick head. The horrific reality of what had happened the night before was starting to sink in. I never mentioned to anyone what went on that night, and I did not see my assailants before I left. Being Sunday, it was the final day of my weekend visit, so after a few very brief good-byes, I got in my car and made the four-hour trip home.

The journey down had been very different. I was full of anticipation, singing at the top of my lungs to Aerosmith on the radio. Going home, I drove in complete silence. In the space of those four hours, I made the foremost decisions that were to completely alter the course I had previously chosen for my life. I accepted the fact that I was partially responsible for what had happened to me because *I had made the decision to drink that night,* unable to take care of myself. Accountability had been drummed into me my entire life, so when I arrived home, I marched into the house, a big smile on my face, and announced to my parents: "I'm starting Coker College in the fall!"

I never told my parents what happened that weekend; I know that Mom and Dad would have been devastated, so hurt for me, yet fully supportive. As far as I was concerned, I had gone from teenager to woman overnight. It was my responsibility to clean up my own mess. At the time it all happened, I suppose I was disappointed in myself for straying so far from the thoughtful and loving boundaries in which I had been raised and for being so naive as to have allowed my safety to be compromised.

I didn't permit myself to wallow in these feelings for long though, because I had also been taught that living in remorse and regret stood to destroy me quicker than any lapse in good judgment ever could.

What, you may ask, does this event have to do with my developing clairsentient abilities? Quite frankly, everything. This incident became a pivotal moment for me on many levels. I came to understand that just because I "knew" things pertaining to other people, world events, and those in Spirit, it didn't mean I was immune to facing the difficult challenges that were destined to unfold on my own life path. I also became acutely aware that chemical substances, such as alcohol or even prescription medications, had an exaggerated effect on my unique energy body, and if I chose to abuse them, the outcomes could be disastrous. I eventually found that the lessons I learned in accountability during this time would become the underlying theme used in the healing sessions I would facilitate in the future. If first and foremost an individual cannot take stock and accountability for their physical, emotional, or spiritual crises, not only will the path to healing be long and arduous, it will be next to impossible.

# Chapter 6

IN AUGUST of 1987, I began studies at the small private college in Hartsville, South Carolina. My parents went with me to help move me into my new home on a sweltering, late-summer evening. When I was all settled into my dorm room, I bade my parents farewell and began a new chapter in my life as a college student. They were going home, for the first time in thirty-five years, with no birds in the nest.

My first year of college was a blur of parties and wasted time; I enjoyed myself thoroughly and got into my fair share of trouble. My sophomore year of college, however, proved to be very interesting in terms of revisiting my ongoing psychic development. That year, I began to have numerous dreams that would eventuate into reality. At first, they were simple enough. I would dream the scores to the basketball games, and they would be accurate. It became a bit of a pastime for my roommate and me. I would dream the scores; we would write them down and seal them in an envelope; go cheer at the game; then come back and have a look. Wouldn't that have come in handy if I was a gambling kind of girl? Even at that early stage in my growing awareness, I instinctively knew that gifts like these were never to be used for personal gain, such as acquiring large sums of money by gambling or picking lottery numbers.

As they progressed, my dreams didn't limit themselves to basketball. There was a girl who lived on the floor above me named

Kelly. She had lost her father when she was a teen. A sudden illness had taken his life, leaving her quite guarded and terribly serious at a very early age. One day, Kelly came down to my room to ask if I could help her find something she had lost—an earring from a very special pair, given to her by her late father. We went to her room and turned the place upside down, but couldn't find the missing piece of jewelry. Needless to say, she was very upset to have mislaid something of such sentimental value, because it could never be replaced.

That night as I slept, I was visited by a man in a uniform. He politely identified himself as Kelly's father. He told me that he was aware that he would be able to communicate with me, and that he knew that his daughter was very distressed about losing the gift he had given her so many years ago. This lifelike apparition told me that the earring had fallen between the floorboards underneath the old radiator in her room. He thanked me for my help, and the visit promptly ended.

The next morning I went straight up to Kelly's room and told her about my "dream." She was skeptical, but at this point she was so desperate to find the earring, she went and had a look anyway. Sure enough, there sat her prized possession, exactly where my visitor had said it would be. The interesting thing was, when I explained to Kelly how this man was dressed in uniform, she replied, "Well, of course he was. My father was an officer in the military."

It became quite a regular occurrence for me to dream that someone was in trouble or had died. My mother would always be amazed, yet never really surprised, when she would ring to tell me about someone's passing and I would invariably tell her who it was before she could get a word in. As cool as it sounds, knowing these things was, and remains, very unnerving. I began to worry that I was going to dream the demise of one of my family members or close friends. I had always known about Mom and Dad; however, there were any number of relatives about whom I could still get disturbing news. Since the only time that this was happening was when I was asleep, it seemed logical at the time that if I refrained from sleeping, I wouldn't get this information. So for the remainder of my second year of school, I became a self-inflicted insomniac, catching catnaps during the day, and sleeping little to not at all during the night.

One can only imagine the effect this had on my schoolwork. I was majoring in graphic design as well as communications. I spent many late nights in the art department, and the rest of my studies went down the tubes. My creative ideas were good enough, but the ability to implement them when running on fumes began to show. I did very poorly in school that year and did everything I could to hide this fact from my parents.

I returned to Virginia for the summer in 1989 and lived at home, worked, and took courses at the community college. I now had to make up for how poorly I had done the previous school year. I was dreading going home, mostly from embarrassment. Relations were a touch strained between Dad and myself. When I first arrived home, he was disappointed, and rightly so, at the situation I had gotten myself into at Coker. He knew I could do better. I had let no one down but myself and was feeling a little worse for the wear due to the trouble I was in, as well as from the effects of living with the waking nightmare of insomnia. *I was feeling a little too sorry for myself to see the lesson that was right in front of my eyes.* After arriving home from work one evening, I found a note from Dad on my bed. It read:

> *If you let continuous regret, remorse, self-persecution keep you from functioning now; if you persist indefinitely in feeling guilty and upset over something that is over, then you are behaving in a non-productive manner. Feeling guilty is not going to make your life any better. You can learn from your mistakes, vow to avoid repeating them, and get on with living NOW.*

Eckhart Tolle hadn't even begun writing about *the now* when Dick Hensley popped out with this little gem! That note meant so much to me that I still have it tucked away in my diary, all these years later.

I made a major attitude adjustment that day and proceeded to have an amazing summer. I reconnected with one of my closest childhood friends, I had a lot of fun at work, and I managed to excel at community college.

# Chapter 7

I RETURNED to Coker in the autumn with a new attitude *and* my own apartment. The previous year of poor performance with a few "misunderstood" campus pranks had meant that the only way I was allowed to return was if I moved off campus and got my act together. I dreaded the thought of being on my own, away from all of my friends. It turned out to be a life-changing experience, introducing me to a whole new level of freedom. I met an entirely different group of friends, locals from the town of Hartsville. I met a family who took me in as one of their own, and had many strange and wonderful adventures with Mr. and Mrs. Cannon and their clan. Mr. Cannon was a lawyer and a good old Southern gentleman. Mrs. Cannon was an absolute gem. She always loved me because I was a fellow Coker-nut, she having gone to school there when it was still an all-girls' school back in the 1940s. I was also forty years younger than her to the day. Even more bizarre, she was from South Carolina and my mother was from Kentucky. Both had lived in Coral Gables, Florida, as teens. Not only did they live in the same town, they also were the same age and went to the same school. Oddly enough, they never met until I was at Coker. It was as if the Cannons had been strategically placed on my path to watch over me.

I will always be grateful to the Cannons for the introduction to a form of health care, which until I had met them, I didn't know

existed. The entire Cannon family were avid believers in chiropractic, and when I injured a shoulder in rowing practice during
my senior year in college, they took me to see their chiropractor,
Dr. Jim. From that day forward, chiropractic became a part of my
health-care regime, particularly following my car accident in the
not too distant future.

I managed to actually study in my junior year and stayed, for
the most part, out of trouble. The summer before my senior year
at Coker, I had remained in Hartsville to work in a local restaurant.
I met a fabulous new friend with whom I would paint the town
red on a regular basis. Maggs was a free spirit, had a very large
personality, and was well traveled for a girl from a small Southern
town. She actually owned a passport! We had a blast together and
went on many adventures that summer. One evening, as I was preparing for another night on the dance floor, Maggs arrived at my
door and announced that she had met the guy I would marry. She
also demanded that I promise to make her a bridesmaid. She had
been out the night before and met a student from the university
in the nearby town of Florence, who was tending bar at a hotel for
the summer. "Change of plans!" she yelled while I finished getting
dressed.

We jumped in her car and drove to Florence to meet my be-
trothed. I had to give it to her: Ben was cute and friendly, he had
short brown hair, the sweetest smile, and a muscular build that
would make any young lady swoon. We immediately discovered
that we shared a common bond. We both loved our food! We
would hit the all-you-can-eat buffets, sop up gravy with a big slice
of bread, and wipe a dinner plate clean. It was love at first bite! He
had a delightful Southern drawl and was always laughing at his own
jokes. I soon learned that he loved the water, loved to ski and fish,
and was very much the outdoorsman.

We began dating *the very next day* after we met, and due to the
fact that I spent most of my time with him rather than out on the

town, I managed to keep myself focused and sailed through the last year of college. I graduated with very high marks and a clear plan to move to Charleston, South Carolina, Ben's home, to start my new life.

*

Getting a job, even with a college degree, isn't as easy as young graduates foolishly think. Ben and I had moved to Charleston with high hopes of landing the perfect job and working for big money. After many interviews in my chosen field, with just as many responses of "Sorry, we need someone with experience," I finally took a job with a franchise company that made signs. I thought I was interviewing to design signs, or at the very least to sell signs, but my new boss had other ideas.

Having a seventh-grade education and more business savvy than most I've met, my boss proceeded to tell me that he felt it was his duty to give me a gift that would last a lifetime. He was going to *allow* me to start at the bottom, and I mean the very bottom: sweeping, mopping, and cleaning up after those who actually made the signs. I was less than excited that, as a college graduate, I would be spending my day cleaning up someone else's mess. Reluctantly, I took the job. I really needed the money, and no one in the fields of communications or graphic design was beating the door down to hire me. This turned out to be one of the best moves I ever made.

Frank and his wife, Teresa, were always kind and respectful as employers, but more than that, they took the time to teach me a few of the key lessons for success. Lesson number one: Learn everyone's job. With that, I swept, I mopped, I made signs, I designed signs, and eventually I sold signs. I might not have been the best at any of these jobs, but I tried really hard. This couple taught me that you don't always have to be the most skilled or the most educated to learn a job and do it well. I also learned that when you accept a position of employment, in order to truly excel, you must treat the place as if it belongs to you. Eventually, a business may belong to you, and you will want your employees to treat it as if their own money, sweat, and tears went into its creation. I have taken that lesson with me always and use the example every time I interview a potential team member for one of my businesses. I am forever grateful to Frank and Teresa for caring enough to *teach* me rather than just give me a job.

*

The summer of 1991 was an unusual one. I was finally out of school, I had moved to a new city, started working in the real world, and I found myself living with my college sweetheart. We had talked of marriage, but Ben wanted to wait until he could save enough money to buy a ring. We couldn't afford to live independently of one another, so we rented a cheap town house. I had to make up stories to my parents that Ben was living at home with his family. I had become quite accustomed to "stretching the truth," as I had strayed, somewhat, from the rules of life that my folks had given me. It wasn't that they wouldn't handle, or discuss rationally, any and all events of my life: it was *my* own issues with letting them down that prevented me from being 100 percent honest about my living arrangements, and my life, as a whole.

The last four years had been far, far away from the fairy tale that I had thought was my birthright. I was learning that life, and its experiences, were forever changing at the drop of a hat, and sometimes these lessons left me feeling pretty good about myself, but more often I was left feeling disillusioned. It's amazing how I felt so sure that I was marriage material at twenty-one and became focused on getting engaged and wearing the ring of my dreams. Talk about pressure on a man—especially when you get someone with my intensity and drive, focusing on the goal of marriage.

I, of course, dropped numerous hints, as to the "perfect" ring.

It had to be this, couldn't be that, and I expected no ordinary proposal—it *had* to be unique. I shudder as I think of it now. Poor Ben was a lamb led to the slaughter: young and naive, with his whole life ahead of him. I know there are no mistakes, and that every circumstance is a learning experience, but this guy had no idea what he was getting himself into, at least not on a conscious level. Ben was such a lovely person, with a great sense of humor and cheerful disposition. He took the news well when I found my own engagement ring in a fabulous consignment shop in downtown Charleston. We could in no way afford to buy it, but the girls in the shop set up a fund, charging me a small fee every time I went to visit my ring. As one could imagine, that fund was considerably large by the time he finally purchased it.

Ben's family lived on the Intracoastal Waterway, just outside Charleston. They had a dock and a boat and a view like something from a picture postcard of the South. For a girl from the foothills of Virginia, this place was heaven. We swam, fished, went crabbing and shrimping, and I quickly became addicted to the heavenly dish of mullet and cheese grits. These people took me in as one of their own, and I genuinely felt that I was part of the family. Oyster roasts and corn boils were common occurrences: great excuses for the friends in the community to get together on a regular basis. I have to say, this really was a happy time in my life, and I treasure the memories of being a part of their world. There were challenges, of course, as their way of life was dramatically different from that to which I was accustomed. Ideas and personalities clashed on the odd occasion, but when the going got tough, and when I needed support, especially in the months that followed my car accident—Ben's family was there for me.

# Chapter 8

FEAR DOES strange things to people. For my boyfriend, the fear of nearly losing me in a car crash, just before Christmas, prompted him to propose, and that very same fear led me to accept. It was New Year's Eve, 1991, when I became engaged to be married to my best friend, Ben. At twenty-one, I had no business entertaining marriage, but at twenty-one, *I knew everything.* No one was going to tell me anything different. And come on, how could I resist the "surprise" of a ring with which I was now on a first-name basis. It had been lovingly wrapped in toilet paper and stuffed in Ben's sock until it was produced at the stroke of midnight, as the band played "Auld Lang Syne" at a Holiday Inn on the James Island beachfront.

I spent the next ten months visiting the wedding band in the jeweler's, since Ben's salary had not yet been able to liberate and reunite it with my engagement ring. Is anyone beginning to see the direction my life's priorities were heading? The ring and the pursuit of marital bliss actually became a distraction from the fact that I had turned my back on the instructions and guidance given to me by my guardians at the time of the accident.

Over the course of the ten-month engagement, there were many times that I second-guessed my decision to marry, but I never chose to figure out what was bothering me about the whole arrangement.

On October 24, 1992, I marched down the aisle, dragging

my unsuspecting new husband into a life that no normal person would find sane or easy. The wedding, itself, was a dream come true. I had always wanted a medieval wedding, a throwback to some past life, no doubt, complete with full regal attire, banners, and a giant chocolate cake in the shape of a castle. There were eighteen in the wedding party, including a ring bearer, dressed as Robin Hood, and two flower girls in cone hats and flowing veils. I had visualized my dream wedding gown and my dear friend, Cookie Washington, took on the task of bringing it to life. It was white velvet with a gold-and-pearl bodice and a giant upright collar that would have fit right in at Buckingham Palace. Yes, I even wore a crown of pearls!

I floated through the church to a song I had chosen when I was only eleven years old. I had seen the movie *Chariots of Fire* and had decided on the spot that the song that had accompanied Scottish sprinter Eric Liddell to Olympic gold victory was to accompany me on my wedding day. I had perfected the march for years in my parents' sitting room, playing the album on high volume, over and over again. I owned this image of my wedding day and had reinforced it with a powerful musical piece that was now manifesting, exactly as planned, eleven years later. I was ready, as I stood at the entrance of the church, to make the walk I had practiced so many times before. At this stage, I believe I had completely blocked out the fact that there was another human being waiting at the end of the aisle, ready to pledge his troth, even though we didn't really know what *troth* meant.

As I took my father's arm, a wave of panic swept over me, just as it had on the way to the church. I didn't want to do this! How could I leave him standing there? What about the three complete sets of china—everyday, good, and holiday—sitting in my parents' basement, along with countless pieces of sterling flatware and stems of crystal goblets? *What had I done?!* How would I return all of the presents? What about the five hundred plus people waiting for me to make my way to the front of the church? What about the roasted pig and the castle cake, waiting at the country club?

All of the money my parents had spent—the bridal showers, the flowers, the food! My father looked at me, as if to say, *you don't have to do this,* but instead of backing out, I continued on, committed to seeing this thing through for as long as it was meant to last. I thought I would be sick! How's that for romantic? I would have dropped dead if someone entered into marriage with me with those thoughts in mind, but that's *exactly* what I did. I laughed nervously, nearly until I shook, the entire way through the ceremony with Ben—my best friend, my greatest challenge, and now my new husband—by my side.

# Chapter 9

MARRIED LIFE was ticking along nicely, at first. When supernatural events would occur, Ben actually handled them quite well in the beginning. One rainy afternoon during the winter of 1993, I was at home, sitting on my bed, reading a book. This book had been recommended to me by a friend with whom I had felt comfortable enough to share part of my accident experience a few months earlier. The reason she had given this particular paperback to me was because it told the story of a woman who had also experienced a brush with death, revealing some memories that were very similar to my own.

The distraction of planning a wedding and actually getting married had diverted my attention from the inevitable—*the reality that I must face up to the information I received at the time of my journey beyond life in this world.* I knew that in doing this, it would change the entire way in which I was to live. I was also aware that opening up to the enormity of what I had discovered would not only transform the course of my life, but the key people in it, as well. Honestly, I knew that delving into this issue would be the beginning of the end of my relationship with my new husband. Deep down, I had known this all along but just hadn't developed the maturity, *or the guts,* to face it.

The clock said 4:03 p.m. It was a rainy winter afternoon. The only way I can describe what happened next was as if a protective circle of light had been placed around me. I felt perfectly at peace within this bubble of bliss. With a whoosh and that strange but memorable buzzing noise that had accompanied me during my death, I was transported back to the incredible surroundings of the other world I had visited during my car crash. Lights, colors, and the Music of the Spheres; all sensations seemed to envelop me, filling me with an indescribable joy. This time, I was *surrounded* by "old friends," spiritual companions, instead of only the two who had greeted me as I transitioned from this world to theirs. It looked like the tornado scene from *The Wizard of Oz*, as information in the form of thoughts, words, symbols, and images began flying right through me—I was no longer a solid substance.

Suddenly, I found myself filled with a buzzing sensation, similar to the vibration I feel each night before falling asleep, only dramatically more intense. All I knew was that the influx of information that I had been given before, but chose to ignore, was now becoming part of me, integrating and vibrating within my being, along with the consciousness that sometime in my near future, I would become enlightened enough to use it. Once again, I remembered why I had chosen this life and its challenges. I clearly remembered myself in Spirit, making the decision to return to this life to serve. All lifetimes were clear, particularly the thread of lives that revolved around safe-housing a group of symbols from a time long forgotten. I wasn't sure what they meant, but knew with every fiber of my being that someday I would. I was filled with a deep understanding of what it means to become human and how the Universe and its vast array of spiritual beings are always present, supporting and guiding our every move. The pain and suffering, as well as the joy and elation, which are part of the human condition, once again made perfect sense. Our capacity to evolve, even in one lifetime, to reconnect with the ability to see ourselves as pure energy, manifesting, creating, and healing ourselves, was so evident that I felt entirely foolish for having forgotten.

*I could no longer resist my destiny.* Lovingly, but firmly, it was made crystal clear that I was to embark on my life's work— NOW—fulfilling the contract I had agreed upon before entering this incarnation. It was as if my car crash had only been preparation for this day: my true life after death.

Now it all made so much sense; a second look beyond the veil and the privilege of remembering it. My spiritual Guardians made certain that this experience was to stick with me. I had spent too long, nearly two years, turning a blind eye to the events of my previous voyage home. This time, there was no escaping it. My perception had just been altered—*again*. My memory was refreshed as to why my thinking, my actions, and my life *must* change. I was being given the formula that would make the work that I was to do in the future effectively powerful and beneficial to those in need.

Just because we have the knowledge to transform our lives does not mean that we always choose to use it. We can literally "see the light," yet make the choice to remain in the dark. Changing our perceptions and actually doing the work to integrate those new concepts is far more painful than the mediocrity that binds us. This time, I *promised* to embrace what lay ahead.

I knew this would not be the last time I would hear from my Guides. I now accepted the help that had always been readily available, and I vowed to listen intently from that day forward. Armed with wonder, compassion, and a direct line of communication with Spirit, I felt the burning desire to use the new gifts that had just been bestowed on me. A deal was made: If I looked within, embracing the lessons that every aspect of my personality had to teach me, my abilities to assist the healing process in others would increase. I was to look out for signposts and messengers, taking heed of their direction without fail. Once again, I had been *promised* to be guided in the direction that would ultimately lead me to my life's purpose . . . and I *promised* to follow.

Back on the bed again, I looked over at the clock, and exactly one minute had passed. *One minute!* Unsure of what to do next, I rang my mother and told her what had just happened. Rather than try to explain it away as anything but a Divine moment, Mom comforted and reassured me that this was all good—all part of God's plan. She knew that I had been blessed with a very special gift. Indeed, I had, and it was having her as a mother. Faith, not the need for proof, has always guided her life, and this has been her greatest gift to me. We talked for several hours that afternoon and it was during this conversation that I finally revealed all that had happened during my car accident in December of 1991. My mother and I have always had a special bond, but on this day, she became my closest and most trusted confidant, as she expressed a depth of belief and understanding far beyond my wildest expectations.

My husband came home that evening, and he could tell by the look on my face that something monumental had taken place that day. While he didn't really understand what had happened, he supported the possibility that something extraordinary was at hand. I was very concerned that he would get spooked, or think that I had turned into some sort of religious fanatic. I had given him a very watered-down version of my experiences over the last few years, but I could no longer hold it all in and be true to myself. The next few days were difficult, to say the least. I began to doubt my experience, even making excuses as to why something like this could happen to me. Who was I to think I could have possibly left this Earth, returning to the spiritual realm *again*, this time without the trauma of accident or illness?

Slowly, but surely, I made peace with those feelings, knowing that they, too, had something to offer. I regained the sense that life was changing for me in a way that would reveal itself, all in due time. I knew that I was "shifting" when my mother rang the following day to tell me that a very dear family friend had passed away the day before. Although I was already aware of his passing before she uttered the words, I dealt with this news in a much different manner than I would have in the past, grieving my own loss as opposed to celebrating what was in store for whoever had just died. I became wildly excited, because I knew exactly what awaited him, and for the first time, I attached no sadness or fear to the news of a loved one's crossing.

＊

To look at me now, one would never suspect that I had been in a very serious car accident all those years ago. Apart from a quirky head tilt and a posture very unbecoming to a chiropractor, I appear unscathed on the outside. The inside, however, is a different story. I damaged the retina in my left eye, developed a severe hearing loss in my left ear, and sustained quite serious spinal trauma, including a break in the neck, resulting in very painful symptoms that I will deal with for the rest of my life. After my accident, I began to regularly see Dr. Ross, a chiropractor on John's Island, who came highly recommended by the locals. My spine had been bashed into the shape of the letter C, and the resulting health problems were immense.

I quickly learned that chiropractic is based on the premise that the health and balance of the body depends on a nervous system that is free of interference. This interference occurs when physical, chemical, or emotional stresses cause the vertebrae of the spine to move slightly out of position or to subluxate, resulting in a decrease in normal function within the body's many delicate systems. I had become a walking subluxation, both physically and mentally, with a list of ailments too long for this book, and too many for a girl of twenty-two.

My chiropractor embarked on the long and difficult task of assisting my body to heal. He gave me a gift that would prove to be just as important as each life-enhancing adjustment of my spine. Interestingly, during a visit from my grandfather, in spirit, I was told that in order to know the inner workings of the human body, as well as the dynamic between the emotional, physical, and spiritual state, I would become a chiropractor. Not a medical doctor, as he had been, but a chiropractor. He stressed the importance of how the vitalistic approach to the human form would be crucial as I progressed with my extrasensory abilities. The passion with which Dr. Ross practiced led him to educate me every step of the way, so much so that I woke up one morning, and in my mind I already was a chiropractor. After just having finished four years of college, I wasn't sure how receptive my husband, or my family, would be to the idea of another five years in school, along with over one hundred thousand dollars of investment in this new future.

*

Not long after my "reawakening" spiritual experience and the visit from my grandfather declaring that I would become a chiropractor, I was out making sales calls for the sign company. I stopped to have lunch in a restaurant close to home, beautifully situated on one of the local creeks. I had been there for supper a few times, but never before had eaten there at lunchtime. I sat at a table on my own and contemplated what I would do. Was this just a passing fancy, or was I ready to commit all of my time and energy, not to mention the finances, to becoming a doctor of chiropractic? Just then, I looked over at a man sitting a few tables away from me. He was fiddling with a contraption that had an outline of a human form, painted on wood, with little lightbulbs strategically placed on different points in the body.

Curiosity got the better of me, so I went over to the man and asked him about the device. In a thick New York accent, he proceeded to introduce himself and show me the tool he had invented to educate his patients about the impact that interference within the spine had on the function of the systems of the body. I nearly fell over! This man was a chiropractor from New York, who had stopped in for a seafood lunch, taking a break from his long drive home from Florida. He spoke to me about his many rewarding years as a chiropractor with such conviction and passion that I walked out of the restaurant and enrolled in the local technical college for the following semester, in order to get the prerequisite courses necessary for chiropractic school.

Something magical happened that day. It was well after lunchtime when this man and I both landed in the same restaurant. The tables were all empty, except for the two of us and a few stragglers at the bar. Funny, that he would have brought this box, a prototype that he had been working on, to lunch. Why that day and why at that time?

Most people bring a book or the newspaper when they are dining alone. I am sure that our paths were meant to cross, to solidify my decision to take my life onward and upward to a new career and, more importantly, to a life of service. Even better, heaven had just made good on its promise of sending messengers to guide me on my way.

The excitement and buzz of making a life-changing decision quickly succumbed to reality. I will never forget the moment of silence when I rang my parents to tell them the big news. In fairness to them, those poor souls never knew what was going to come out of my mouth each time I phoned home. So the pregnant pause before "Are you sure?" was a reasonable response, indeed. My prerequisite courses would take nearly two and a half years to complete, as I had little or none of the science subjects necessary to enter the world of health care. I look back at this time and can see the grand plan as it unfolded, giving me the tools I would need to assimilate the information and to create the foundation I was to have before and during chiropractic school.

## Chapter 10

SYNCHRONOUS EVENTS were now occurring on a regular basis. Someone or something was definitely attempting to get my attention. Things began to happen so frequently that I often wondered if it was my active imagination, or if I was somehow *willing* these encounters to take place. Doubt slowly turned to wonder, quickly turning to gratitude, as these small miracles began to reshape my very perspective of the world.

I walked into a grocery store one day, stopping dead in my tracks, as an old man approached me with a very peculiar yet somehow familiar glint in his eye. He gently took my arm, pulling me close as he whispered in my ear, "I know who you are."

I stepped back. He seemed to look through me as he winked.

"You've been 'there' and back, *haven't you*? Don't worry; you'll soon be able to recognize them, too. You'll know by the glow, little lady."

He chuckled and walked on, leaving me absolutely flabbergasted, but strangely comforted. I had just received a message that the cascade of paranormal events now going on in my life *was* actually happening. No wishing, no willing, no flights of fancy, imagination, or delusions. He was yet another messenger of reassurance, just as promised, and he was certainly not to be my last.

*

Several months after my wedding, I was in the shower one morning, when I came across a lump in my breast. It was quite by accident that I happened to feel it at all, discovering it while doing a routine wash, not self-examination. I was only in my early twenties and the concept of breast cancer wasn't a part of my reality. Several trips to the doctor and a mammogram later, it was decided that I had a tumor that would have to be removed. Now, for the average pseudo-hypochondriac, this would have been earth-shattering news. For me, something happened that day. I went from someone who had practiced using illness for personal attention, be it to escape stressful situations or to gain sympathy, to someone committed to healing herself. I knew I wasn't going to die. I had known all of my life how and when that would happen and it wasn't like this. Deep down, I knew that my body was trying to tell me what my mind had known from day one. I had married my best friend, hoping against hope that I could override the feeling that I knew this would never last. My body knew better. . . .

Overnight, I became obsessed with alternative healing, deciding that I would find some way to take care of things myself. I was beginning to focus on the possibilities, not the drama, of what this illness had to offer. This was a definite change from my pre-accident personality. For the very first time in my life, the concept of self-created illness was becoming my new perception of reality. Rather than scaring me to death, this new challenge *awakened me to life.*

Ben was working for the Department of Agriculture, tending to strange-looking plants and supersized veggies; the birthplace of GMOs. It was an interesting enough job for the time being, but not what he aspired to do permanently, thank God. For Ben, that was the great unknown. It was a quality that used to really annoy me, no goals or plans, no vision. *Or so I thought.* In my naiveté, I never appreciated that he was simply doing something that would take me years to comprehend. *He was living in the present.* Enjoying being a twenty-two-year-old newlywed who spent his days off waterskiing or fishing, not struggling with the burden of how he was going to save the world or amass his fortune. He didn't overthink or stress himself out. He simply lived for the moment. Really, what better time to do that? There were absolutely no other commitments, like children, a mortgage, or a high-pressure job. It was exactly the time to perfect the skill of *living in the Now*. What a wonderful and completely unappreciated ability he had. As for me, he was exactly where he needed to be at precisely the right time, especially for the next challenge I would face in learning about the healing process.

I was visiting Ben one day for lunch, as I often did, when I had the good fortune to meet one of the scientists who worked with my husband at the facility. He had a wonderful burr, Dutch, I think, and it was enough to make me listen to him, no matter what he had to say! But lucky for me, his curious accent told a story that was well worth my time and attention. This man had come across some information within the department about a concoction made of four fairly common herbs, alleged to have amazing results with cancer. *Coincidentally*, we got into a discussion about this "cancer tea." He had just returned from overseas where he had successfully used the potion on his father.

A most interesting topic for him to casually bring up to a girl just diagnosed with a breast tumor. Of course I wanted to know how I could get my hands on the stuff. He said it wasn't quite as easy as running down to the local supermarket and buying it off the shelf. The four herbs had to be steeped in stainless steel for fifteen hours, and *nothing* but stainless steel could touch them in the process. The mixture had to be bottled in dark glass and used immediately, as it had no preservatives. It was only beneficial when fresh and that was roughly five to seven days.

My first question was how come everyone didn't know about this? If it was so successful, why wasn't the government using this to treat the multitude of cancer patients in America? He chuckled at my bewilderment. My age and lack of life experience had never led me to question the motives of the government and the power of the almighty dollar. I was shocked as he proceeded to explain that cancer was an enormous moneymaker, and it would not be in the interest of the pharmaceutical companies or their investors to *ever* find a proper cure for the disease. I was never one for conspiracy theories, but I was captivated by the concepts and all that this doctor had to say.

It was much later before I fully grasped the idea that people were responsible for their own illnesses. Therefore, people must also be responsible for isolating the causes, making peace with them, then resolving the physical manifestations of these issues. *On this day, I was simply a girl with a malignancy in her breast, looking for a miracle. This guy had just answered my prayers.*

I was told that there was a shop in downtown Charleston that sold the herbs necessary for the tea. I went straight down that afternoon and was greeted at the door by the cheeriest, most approachable Jamaican guy. His charismatic nature made me temporarily forget why I was actually there, as he bounced his way through the shop. Everything was "Irie" and "No worries, mon." He put me instantly at ease. I was beginning to wonder just what sort of "herb" this scientist had sent me to get!

When I explained my story, the guy chuckled and said, "Relax, no worries, mon, we have de 'erbs for de cancer tea. You should see what it does for de AIDS, mon."

"AIDS?! Did he just say AIDS?!"

My heart began to pound at the sound of it. My mind shot instantaneously back to the past, the rape, and for a moment, I experienced a terror that I *thought* had been completely put to rest.

He went on to explain that the combination of these herbs was able to "break down de badness, mon." I have come to understand, years later, that the compound created by these herbs is able to somehow crack and disintegrate the outer shell that surrounds the cancerous cell, much like chemotherapy and radiation do, only without harming any healthy cells in the process. The body would then gobble up the weakened cell, essentially ridding itself of the cancer.

With bags of herbs in hand, a car full of stainless-steel utensils, and brown glass bottles, I set off home to start preparations. I looked like a witch toiling over her cauldron for the rest of the night. The next morning, I was a little more than nervous before taking the first swallow of my creation. In true chivalrous fashion, Ben decided that he would drink the concoction as well, for moral support. We hammered back the strange brew and wondered if we were going to feel anything straightaway. It wasn't until that night that the fun began.

What the tea actually does is take the body through an intensely rapid detoxification. The system goes from acidic to alkaline— literally starving the cancerous cells—creating all sorts of interesting reactions! I must have peed fifty times that first day. I can't remember which one of us actually wet the bed that night, *but one of us did*. The dreams were vivid and frequent. We sweated; oh, how we sweated! We spewed up mucus, and worst of all, we stank to high heaven! Our breath and our body odor were embarrassing, but we figured that something good must be happening—and sure enough, it was. Three weeks later, I went for my pre-op checkup. My four-centimeter lump was nowhere to be seen.

"Impossible," the doctor huffed.

After a few more attempts to locate the tumor, including a mammogram, he decided that maybe they would do a little exploratory surgery, *just to be sure*. I attempted to tell him about the tea, but his hand went up and I was silenced before I could even finish my sentence. I smiled, shook that same hand, and bade him good day. That was the last I ever saw of him.

I have often wondered, over the years, how I managed to rid myself of this disease without the working knowledge of health and healing that I have today. I assist sick people every day, pinpointing the frequency and location where they left part of themselves behind to fester in grief, bitterness, or disappointment. Discovering that point in time and space, releasing the part of the spirit that has been held hostage there, is an integral part of the healing process. How is it that I managed to heal myself without knowing this?

I am now aware that just as there are many roads to heaven, *there are just as many ways to heal.* It all depends on the occasion, and the circumstances, and most importantly, *where* the person is on their journey. Spirit would never leave us without the means to repair ourselves, if that's what we truly wish to achieve. While I didn't have the same understanding I have today, I had something equally as powerful. I had the *time,* and the *energy,* as well as the *love, support,* and *undivided attention* of my husband. We laughed and loved our way through this challenge, which in the end seemed more like an adventure as opposed to a battle. In our ignorance to the complexity of healing the body, we completely surrendered and let nature take its course. It was an invaluable lesson for us both, and it ultimately led us toward our next destination.

# Chapter 11

A FRIEND had told me about how great kung fu was for flexibility, strength, and concentration. Although it had been many months since the accident, I still walked like a rusty robot and looked like an old lady of ninety when I bent over and tried to straighten up again.

"Are you kidding?" I sneered. "I can barely tie my own shoes and you want me to break concrete blocks with my forehead?"

I would soon find out that I couldn't have been more wrong, and my complete ignorance as to the basic premise of kung fu was telling on me. I went to a dojo not far from where we lived and met its most remarkable owner. Apart from being an absolutely fine-looking being, he was interesting; incredibly knowledgeable about all things alternative, he was very serious about his martial arts.

From the time of the accident, I had struggled with a complete lack of mobility and flexibility in every square inch of my body. And so, over a bright green vitamin-enhanced health shake, my friend and I discussed my story and what it was I wanted to accomplish with my body. After listening patiently to what, by now, was a fairly well-rehearsed epic saga, he gently let me know that there was no way he would allow me to join his kung fu class without first completing a year of Tai Chi.

"Tai what?" I said, showing just what a novice I really was.

"Tai Chi," he replied, enduring my complete ignorance about his passion.

"Is that some kind of supplement?" I asked.

He laughed and began to explain to me why Tai Chi would be so important in re-centering my body. I had no idea that it was my mind that he was really planning to reshape. The body changes would simply be a pleasant side effect.

The time spent in that little dojo over the next year or two was responsible for changing the way I would create my future. I learned the art of meditation and eventually went from the immature girl who giggled and disrupted the rest of the class to using the time to switch off and center myself. Not only did I have the pleasure of knowing this man, and his amazing wife and family, but I gained the knowledge he shared so freely with both Ben and myself. He fast-tracked us through what must have taken him a lifetime to acquire. I was hungry for more, and he was there to feed my mind, body, and soul.

I am so grateful for the day he handed me a copy of Dan Millman's classic book, *Way of the Peaceful Warrior*. It was a class requirement and my first formal introduction to metaphysical literature. I devoured the book in one day and, on my teacher's recommendation, began to read everything I could get my hands on in this field. My mind was expanding at an exponential rate, and I was truly in my element. Ben was attending the classes when he could and was interested enough in the subject matter, but I was already beginning to notice the difference between my passion and his interest.

In hindsight, I will admit that my passion was probably more like obsession, as I was trying to bring all of the pieces together. I was on a mission to carry out what my Spirit Guides had rolled out before me. This time in my life was dedicated to gathering educational tools, as well as momentum, for what was to come next.

*

Though it seemed like an eternity, I finally completed the pre-requisite subjects necessary to enter chiropractic school. I had made it through Organic Chemistry and Physics by the proverbial skin of my teeth. An incredible feat for a right-brained, esoteric thinker, who was incapable of balancing her own checkbook! On October 1, 1994, it was time for Ben and me to leave the comfort and safety of the lowlands of Charleston and make the move to the hills in the northwest of South Carolina. I would say that Ben never thought in a million years that he would land in Spartan-burg, so far removed from his coastal home. He was a good sport about it and held fast to the hope that when my schooling was over, we'd be back in good ol' Charleston again.

*Man plans, God laughs.*

# Chapter 12

IN JANUARY of 1995, I walked into Sherman College of Straight Chiropractic, wearing a bright-pink top, pink leggings, pink cowboy boots, and big pink dangly earrings. With a personality as loud as my outfit, I was determined to make a lasting impression on my teachers and fellow students. My big day had finally arrived.

Sherman College was a fascinating place, with a history littered with struggle and strife. It was the kind of environment that attracted a very unique selection of people. Most of the scholars were mature students, people who had experienced a life change because of chiropractic, choosing to drop everything to return to school and study their newfound passion. There were those who had rid themselves of lifelong ailments, like migraines or allergies, others with miraculous recovery stories from serious injuries, and then there was me: the girl who had been told to attend chiropractic school over medical school by her grandfather, a surgeon who just happened to be dead.

Sherman was the underdog of the chiropractic schools due to its philosophy that chiropractic should not be mixed with any other type of therapy, such as physiotherapy or massage, for example. The education of the patient, and the assessment and adjustment of the vertebrae of the spine, if necessary, is the principal contribution to a person's health made by a chiropractor. While other types of therapy are valuable, the "straight" chiropractic philosophy supports the premise that these adjunct treatments should be performed by therapists who have specialized in those therapies. At the time I joined the school, graduates were only allowed to practice in fourteen states, due to legalities surrounding the school's unwillingness to conform or compromise its mission statement. The people who chose to attend this school were there because they wanted the real deal—pure, unadulterated, spine-tingling chiropractic education, unaltered or watered down by other forms of health care The fact that the students had no idea of the future or their ability to practice didn't seem to matter. These were people with conviction, ideas, and lifestyles that were completely foreign to me. They were fueled by passion, eager to serve, and I fit right in.

There were philosophers, medical and philosophical doctors, vegetarians, gay couples, married and single parents. There were those who had obviously come down from the mother ship to study, along with the children of movie stars, famous authors, and representatives of every religious and political organization under the sun. The students were from all over the country and around the world. I was absolutely in my element, and I thought I would burst with delight in this rich environment of total diversity. I was voted in as class president the first day of school—*I'm sure it was the hot-pink outfit.* From there, I aspired to be president of the student body as soon as the position became available. As far as I was concerned, heaven was on top of a rolling, green hill, at a school called Sherman, in the town of Spartanburg, South Carolina.

A few days after school began, Ben and I were walking through the front door of the school when we ran into the school's president and founder. Dr. Thom Gelardi was an amazing personality. A man of vision and unwavering faith when it came to teaching the philosophy of chiropractic, he had a great talent of interjecting "food for thought" into any conversation. On this particular morning, he chose to tell us that many people came to Sherman single and left married, and just as many people came to Sherman married, and left single *or* with a new partner. We laughed nervously and walked away hand in hand. I remember Ben saying that *we* were different, and that would *never* happen to us.

*

Chiropractic philosophy started every morning at 7:30 a.m. sharp (I think I would have loved it an awful lot more if it had started at 9:30 sharp). It was a great way to wake up the mind on a good morning, and the cruelest of punishments after a late night. The walls were painted with things like A=A and AS ABOVE SO BELOW AS WITHIN SO WITHOUT. It was a suitable atmosphere for absorbing Ayn Rand's mind-bending book, *The Fountainhead*. The class was *all* about committing things to memory, like the basic premise of chiropractic, the exact definition of a subluxation, and the difference between mechanistic thinking and a vitalistic approach to life and health. I was seeing the world in a whole different light, and this new way of thinking made absolute sense to me.

I began to see the human form as an incredible vehicle through which to experience life, as opposed to a bag of protoplasm that should only be repaired when broken down. I had a newfound respect for my body and all that it was capable of, if given the chance to function free of interference. The impact of stress—be it chemical, physical, or emotional, was being presented in a tangible way. It changed the way I was to think about life and health forever. I could now understand why I had been guided to this profession by my own DC as well as my grandfather. As a doctor of chiropractic, I would be able to contribute to people's lives in such a way that it would empower them with the ability to live at their personal best, whatever that meant for the individual.

I was also learning a new language. This developed my skill to communicate with an infectious enthusiasm that got people all fired up about their own journeys through life. I was experiencing the *magic* of being human and the gift of our physical structure. I was moving from a body that had discovered its spirit to a spirit embracing the potential of its body. It is the latter of the two that has proven to be the most incredible aspect of my work as a healer. Spirit takes on the confines of physical form for growth and understanding. A long time ago, a much better author than me simply stated: *"Know thyself."*

My class was small, less than twenty students, so we got to know each other very quickly and became a close-knit family. It's hard not to know your neighbor when inevitably you will bare your back on a regular basis in order to learn how to palpate, or feel, the spine. We all got along well, and it didn't take long for us to know who the real academics, the slackers, and the class clowns were going to be. I'll let you guess which role I easily adopted.

The environment was so different than when I had been in college at the age of eighteen. My goals were more focused: I was now married, and *I* was footing the bill! The tendency to waste time, or not turn up for class, was much less of an issue than it had been in 1987. I did, however, promptly become the one who was sent to negotiate with the teachers for extra time before an exam or any other general requests from my classmates. Usually, I was very persuasive and ultimately successful. I took my work seriously, but I was also having more fun than I had ever had in my life. I truly loved being a student again and was absorbing the experience with every ounce of my being.

During this time, I developed a wonderful friendship with one of the most genuine people I have ever met, a former postal worker named Dan. He and his wife, and their two daughters, had moved from Missouri for Dan to pursue his dream of becoming a doctor of chiropractic. Dan was in his early forties at the time, but by no means was he the oldest student at the school. We had a few in their fifties and sixties as well. Dan was always smiling, had big dimples, and he and I were inseparable. I loved him dearly, I loved his family, and we became the best of friends throughout our entire time at Sherman. Dan was the first person I shared my unusual life story with, in its entirety, without being prompted to by Spirit. I trusted him implicitly.

Dan became my confidant. He also was a great man to keep me in check. He would get excited right along with me, as each new adventure unfolded, but was rock steady, always helping me to *keep it real*. Because of Dan's friendship I was able to keep all of the wild and wonderful things that were happening in perspective, without allowing my ego to take over, potentially ruining the genuine nature in which these events actually occurred. Dan was forever looking after me. There were many days when he bought my lunch knowing I really couldn't afford it, and every day he kept me filled with iced tea and lemonade. We sat next to each other in nearly every class. How he managed to get the grades he did was remarkable. I never shut up. Not before class, especially not during class, and certainly not after class, but he took me in his stride and was genuinely a loyal friend, or perhaps "guardian" would actually be more appropriate

*

In our second quarter of school, we moved from the rigor of Philosophy 101 into the more high-spirited classroom of Dr. David Koch. Dr. Koch brought philosophy to a new level for me, and I'm sure for the rest of my classmates. The discussions were lively, the information immense, and he was extremely easy to distract from the day's agenda, if you got him on a subject that ignited his passion. I adored this class. I thought the world of Dr. Koch as a teacher, and later as a friend. I think he got a kick out of my get-up-and-go attitude, and he was a very willing victim of my distractions, because he ultimately knew that we would learn something powerful, no matter what topic of discussion he was thrown into.

One day, we were all sitting in Dr. Koch's class, listening to him tell an amazing story of an old chiropractor he had known many years earlier. He explained that this old doc seemed to be able to run his hand up the back of a patient without touching him/her and know what was wrong. "You know," he said, "he was just sort of special. Kind of like those people who can see light around other people."

I didn't hear another word of the lecture because I was so utterly perplexed by what he had just said. I waited until the end of the class, and I went to speak to Dr. Koch with Dan by my side.

"Yes, Mary Helen, I saw by your face that I've puzzled you in some way?"

I asked him to repeat the bit about the old doc being special like the people that saw light.

"You know," he replied. "Like people who can see auras."

Now I was really confused. I had heard of an aura before but generally thought that term was reserved for those schoolmates who ate nothing but green, chanted mantras, and had direct contact with their stellar origins. Dr. Koch asked me if I was one of those people.

"Of course not!" I snapped back. "But why did you say 'like the people who can see light'?"

Now he was really amused. "But, Mary Helen, that's what auras are!"

Dan was having a fit watching me squirm! Dr. Koch suggested that we pop in to see him for a few minutes between classes.

When we got to his office, there he sat behind the desk, smiling out at me like a Cheshire cat. He, too, was enjoying the opportunity to see me so uneasy! Dan and I stood at the door, and he said, "Now, talk to me."

In a voice that was much meeker than either Dan or Dr. Koch had ever heard from my boisterous mouth, I asked him if he was trying to tell me that everyone doesn't see light around everyone else. Dr. Koch had this amazing laugh; nothing was sweeter than when he cracked himself up and started to chortle. He was laughing like this now, and his chuckle turned into a big smile when he realized what was going on.

"Mary Helen, how old are you?" he asked.

"Twenty-six," I replied.

"Are you telling me that you see auras, and in twenty-six years have never discussed this with anyone?"

Well, that was *exactly* what I was trying to tell him. I was now freaking out as my mind retreated to my childhood, when I used to love gazing out the car window, looking at the trees and plant life as we drove along. I was now being told that the beautiful glow that I saw from the vegetation wasn't something that everyone could see. Honestly, I was never aware that the ability to see fluid colors surrounding every living thing was not a normal part of life for most. I never paid a lot of attention to it, unless I saw something that really intrigued me, or on the flip side, made me feel uneasy. I would lie in bed as a child, avoiding the sandman, entertaining myself by putting my two index fingers together, and then slowly pulling them apart, watching the trail of color and sparks in between them. I now found myself trying to come up with a reasonable explanation as to how I had made it to adulthood without discovering the uniqueness of this gift.

"Dan, what color is the shirt that Dr. Koch is wearing?" I stammered, attempting to make sense of it all.

"It's white with stripes."

"Now, that's what I see, too," I said. "Why on earth would I discuss with Dan, or anyone else for that matter, what color your shirt is, if I assume that he is seeing the same thing as me? I imagine that when he walks outside, he is seeing the same green grass and the same blue sky that I see. I can honestly say that I have never thought twice about the glow, or the colorful lights, because I thought we all saw them!"

Dan stood there, mouth agape, and Dr. Koch was absolutely

delighted to have been a part of this discovery. Neither was able to argue the point, and I think even if they could have, they knew that I had enough to chew on for one afternoon. My mind was blown! This was to be the beginning of a very exciting relationship, full of great stories, tremendous support, and the joy of a teacher watching his student blossom, bathed in the light of his wisdom. It was about understanding, and the constant challenge to shift the old paradigm and embrace the endless possibilities that lay ahead.

I'm not so sure Dan was buying the whole aura thing; he never said so, but I think it was all a bit much for him to digest. I, on the other hand, was now plagued with the fact that something that had been a normal part of my entire life had now been pointed out as unusual. Up until that time, the lights and colors had always seemed to blend into their surroundings. Now they seemed to be on high voltage, staring me in the face everywhere I turned. I was surrounded by auras, wondering why in the world everyone couldn't see them.

Something extraordinary was beginning to happen, and I could see it coming. My visions were becoming crystal clear, and I had begun to develop a strange tingling sensation in my hands when I touched people. A few weeks after our conversation with Dr. Koch, Dan and I were sitting in the back of a classroom that was used for reading X-rays. The teacher was at the front of the class, when all of a sudden, I was certain beyond a shadow of a doubt that I could help Dan see an aura. I put my hand on his and felt that funny tingling sensation. I told him to look to his right and tell me what he could see.

"Holy smokes!" he yelled out, loud enough to stop the lecture.

We went into hysterics because in an instant, after forty-two years of never seeing "the light," he saw it. Dan was amazed; however, he was also perfectly content to leave the *weird* stuff to me.

# Chapter 13

AFTER TWO terms of retraining the muscles in our upper torsos and arms, using strange exercises that looked like something out of a cheesy aerobics video, we began to learn the art of palpation. This started with taking a hair from the head and placing it between the pages of a phone book, then tracing it with the fingertips. We were developing the sensitivity to feel what bones and muscles were doing in and around the spine, with the goal that by graduation, we could feel a "disturbance in the force" through a concrete block!

There was a day in palpation class that had started out like any other, as we moved from person to person, feeling as many spines as we could get our hands on. I was working on the neck of a girl in the class called Lisa. She was all choked up with a summer flu that had her temperature up, her nose running, and her two eyes ready to fall out of her head. It was the first week back to school, and she didn't want to take time off so soon in the term, as we were only allowed a limited number of days off.

I stood behind Lisa, the same as I had with everyone else that morning, when suddenly I noticed something very peculiar. The heat coming from her back was literally burning my stomach.

*That's a wicked fever*, I thought to myself, until I realized that this was no ordinary body heat. I looked around to see if anyone was watching. My left hand had begun to get that weird tingling sensation, so I slipped it down to the middle of her back and held it about two or three inches away from her.

All of a sudden, my hand began to shake. Recognizing that something out of the ordinary was happening, Lisa kept looking forward but whispered, "It feels like something is shooting through my body."

I asked if she was okay, because I had absolutely no idea what was happening to either of us. She told me not to move, just go with it. The rest of the class seemed to carry on around us as if we weren't even in the same room. After two minutes that seemed like two years, my hand stopped shaking, but my heart continued to thump wildly. Lisa turned around and was drenched with sweat. She had a strange look on her face, but the sparkle was back in her eyes. *Look at me!*

I knew what she was about to say. Her fever had gone, her throat was no longer sore, she had no red eyes . . . no nothing. Speechless, I sat on the chiropractic bench beside her, trying to absorb what had just happened. We decided to keep this one to ourselves, as neither of us really knew what had just happened. Her symptoms didn't return, and I spent the weekend trying to accept the fact that the heavens were continuing to make good on their promise. I had been told in great detail by my friends in Spirit about how this energy would course through my body when the time was right. It looked as if that time had arrived.

Lisa had, in fact, felt so well that she spent the weekend working on her house. She hobbled through the door on Monday morning, after badly damaging her knee while doing some DIY. It was red, swollen, and very painful, causing her to walk with a considerable limp. She pulled me aside and asked if I would try "it" on her knee. I told her I didn't know what "it" was, but I would sure give it a try! Could I actually conjure this energy on demand?

That day after school Lisa, Dan, and I met in the first-aid closet. It was literally a tiny, converted storage closet with a massage table covered with a starched white sheet, boxes of bandages, and gauze on the shelves and it smelled of antiseptic. I propped Lisa's leg on mine, and put my hands around her knee. This time I felt no heat, only an intense tingling sensation as I moved my hands around her leg. When my left hand went under her knee, we watched, wide-eyed, as her muscles began to twitch and jump. We heard a loud pop, which I also felt in my hand, and I wasn't even touching her at all! Lisa stood up.

"What pain?" she laughed.

She walked with a completely normal stride out the door and down the hallway. Dan and I were giddy and marveled at what had just taken place.

Overnight, I had seemingly developed this ability to place my hands on someone or in their "energy field" and facilitate changes. I didn't and still don't think I personally healed them because I was quite aware, and had been from day one, that this was not about me. To be perfectly honest, I think that the Universe was trying to show me how I could serve, if I was willing. It seemed a natural progression, and although I didn't yet own the language to adequately explain what was happening, after a lifetime of dreams, "imaginary" friends, visions, and several trips beyond the veil, facilitating the healing process was becoming my new norm. I was well aware that I was being groomed for something other than chiropractic and my Guides had told me that this and more would manifest. But the preparations for the next leg of my journey were to first take place within the confines of my formal education.

\*

Around the same time that these healing sessions were taking place on the sly, something on a much larger scale was happening in the constant drama surrounding Sherman College. The school had been fighting an uphill battle for over twenty-three years, for the right to be accredited by a particular scholastic agency without compromising its mission statement. Recognition by an agency should've had nothing to do with the school's mission statement at all, other than the fact that it was providing a safe and sound education within the limits of the law. It was, after all, the only school in the world that offered a doctorate in chiropractic based solely on an all-chiropractic education. Many wonderful people had fought over the years to ensure the right of the school to teach the art, science, and philosophy of chiropractic without diluting the education with course work that had nothing to do with the basic premise of the profession. There were other schools to attend if a student wished to learn other modalities in addition to chiropractic, and Sherman constantly fought for the right to adhere to the origins of the profession. With all of the ridiculous politics involved, there were several times when Sherman was on the brink of closing its doors. Sherman's founders respected the rights of the other schools to educate in the manner in which they chose and all that they asked in return was to be allowed to teach a curriculum based on chiropractic alone. Ever-increasing government rules and regulations, especially concerning standardized testing, made this seemingly simple goal nearly impossible. In January of 1995, we got the news that Sherman would be accredited by a particular agency, without having to make any major changes to the curriculum. This was a tremendous accomplishment for the school, and it looked as if decades of obstacles had finally been overcome. Unfortunately, a court order, later filed by our previous accrediting agency, almost brought us to our knees again. The court order would mean that students would be unable to receive federal funding for a period of two years. I could probably count on one hand the number of students who were not dependent on federal funding. This would surely be the kiss of death for the college.

I had become friends with the president of the college, and visited his office regularly for chats (actually I was always eyeing up his desk, as I fancied myself president of the college someday).

I happened to pop in the very afternoon that the news had come in about the funding. As it was explained to me, we were dangerously close to closing down, and I was sworn to secrecy. I felt ill inside. I was sick at the thought of losing what had become my new home, the institution that had provided an environment that made me want to learn, express myself like never before, and soar as an individual. I was devastated for all the other students whose dreams would soon be dashed. I walked out of the office into the sticky Carolina heat and sat at a picnic table and cried. No sooner than my first tears fell, I heard in my head a very distinct voice, the same voice I had heard so many times before—the voice inside my head that would give life to waking premonitions, direct my inner guidance, as well as narrate so many of my prophetic dreams. I listened with great anticipation to what I knew would be an important message from the Universe.

*Get the document, get into your car, and drive through the night to Washington, DC.*

"What document?" I asked, out loud, looking around to see if anyone had seen me talking to myself.

*All will be prepared when you arrive.*

"You've got to be kidding me!" I argued aloud.

"The voice" repeated itself without changing its tone. I got up from the table and went back to the president's office, and closed the door behind me.

"What's going on concerning some document?" I asked directly, as a matter of fact.

With a deeply curious expression as to my knowledge of the document, the president began to explain. Apparently, there was a file that the school had spent a lot of time and money, in vain, to get into the right hands at the Department of Education in Washington, DC. It outlined why the school should never have been in this situation in the first place. There were forces at work, people involved, trying to unjustly have the school shut down. I briefly explained why I needed this paperwork and, finally, a very nervous president produced the goods. My attitude at this point was . . . what in the world do you have to lose?

I went home and waited for Ben to arrive so that I could tell him that we were going on a road trip. Oddly enough, he had been reading *The Celestine Prophecy* and had just come to the part where the main character had made a decision to take a trip, following a series of "coincidences" that involved ancient manuscripts. No more explanation was needed, as he felt that the book seemed to be coming to life.

"Let's go!" he exclaimed with surprising enthusiasm.

Just as we were about to pull out of the driveway, a booming tone spoke clearly. *Do Not Go.*

Again I yelled, "You've got to be kidding me!" I was disgusted and very confused, but I *knew* that I had better listen.

I hardly slept a wink, mulling over the day's events. Should I have gone anyway? What in the world was going on? I was perfectly willing to do as I was told, and risk looking like a fool, but why had the plans been changed at the last minute? I must say that I was devastated, not to mention absolutely furious. Ben had taken it in his stride and didn't seem to be as concerned as I was. His snoring throughout the night attested to that.

The next morning I got up and went to class without a clue as to what I would say if the president saw me and asked why I was there. *And then it happened again.* Sitting right in the middle of class, *it freakin' happened again.*

"Seriously?" was all I could say. Again, I was conscious that I had just answered this voice out loud, and yes, people were starting to stare.

*GO NOW!* the voice commanded, and as if I hadn't heard it the first time, it said it again.

I called Ben and told him the story. Half an hour later we were on the road.

*

We made it as far as Richmond, Virginia, where we spent the night at my sister's house. I didn't know what to say to her, because she knew absolutely nothing about the strange goings-on in my life . . . ever. Those were secrets that my folks and I had refrained from sharing. I was just *so different* from my brothers and sister, that Mom and Dad felt it was probably best to keep any of my "interesting behavior" to ourselves. My sister had always known that I was a bit wild and adventurous, so it wasn't that far-fetched that I was simply delivering some documents to Washington for the school. Without divulging too much information, we hit the road very early and quite easily made our way through DC, in spite of the early rush-hour traffic.

At nine-thirty that morning, we arrived outside the Department of Education. Bear in mind that this was a government office, where no one was allowed in unless they have an appointment concerning official business. There were metal detectors at the door and guards on duty. I had absolutely no idea whom I needed to see or how I was going to get in there.

We walked through the front door easily enough, and as *fortune* would have it, the desk clerks were changing shifts. I quickly scanned the board with all of the names of the offices and the people working in them. I chose one, and when no one was looking, put my name down as having an appointment with the director of Secondary Education. We slipped over to the elevator and made our way up to the office. My adrenaline was pumping and I felt like the cameras were rolling and I was the star of an awesome action adventure!

It seemed that our mission was about to be cut short when we were informed that the director had taken a personal day. We spoke to someone else in the office and were told, in no uncertain terms, that we had wasted our time. How did we think we were going to speak to anyone without an appointment set up in advance? We were shown the way out, but a gut feeling would not let me leave the building. We snuck back on the elevator and decided to go *straight to the top.* And at the top, we ended up in the office of the chief of staff and made a beeline straight toward the secretary.

We blatantly lied. I was just following orders from above, so I didn't feel too guilty about it. We told her that we were touring Washington and wanted to stop by and thank the chief of staff for something wonderful she had done for our school. *(She was simply unaware that she just hadn't done it yet!)*

We waited for a few minutes, when in walked a beautiful woman, not much older than Ben or me. She had a quick word with her secretary, and then came to greet us with the most welcoming smile. When we got into the office, we had to confess our real agenda. I tried to keep myself from talking too fast, as I do when I get overly excited. I knew I was on borrowed time and I had to get the severity of our problem across to this woman. She listened intently, with the periodic "Oh my gosh!" and "You poor things."

She applauded our efforts to deliver this document, and our humble attempt to try and save the school we loved so dearly.

The chief of staff was a far cry from the woman downstairs, the one who had sent us packing without a second thought. She took notes and even used a highlighter to mark the important points in the document. She sincerely thanked us for bringing this to her attention and promised that she would do all that she could to help. Her exact words were: "The day a *student* can't walk into the Department of Education is the day they need to shut the damn doors."

As we were leaving, we watched her walk out of her office, with our papers in hand, into the office of the assistant secretary of the department. We felt satisfied, and we also knew that our mission was complete.

It all became clear as to why "the voice" had initially directed me to go, and then to wait. If we had gone a day earlier, we would have arrived in DC, only to make it as far as the director of secondary education. By waiting to leave until the following day, we skipped right past him, because he had taken a personal day, allowing us to get the papers into the hands of the chief of staff.

After inquiring about her, we found out that she had only been in the job for about three weeks, hired by the Clinton administration. She was fresh, unscathed by burnout, and she really wanted to make a difference with her work. The following night we arrived back in Spartanburg to be greeted by one flashing light on the answering machine. It was a message from the chief of staff, herself, our angel in DC, telling me to ring her first thing in the morning.

The next day at the college, an assembly had been called to inform the students that things weren't looking good for the school and we would most likely be closing down. Just before the president went to address the assembly, I came running in to tell him to wait before he made any announcements. I had just been on the phone with the chief of staff, and she had organized a meeting for twelve o'clock the following day, for our president and the school's legal advisor. Finally, we had a proper audience with the right people.

As a result, the decision to cut federal funding was reduced from two years to six months. That, for us, was doable. The students had to seek alternative funding for half a year, but almost everyone could be accommodated with short-term alternative funding. There was a bit of griping and moaning among the students because no one really knew *just how close* they had come to having no school at all.

I have never yelled back at "the voice" again for doing or saying things that I don't understand. I was told that all would be in order, and so it was. The courage to do something risky is not the absence of fear, but the presence of faith. My faith in the guidance that I had been promised has never wavered . . . okay, almost never.

# Chapter 14

OPPORTUNITIES TO facilitate the healing process were presenting themselves at an astounding rate. I was careful never to seek out "subjects" to work on, but always waited for guidance as to where I could be of service. It was such a wonderful buzz, to watch people who were often dealing with very frightening health challenges miraculously recover and get on with life. I know now that these initial experiences and their success stories were not by accident. They were steadily building my confidence and my willingness to listen to direction from my guides.

I was soon to learn, yet again, that the outcomes of these incidents were *not* actually in my control. I was, in fact, serving a higher power who ultimately knew what was best for all concerned. It was easy to fall into the trap of hoping, and praying, that everything would always have a happy ending, but as I soon found out, the happy endings were not always on the personal agenda of the soul I was working with.

I began to see the enormity of how a person's death could have as much or more influence on the growth and understanding of those around them than the entire life they had just lived. I was being shown that a true facilitator of healing needed to be as clear about the beauty of the death process as they were about the prospect of creating more time for life. At the end of the day, a person can only be healed if that is what best serves the life path they have chosen.

As I have witnessed on numerous occasions, the clarity and growth that has eluded some for an entire lifetime can come together like the pieces of a perfect puzzle at the time of their death. I also know, beyond a shadow of a doubt, that all deaths are perfectly timed, even when they seem to make no sense at all.

I received a phone call one night from a very distressed friend. Her boyfriend's grandmother had been a perfect specimen of what it means to mature rather than age. She was in her seventies, in great physical condition, and was a competitive synchronized swimmer. Very unexpectedly, she suffered a stroke and fell into a coma. My friend told her family about me, and as a last resort, they asked if I would work with their loved one. If there was no change, they decided to pull the plug on her life support, rather than see her remain in a vegetative state.

I drove several hours downstate, and late that night was brought up to see her after visiting hours, as a "relative" who had come to say her farewells. The room was darkened, and the grandmother looked lifeless, hooked up to all sorts of monitors and machines. I went over to her and placed my hands over her chest. This was quite a remarkable moment for me, as it was the first time I had ever seen the effects of this energy exchange register on a machine. Okay, I could never wear a watch and I always set off the alarm in airport security, but we're talking life-sustaining hospital equipment here. Before I began, her blood pressure was 80/30, and her temperature well below normal.

After a few minutes, her blood pressure began to climb, and her temperature regulated. By the time I had finished, her blood pressure was 130/70 and holding. The next day, my friend rang to tell me that the grandmother had awakened. Later that day, the news I received was absolutely shocking. The doctors were so astonished at her recovery that they decided to open her up and do an exploratory surgery to see exactly what was going on. After the surgery, infection immediately set in, and she died the following day.

I must admit, I had to sit with this for a while, before I got it. Why bother with the healing if she was just going to die anyway? But it slowly became clear to me that the fact that she died was not the issue. The feelings, emotions, lessons, and growth for those she left behind, by the *way* she died, was key. I had been there to help create that exact scenario. I was not there to determine whether she lived or died. Maybe it was in her Divine plan not to die from the initial stroke, so that the time she lived after it might raise questions, issues, and a plethora of emotions for her family to explore and deal with. Her parting gift was to create an amazing opportunity for her loved ones to question the very rocks upon which their own spiritual foundations had been built.

As far as I'm concerned, she did it with style. Not only did she do this for her family, but for me, as well. I was so grateful to have been invited to her passing, and for the insight and understanding that came with it.

*

Venturing out to hospitals at odd hours was not uncommon for me in those days. After the last experience with the grandmother, my Guides must have felt that I needed a better understanding of what death and dying actually meant. I can recall one occasion where "the voice," now as familiar as my own, awakened me in the middle of the night, telling me where to go, and whom to see. It's much like reading the lines of a book. You are reading in your mind, and the sound of the words are crystal clear and audible inside of your head. They are not loud, nor are they frightening, they are words coming from a page, telling you a story. "The voice" sounds much the same way, only the words are coming from a different source and are telling me things that my conscious mind would have otherwise not known. The instructions were always so clear, so matter of fact that I never found myself doubting whether I should act on them. This is where my own personality is a big plus. I'm the type who would hate the thought of missing another adventure, so fear of participation has never been an issue.

Late one night, I arrived outside of the hospital room of a once thriving young man who had been involved in a very serious motorcycle accident. He had been there for some time, comatose, making no notable progress. His family could not bring themselves around to the idea of unplugging his life support and letting him go. I was met at the door by the young man's mother, who simply looked at me and said, "I've been waiting for you."

She was so tired and distraught, facing any parent's most unthinkable challenge: to make the decision to let her child live in a vegetative state or to let him die. She had prayed for help to be sent, believing with all of her heart that Spirit would oblige. So when I arrived outside of her son's door, unannounced, in the middle of the night, she wasn't the least bit surprised. We had never laid eyes on one another before that moment, but were kindred spirits, all the same. I smiled at her, saying nothing, and took her by the hand. The two of us stood at the foot of her son's bed and she nodded for me to proceed. We placed our hands together on top of his feet, and a wave of energy that was unlike any I had felt before seemed to gently move through us both. In a matter of seconds, we heard the machines indicate what we already knew to be true. She cried quietly, and then hugged me, and I walked away in absolute awe of the power of the Universe.

The work I was doing, with the help of my Guides, was becoming more diverse and incredible by the day. I was a grateful participant, awestruck by the mystery and the miracles that life had to offer. With each new challenge, I was conscious of balancing my time between being healer, student, and wife. Unfortunately, it was in that order. I managed to maintain a fairly even keel between healing and school, but the more that was required of me away from home, the less understanding Ben became. He was looking for his own path, so hard, I'm afraid, that I felt he wasn't listening to the guidance available to him. I had stopped trying to explain what I wanted to do with my life and he had stopped listening. We still maintained a friendly atmosphere, but our relationship as husband and wife had seen better days.

The next "job" that heaven sent my way was a very trying time for both Ben and me. Despite the toll it took on our already strained marriage, I wouldn't have missed it for the world. I was leaving my life in the hands of Spirit, trusting that all would be well and as always, that everything had its purpose.

There was a great character I knew named Stephen who brought a smile to everyone he met, because he was always smiling. He was the type of personality that would be missed if he wasn't around, so when he hadn't been seen for a few days, I asked around school to see if anyone could fill me in on his whereabouts. I was told that his sister, a primary school teacher in her late twenties, had suddenly taken violently ill the previous week. She had been teaching when it happened, and within twenty-four hours, her terrible headache had deteriorated into a coma. It was determined that she had developed encephalitis, but no one could seem to figure out how, or why.

Although I had never met her, I became acutely aware as to why she had become ill, and exactly what needed to be done in order for her to come out of the coma. I was becoming quite adept at "downloading" information about people, sort of like plugging into their spiritual hard drive and accessing their data. This data allowed me to see into the spirit's agenda and assist in bringing it to fruition. Always, of course, with the spirit's permission—my role was to lend a hand, *not to interfere*. This was yet another gift foretold during my death experience, now coming to light.

I went to the hospital and told Stephen that I had been called to help. He had known me for a long time, but was completely unaware of this aspect of my life. So after a brief rundown of what "the voice" had asked me to do, Stephen and I sat down with his family and had a chat. With no hesitation at all, I was given their blessing to do my best. I went into the room and faced what had become a very familiar sight: a beautiful person hooked up to a host of machines, needles, and fluids, fighting for life. Only this time, Stephen's sister, Jane, looked different to me.

The aura or energy surrounding her was exceptionally vibrant and very much alive, no sparkling, popping fireworks in the energy field, like what I had seen around a person who was winding down, preparing to take the journey home. She appeared to be in suspended animation. When I walked over and placed my hands on her, my feeling and intuition for the reason behind her illness was confirmed. I could hear her speaking to me, one soul to another, and in an extremely articulate fashion, she explained *exactly* why she was there.

Her family was very close-knit, and all appearances would suggest that their lives were in order. According to Jane, each of them was at a major crossroads, some with exceptionally serious issues. She went through each of these concerns with me and told how her illness was part of her contractual agreement with these members of her soul group: she was to be the catalyst of change for her family members.

I was fascinated and blown away. Number one, by the fact that I was having this conversation with a woman in a coma, and number two, at the idea that I was witnessing a soul fulfilling a promise made prior to this incarnation. I asked her if these changes could have been accomplished without her having to take such drastic action as going into a coma. She responded that only something as radical as a coma would create the necessary momentum for change that her parents and siblings so desperately needed. I thanked her for allowing me to be a part of this incredible undertaking, leaving her side to complete *my* role in the process.

I sat down with the family, and as could be expected, was met with nothing short of disbelief, a little bit of amazement, but mostly skepticism. I stressed that Jane had made it quite clear that she had no intention of coming out of her coma until each of them had made real and lasting steps to change, regarding the issues that we had discussed. The only way I could prove to them that this was actually happening was by speaking to each one individually and sharing a few *personal* secrets about their individual issues that Jane had shared with me in order to convince them that I was for real. *Now they were listening.*

For thirty-four days I went to the hospital and checked in with the family, and with Jane. Not because I had to be there, but because I wanted to be there to support them all. I could hardly dump this kind of information on them and then leave them hanging out to dry, with no backup. Gradually, each and every one of them made genuine commitments to personal change. Funnily enough, it was my friend Stephen who was the last to get himself sorted out. The very day that he did, *Jane woke up.*

She was like a child when she awakened from her self-induced sleep. She had lost so many skills, such as the ability to read, most difficult for one who teaches others to read for a living. Her speech was slow and slurred, and her vocabulary very limited, but with time and rehabilitation, the doctors said that she would eventually be able to lead a somewhat normal life again. She was moved to a rehabilitation facility, where she would learn basic life skills *all over again.* The day she settled into her new room at the treatment center, I went for a visit.

I had stayed away from the hospital when she first regained consciousness, because that was a time for her to be with the family who had prayed so hard, and done so much soul-searching, to bring about her recovery. I was very curious to meet the girl who had called to my spirit. I couldn't wait to speak to her face-to-face. I went to her room and was greeted by her mother with a grateful smile and a big bear hug. We all sat down, and her mother began to explain in very simple words who I was, and why I was there.

Jane responded in a very sluggish, childlike voice, "Momma, will you leave for a minute?"

Her mother said she would go for a cup of coffee and come back shortly.

The door closed behind her and what happened next still gives me goose bumps to this day. She took my hands, and in a voice as sharp and clear as my own, she said, "Mary Helen, I want to talk to you now because I know that I probably won't remember this when I am back to normal again. The very first day that you came to see me you put your hands on my heart. I could feel everything you were doing. It was as if electricity was coursing through my veins. I thought at first that it was the machines, but then I realized who you were and why you were there. I knew you could hear me when I was talking to you, and I am so grateful that you helped me to carry out the plan. I just wanted to thank you from the bottom of my heart."

Before I could pick my jaw up off the floor, the door opened and Jane's mother walked in and whispered, "Are you all right, baby?"

In the polar opposite of what I had just witnessed, she responded with a slow and slurred, "Yeah, Momma."

I sat there, like a deer in the headlights, but managed to pull myself together enough to kiss her on the cheek, hug her mother, and fumble my way toward the door. I stood in the hallway, back pinned against the wall, trying not to hyperventilate. I could hardly believe what had just happened.

I never saw her again, but Stephen said that when she spoke about me, she always referred to me as her angel. He would ask her why, and although *he* knew what had taken place, she had absolutely *no recollection* of why she called me that or of any conversation that we had ever had. That moment of lucidity had been for me, not her, as there was no need for her to hold on to those words in order to move forward with her life. The words she spoke meant the world to me, *and made every difference in how I moved forward with mine.*

# Chapter 15

I WENT to school during the day, and in the evenings, I had work experience as a student intern, several days a week in a chiropractor's office. On the other days, I worked in a local health food shop. A woman in the chiropractic practice where I worked had been plagued with a lifetime of gynecological problems, including very infrequent menstruation and ovarian cysts. She and her husband had tried on numerous occasions to get pregnant but were facing the reality that adoption might be the only hope they had for a child.

One particular afternoon, I got the urge (more like a celestial shove) to help her out. Desperate enough to try anything, she lay down on a table, and I ran my hands over her lower abdomen, feeling that searing heat and tingling sensation in my hands that had now become second nature. A few minutes later, she had a sensation as if something had popped. She said it was very similar to what she had felt when having difficulties with her ovarian cysts. We had a laugh and never said anything else about it, until I met her in the office a few weeks later. "The voice" spoke and I smiled knowingly as I told her she needed to go and get a pregnancy test.

She was defiant, explaining to me that she'd taken countless pregnancy tests over the years and been so disappointed.

"You *really* need to go," I said, emphatically.

The data had been downloaded the second I set eyes on her,

and I *knew* she was pregnant. I finally convinced her to go, and to make a long story short, she's now a mother.

This wasn't the last time I would deal with someone who had been told that children were not in their future. A good childhood friend was passing through a nearby town on business one evening. We caught up over a cup of coffee as she filled me in on the recent dramas in her own life. Endometriosis and cancerous cells in her cervix had left her unable to conceive—according to her doctors. Immediately I was aware that this most definitely was not the case. I gave her a brief rundown on what had been going on in *my* life since we had last seen one another.

Eager to see if I could help, we went back to her hotel room and I facilitated a healing session. It was interesting to see her reaction as she could feel something going on inside of her, unsure of what it actually was. When I knew that all was well, I said my good-byes and didn't see her again for a very long time.

The next time that we met, several years had passed. My friend beamed as she introduced me to her husband, and their two beautiful children.

My ability to facilitate change in another person's biology had taken yet another interesting twist. I was beginning to see that being a conduit for energy from Spirit meant providing the *potential for change*, then allowing nature to take its course.

## Chapter 16

SO MANY incredible things had happened since I had started school that I should have had rock-solid faith and total belief in what was happening *all around me*. Every time I had a vision, heard "the voice," or felt the vibration of healing energy move through me, it was as if I was feeling it for the very first time. While I was in awe of each and every encounter with the Divine, I sometimes struggled with feelings of loneliness and isolation, even questioning if these things had been real at all. I knew in my heart that it was all happening, but I had yet to come across anyone who could genuinely relate, because they were walking in the same or even vaguely similar shoes.

Even Ben was resisting what was occurring, not sure whether to be amazed or a bit frightened of me. I can still hear him yelling, when he happened to wake up one night just in time to witness his first astral projection. It's not every day you catch your wife's spirit leaving her sleeping body. I remember the feeling of being slammed back into my body because his reaction had startled me so much. I had a lifelong habit of astral travel before going to sleep, because after all of those years, I still didn't like going to bed. It took that long for me to fall asleep; I used the time to work on this skill.

It's not the sort of stuff you go to a marriage counselor with; I mean really, what would you say?

"Well, I know there is no one else she is seeing, not with a body anyway. She does leave a lot in the middle of the night, no, *literally*, she checks out of her body. I know sometimes the spirits have called her to the hospital to do her wacky stuff, and I guess the talking to the dead is a *little* unnerving, but hey, we all have our problems, right?"

So we did our best to work through it ourselves. My path seemed so clear, but Ben's journey in regard to me was getting cloudier by the day. Just as I felt that he had no understanding as to how to help me, I know that he felt equally misunderstood by me. I had talked myself to death, trying to *save* him from his growing apathy toward our marriage, and at the same time working with "the voice" of my Guides. Really, I was attempting to quell *my own* insecurities. Unfortunately, it would take over a decade, and major changes, to break myself of that "needing to save" issue. The delusion that it is our job to save another from life's inevitable dramas is an awful cross to bear.

In truth, I felt like I was making this journey alone, not with my partner. It was like I was married to a good buddy. I'm sure he was feeling the strain, having married into a little more than he had bargained for. Something we were both too stubborn to see when we were dating was now glaring at us. Was our connection deep enough to survive this strange and exciting trip together? Had we reached the end of our time as a couple? I also wondered if both of us were missing out on the heartfelt passion that comes when two souls are singing from the same hymn sheet.

I had never questioned whether or not I wanted my gifts and the wonders that went with them. I knew that by choosing this path, it was going to push my husband and me further apart, and the chances of the relationship surviving were slim to none. Worst of all, I was beginning to accept that it was a sacrifice *I was willing to make.* I longed for both of us to be happy and fulfilled, but at this stage, neither of us was quite ready to make the break, so we remained in our marriage, continuing to settle for its false state of contentment.

You see, at twenty-six, I had not yet discovered that expecting your life partner to meet and fulfill every single one of your needs is the beginning of the end. In actuality, he had done a fairly decent job accepting what was happening in my life. Just because he didn't understand it all didn't mean he wasn't *trying* to support me. In fact, I was probably *less* tuned in to the personal challenges he was facing. I was turning to my friends, trying to find a common thread in the mystical tapestry that my life had become, and I resented having to do that. I thought that Ben should be the one I could turn to, when, in fact, he was probably feeling very left out. Our lack of maturity and growth as a couple was catching up with us, rapidly turning into an unbearable frustration.

✳

Life took another interesting twist when I attended a chiropractic philosophy seminar in a hotel in North Carolina. I had spent the evening halfheartedly listening to the ideas that, at this point in my education, had become second nature. I was preoccupied with a sensation that something mystical was about to happen. I had grown accustomed to this feeling, because it generally preceded a message from Spirit, but this time, *something was different.*

When the seminar had ended for the night, most of the students and doctors who had attended went into the hotel lounge for a bit of socializing before calling it a day. I sat at a table with a few people I knew, when I noticed a guy I had never met but had seen around campus. He seemed to be very quiet. I caught him looking my way a few times, before he finally spoke. The seat between us was empty, and eventually, he leaned over and whispered, "I need to talk to you later."

Was he confusing me with someone else? If this was a pickup line, it was the lamest one I had ever heard.

"Yeah, okay," I replied, not sure why I had even answered him.

As the crowd began to dwindle, I wasn't sure what was about to happen, but I knew that I had better pay close attention. He asked if I would come up to the room where he was staying so we could talk. Ding! Ding! Ding! Ding! Alarm bells, right? I wasn't falling for that one! However, I looked at him again, with his kind brown eyes and quiet demeanor, and I felt in my heart that I was dealing with something and someone on a whole different level.

I went up to his room and walked into what looked like a living room. There was a couch, a couple of armchairs, and a minikitchen. The overhead light was off, and a lamp in the corner dimly lit the room. I was conscious of the pair he was sharing the suite with who were sleeping behind the door to the bedroom, wondering what on earth I was doing there. He sat down on the couch and started to laugh. "Would you relax? Everything is fine."

I laughed nervously at his casual approach and sat down on the edge of the coffee table facing him. The lighting was odd, casting strange shadows around the room, increasing my anxiousness, but in my apprehension, I also found a bizarrely familiar feel to the whole situation. He looked me in the eye and with a very reassuring smile said, "Now, think!"

Oh, I was thinking all right. I was thinking what kind of a lunatic I must be, to sit staring into the eyes of a complete stranger, who was telling me to relax and *think* in his hotel room! Then he said it again. This time, his tone was different and out of the blue, it felt as if something was on the tip of my tongue. It was as if I should *know* what he was talking about; a memory of something long forgotten. As I continued to stare at him, the light from the corner lamp made him appear as if he were glowing, nearly translucent, and this stranger was becoming more familiar by the second. He placed his hand in front of me, as if to give me a high five, and held it there, waiting for my response. I slowly lifted my hand, and our palms met.

The surge of power that shot through me made me feel as if I would be blown off the table and straight through the wall! He had just tripped my circuits, and suddenly, all of my lights were on. I gasped for air as he pulled his hand away, and he fell back into the couch laughing.

"Hello!" he chuckled, through an angelic smile.

My mouth hung open as he launched into a stream questions without taking a single breath.

"How have you been? Tell me everything! How did it work out with the family you picked? You've got brothers and a sister, right? What's it like where you grew up? I want to hear it ALL!"

You could have knocked me over with a feather! I was talking face-to-face with someone from my past, my real past. He was a member of my soul group. The best part was that whatever he had done when he touched my hand, the rush of energy that had coursed through my body, had just removed any amnesia I had regarding who he was, and I could remember him from the place where we reside, *in between* lives! He was from home, and now he was here, right in the same room! The doubt and confusion that had previously clogged my mind was now replaced with euphoria and validation.

His eyes sparkled as he seemed to pulsate light from the inside! I was seeing him now as I remembered him in spirit, as opposed to the body he was occupying while here on Earth. The face was un-familiar, but the essence, the life force behind it, was unmistakable. He was one of my actual soul mates.

The love I felt at that moment washed over any pain or hurt that played on my heart. I soaked up the power and energy that is created when kindred spirits come together. We laughed and I cried, while filling each other in on our biographies to date. This was a reunion like no other I had ever experienced, in this world, anyway. When we finally slowed down long enough to catch our breath, he took my hand, and the next words that he spoke are forever in my heart.

*I know you are wondering why I came to you now. It was actually going to be another fifteen years or so, before we had planned to meet, even though you don't remember that, just yet. I was told that you were having a bit of trouble, that you have doubted whether or not the incredible things that have been going on in your life were genuine. I am here to tell you that this* is very real. *You are following the path that you chose for yourself a very long time ago, and all of these things* are *happening to you, as well as to the people that you are here to help. I was sent now, to tell you this, so you wouldn't lose faith or give up. Stop doubting yourself and trust that you are safe! No matter what appearances may seem,* you are not alone on this voyage. *You are just waking up to who you really are.*

We sat in silence after he spoke, and when I left the room, I felt as self-assured and blessed as one could be at five in the morning. My confidence and faith in the unbelievable had been restored. My heart had been recharged, and I had been reminded what it felt like to live and love in the moment. Once again, the Universe had delivered, *as promised,* and I knew that everything was exactly as it should be.

# Chapter 17

MY MOTHER'S sister has always been one of my very favorite people. She is simply one of those individuals who always has something positive to contribute to any conversation. Her bubbly personality and loving nature make her such a pleasure to be around. Auntie Joyce is also a free spirit. Her formal training as a psychologist never caused her to lose interest in the metaphysical. Being open to all possibilities and her ability to listen and council without passing judgment has always been her strong suit. My mother had kept Auntie Joyce, who was not only her sister but her closest friend, up to date with my unusual adventures, so she was well aware of what was going on behind the scenes throughout my entire life.

In the summer of 1996, I got a phone call from Joyce, concerning my grandmother Elizabeth. Grandmother had moved several years earlier from her home in Kentucky to the house next door to my aunt in DeLand, Florida. She was now ninety, and the congestive heart failure that she had so competently managed for the last thirty years was catching up with her. She had great faith, bold conviction, and absolutely no fear of death. However, time was running out for her, and she still had a few loose ends she wanted to tidy up before she made her journey back to Spirit. Grandmother was now on a portable oxygen feed, and her mobility was extremely limited. She was attempting to finish her affairs and also trying to write and record her memoirs. Joyce said that she wasn't interested in attempting to prolong Grandmother's life in any way, but wondered if it would be possible to give her a little "boost," allowing her to comfortably finish the tasks she was trying to complete. I said I would be happy to help if I could, but that there was one little problem. What would we tell her?

"Just tell her the truth," Joyce said. "She can handle it, you'll see."

I thought back to the time when I was a child and Grandmother had told me she not only believed in fairies but had seen them. I also remembered the no-nonsense woman who used to hold my brother and me in a viselike grip when we misbehaved. She was a devout Christian, and frankly, I was a little fearful of telling my secret, of being rejected, and then having to live with the fact that I had disappointed my grandmother. Even though I knew better, I was still nervous.

Ben and I made the ten-hour trip to Florida during my three-week summer break from school. Although we didn't know it at the time, this was to be the final voyage that we would ever take together. It was so awesome to arrive in sunny Florida, to be greeted by the warm hospitality of my beautiful aunt and her fabulous husband, Billy. I hadn't seen Grandmother in nearly two years, so it was a total shock to see this once vibrant and thriving woman looking so elderly and frail. She was still beautiful though, and her long mane of hair was elegantly wrapped into a perfect bun on the back of her head, just as it had always had been. She had a peace about her, an absolute acceptance that she was going through her death process, and true to form, she was the picture of dignity.

After a reassuring hug and Joyce's trademark *"I'm so proud of you dear heart,"* I went in to talk to Grandmother about the real reason I was there. I wasn't even sure where to begin. How, exactly, do you tell a ninety-year-old woman with a colorful and rich history, who is also deeply Christian, that her granddaughter has visions, talks to the dead, has died and come back to life, and now has some weird vibration coming through her hands that seems to help people heal?

I started with: "I know this is going to sound crazy, but . . . " Then I proceeded to pour my heart out for the next hour.

When I finally stopped talking, I looked at Grandmother, smiling back at me, and waited for something like, "Oh, Mary Helen, you've always had such an active imagination!"

Instead, much to my surprise, she chuckled as she removed the oxygen tubes from her nose.

"So that's where it went!"

"Hmm, Grandmother, that's where *what* went?" I asked, somewhat confused.

"Garland's gift; you have your grandfather's abilities, dear," she replied matter-of-factly.

And there I sat, dumbfounded, relieved, and on the edge of my seat to hear more. I asked how in the world I had never heard this before.

"It's simple," she said. "No one in our family knows about it. I promised never to tell, but under the circumstances, I don't think he'd mind now."

Over the course of the evening, this mysterious man whom I had known as my dreamtime companion throughout my childhood, my confidant and guide as I grew older, was suddenly coming to life through my grandmother's stories.

It had all started when my grandparents had secretly gotten married, just after college. My grandmother was a teacher, and in those days, women were not allowed to be married and still teach, so they took their clandestine vows, never wore wedding rings, and in turn, never took a honeymoon. The time came when my grandfather had a break from medical school, so they decided to take a short camping trip to make up for lost time. They were a young, newlywed couple, and they took to nature to escape the harsh reality that it would be a while before they could actually live together as man and wife.

They had gone deep into the woods to look for a spot to set up camp. As they hiked, Grandmother tripped, hearing a snap that she prayed was the branch she had just fallen over. Unfortunately, the sound was her ankle breaking, and she cried out in pain as she fell to the ground, waiting for her husband to come to her rescue. She said the next moment changed the way she was to live, forever. She reflected on that memory, with a look in her eyes that one only gets when speaking from the heart about true love. She said that my grandfather looked at her, as if he was struggling with the biggest decision of his life. In fact, he was. He didn't speak, walked over to his ailing new bride, and crouched down beside her. He took his two hands and placed one on top and one on the bottom of her throbbing ankle. A burning sensation shot through her leg. After a few minutes, my grandfather stood up, offered her his hand, and looked into her eyes. Grandmother stood with ease, without pain, and in total shock.

Not a word was spoken about what had just happened. She knew that this quiet and unassuming man she had just married never wanted to speak about this part of his life. Grandmother said that she respected what she knew were his wishes, and never mentioned a word to anyone. Now, nearly three quarters of a century later, she was *finally* sharing their secret.

The stories continued to flow from her lips. Some of them even I found hard to believe. Apparently, when my grandfather had passed away, friends and strangers came out of the woodwork, secretly sharing the most amazing personal stories with my grandmother. As a doctor, he had worked with so many people down through the years, and she was told how he had actually placed his hands on dying patients and suddenly they miraculously recovered. He had assisted people with the dying process in ways that most doctors could never fathom, gently taking them through the Light, especially if they were resisting or afraid.

Grandmother was even told about a time that her husband had

been called out during a snowstorm to deliver a baby on a farm in the country. Anyone who knows Kentucky is familiar with the rolling hills of the Bluegrass State. Apparently, the roads were so bad that my grandfather was unable to get his car over a hill, just across the field from the farmhouse. The farmer recounted to my grandmother that he was watching out the window as Doc Clark was trying to get over the snow-covered hill. He said that right before his very eyes, he witnessed the car lift up, several feet off the ground, as if it were floating, and gently set down on the other side of the icy stretch of road. The farmer said the doc skidded up to the front door, just in time to catch the baby.

Now I knew exactly what it felt like to sit in the shoes of someone with whom I was sharing my own history. You want so badly to believe, but it just sounds too far-fetched to be true. I was making mental notes the entire time about patience and compassion for those I would share with in the future. As Grandmother continued, I could see her pure delight. She would barely finish one account before launching into another, as if she were afraid that she would forget one of her long-kept secrets. Imagine holding on to that kind of information for all of those years. She was like a child, bursting to tell everything she knew, and in her excitement, I was feeling as if I finally belonged!

My gifts were my grandfather's legacy. I had discovered them through my own unique experiences, probably just as he had, but now I was seeing that this wasn't by accident, *or* strictly because of my accident. That had only been a catalyst to awaken my sleeping giant—my heritage, and my birthright as one who works for the Light on this planet.

As she spoke, I began to recall several accounts of Grandmother's connection to my grandfather—Judge, as he was lovingly called by my family—which had long been forgotten. Now my fears of sharing my story seemed totally unfounded. I had completely forgotten about the time that Grandmother had been driving back to her home after a trip away, when she had an overwhelming sensation that she needed to pull the car over and pray for her husband. Apparently, she prayed until the feeling left her, and later found out that, at that exact moment, my grandfather's medical practice had been robbed, and he had been held at gunpoint while the assailants tore the office apart looking for prescription drugs.

There had been another time that Grandmother had been staying at our house, several years after Judge had passed away. Due to fly to Florida the following morning, Grandmother walked into the kitchen, picked up the phone, and rang the airline to cancel her flight. We were all sitting around the kitchen table eating our breakfast, curious about the phone call she had just placed to change her travel plans. She explained that the night before she had dreamed that she was sitting on an airplane. She looked up, only to see her husband walking down the aisle toward her. He took her by the hand and whispered, "Come on, Elizabeth, sweetheart, this is not your flight."

Without a moment's hesitation or a second thought, she canceled her booking. A flight went down over Florida that day, killing all on board. None of the family can remember if that was the flight she was supposed to be on, but it *was* Florida that she was flying to, and my mother and aunt both remember the incident well. What was outstanding about Grandmother was her complete and utter trust in the message she had been given by my grandfather in that dream. She didn't care if it cost her a little more to take another flight, or if anyone thought her a fool for following a dream. She took her message from beyond quite seriously, and as far as any of us know, it very well may have saved her life.

It's funny how those things had slipped my mind over the years, when in actuality, Grandmother would have probably found it the easiest, of anyone in the family, to relate to my stories of psychic adventures and healing. I laugh now at how ridiculous my fears were. The chance to share this part of myself with this amazing woman is a gift I will treasure always. Sadly, but with gratitude and a complete sense of closure, I said good-bye. It would be the last time I would see her alive, and the picture of aged beauty and grace is the way I will always remember her in my mind.

*

When Ben and I left DeLand, I knew that I would never see my grandmother again. We had even discussed me singing at her funeral, whenever that might be; however, she said if I allowed singing at her funeral to interfere with my schooling, she would haunt me from the spirit world! No better woman, I might add. The prospect of her ability to rattle my cage from beyond was not even worth contemplating. I gave her my word that I would not sing at her funeral if it clashed with school commitments. It was a promise she insisted I make, so I made it, said my farewells, and headed home.

On the drive back to South Carolina, Ben and I stopped in at the old village of Saint Augustine, Florida. I was well used to getting readings, or energetic impressions, of a place I had never visited before, but this historic old town was overwhelmingly familiar. It was uncanny how well I knew my way around, having the very distinct feeling that I had been there before.

Ben and I went to a candle shop, where they were dipping people's hands in wax, making sculptures out of the finished products. We dipped our hands in the same position as Michelangelo's hand of God touching Adam. Our two waxed hands touching were gently wrapped and placed in a bag for the trip home. Even with the air-conditioning on, our masterpiece took on a twisted, unrecognizable form due to the heat, looking nothing like it did at the start of our journey—a prophetic indication of what we had become as a couple and what was to become of us in the not-so-distant future.

*

Ben and I had become very close over the last year with a group that consisted of three other couples. None of them were aware of our *lack* of marital bliss, so when our friends suggested that they wanted to take us out to celebrate our fourth wedding anniversary, we decided that we would oblige.

It was October 24, 1996, when we went out to a Japanese restaurant in Greenville, the next town over. Something strange was in the air (or the sushi) that night. I don't know if the moon was waxing or waning or if the planets were in some sort of wacky alignment, but some outrageous force was at work. By the next morning, Ben and I, as well as two of the three other couples, had broken up *for good*.

Four years, to the day, after we had tied the knot, our knot *and* the thread that it was hanging on unraveled in a most bizarre fashion. It shocked both Ben and me and everyone that knew us. Because no one had been aware that our troubles had been brewing for quite some time, everyone thought that *I* had just had a little tantrum, and everything would work itself out. It looked as if I had made a spur-of-the-moment decision to abandon my husband and my marriage, and almost everyone saw Ben as the victim of my rash behavior. All I can say is, on that night, exactly four years after saying "I do," I couldn't go another day in the marriage. I knew that, initially, the decision would be painful, especially for Ben, but I also knew that "the work" I had now committed myself to for life had caused me to outgrow the support I could receive from the marriage, and in turn, the time and attention that a healthy union required. I refused to fight, my mind having been made up long before that fateful night, and prepared myself for the inevitable deluge of judgment from the outside world.

It was then that I really learned not to be bothered by what other people think. In fact, at the time of my death, it was the one stipulation I insisted upon if I was to return as a steward of humanity; no regard for what others thought of me, my beliefs, or my unusual abilities. Rumors flew around at lightning speed that I must be having an affair, or that maybe I was even gay. After all, they speculated, I did have a lot of friends who were gay and I certainly knew a lot of married men, so one of them must be true. No mention was made that maybe I had just come to understand that there was nothing left that could benefit either of us from remaining in this relationship for another day. It was a hard time for both of us. Ben even told me that he didn't know that we had a problem. It was *that* conversation that made me aware that, as difficult as this time was, leaving this marriage was the right thing to do.

I went out that same week and cut off all of my long blond hair: a change of energy and appearance. I began to go running again. This was something I had not done in years. I found it very difficult at first, as each step felt as if someone was knifing me in the back. Eventually, I found my pace and began to focus on reclaiming my state of health prior to my accident and my marriage. Ben moved back to his hometown, and bar one fifteen-minute conversation the following summer, I never saw or spoke to him again.

I would have preferred to remain friends, but Ben requested that we not keep in contact, so I honored that request and moved forward.

*

I spent that Christmas at home with my parents. Mom always went above and beyond, elegantly decorating the house for the holidays, and the smell of banana bread reminded me of my youth. The air was crisp and refreshing in the mountains of Virginia, a welcome reprieve from the stale, unseasonal heat of South Carolina. I was happy to be home and enjoyed reconnecting with some of my childhood friends. I had no regrets that I was spending my first Christmas in five years without Ben, because I had already moved on. There's one thing about me: When I've made up my mind and committed to change, I always follow through. I am not the type to wallow in "what if" or "if only I had . . ." Through reading Caroline Myss, my author of choice at that time in my life, I subscribed to the idea that leaving pieces of myself behind in what I or others judged as past mistakes was only laying a template for disease to manifest later in life. I was greatly inspired by her words; to me, it all made so much sense. She was eloquently verbalizing what I knew to be true in my heart. I valued this passage, in particular:

*No matter what the challenge is that we face today, life goes on tomorrow and the way that we handle yesterday can make, or break us in the future. It is impossible to remain healthy and whole, if part of you is still visiting the phantoms of the past.*

I met an intriguing new friend during that Christmas break, who introduced me to the concept of sitting with myself and embracing my dark side. He was a few years older, had gone to the same high school that I had graduated from, yet until now, our paths had never crossed. We became close very quickly, and I had shared with him many of the supernatural happenings that were going on in my life. With great interest and reflection, he gently challenged my intentions, asking me to look at what my ego was getting out of all of this. My first instinct was to turn on my heel and leave, but fortunately, I really listened, and took on board what he was saying. It was as if he had been placed on my path at precisely this time to ask some heavy-hitting questions. He wasn't judging my motives; he was asking me to explore where my ego stood in all of these experiences. It was okay if it made the occasional appearance; the work I was doing with people was incredible. He was teaching me not to fear if my ego was involved in my work, but to embrace the fact that when I saw glimpses of it, I needed to listen to why it was present, and what it was trying to show me about myself.

In telling my story to anyone, I had always been so careful not to come across as though I thought I was something extraordinary in heaven's eyes. In fact, I often made comments like, "This could happen to anyone" or "I'm sure everyone is capable of doing these things if they really want to." I was constantly attempting to downplay my role in these events, so as not to appear arrogant. I never wanted to give the impression that I didn't think that everyone was gifted and special. In reality, I did not want to be judged, or made to feel as if there *wasn't* something special going on, when I *knew* that there was. I couldn't stand it when I heard myself making these comments, but it was a habit that I found hard to break. It all went back to the fact that I was asking people to believe something so incredible that I sometimes questioned whether I actually believed it myself. In short, I did not like the idea of having to defend my calling. The catch was: *No one was asking me to.* The fear that no one would believe me was actually my own fear—that *I* didn't believe me, despite the fact that the Universal truth had *always* backed me up, *as promised.*

My friend had taught me one of the most valuable lessons I have ever learned, and, thank God, I stuck around to listen. He had introduced me to what I considered to be one of my worst character flaws, made me shake hands with it, hear what it had to offer me, and then accept it as a part of who I was. My Guides had said that there would always be messengers. . . .

# Chapter 18

I RETURNED to school in mid-January of 1997, feeling reju-
venated and ready to face the world. I was driving from Virginia,
returning to South Carolina, when I had to make a pit stop, just
outside of Charlotte, North Carolina. The rest area was large and
the building that held the bathrooms was made of brick with no
windows. My father had gifted me with some "pocket cash"' before
I left home. At the time, it was desperately needed, as I was now
a twenty-six year-old, nearly divorced college student, working
several different jobs to make ends meet. I had been driving with
the window down a few inches to keep myself awake, and thought
nothing of it when I locked the car, leaving my handbag on the front
seat. I went into the restroom and literally, just as I was about to
sit on the toilet, it was as if a movie was playing in front of my eyes
on the door to the stall. As clear as day, I could see an older-style
white convertible pulling up next to my car. A guy who looked to
be close to my age jumped out of the passenger seat and as quick
as a flash, had managed to somehow get my handbag off the front
seat and through the small space left in the window. I shrieked as I
went running out the door, barely able to get my trousers back up,
just in time to see the same white convertible, driven by a girl, with
the guy whom I had just seen in my vision in the passenger seat. I
ran as fast as I could as they backed out of the space next to my car.
I jumped in front of the car, screaming, "STOP!!"

The car stopped and the guy looked at me and said with a smirk: "Can I help you with something?"

"Dude! I know you have my bag in your car and I know that you know that I was just in that building and couldn't have possibly seen you take it, so obviously something freaky is going on here! Unless you want to find out just how freaky I can get, you better hand over the bag now. The money in it is all that I have."

Believe it or not, he did. He was so completely shocked by the fact that I knew he had taken the bag, he simply handed it over. The girl driving the car looked at me like I had forty heads before she burned rubber and took off.

I always laugh when I recall this story because it reminds of the fact that the Universe is always looking out for us, and when we're in the zone . . . wonders never cease. Over the years so many people have asked me, "If you're so psychic, why don't you know the lottery numbers?"

I have always known that personal gain is not the objective of working with Spirit, but in the case of having something returned that already belonged to me, it sure did come in handy.

*

Winter quickly came to an end, as it does in South Carolina, and by March, spring was in the air. Spring wasn't the only thing in the air; something new, unlike anything I had ever experienced, began to appear in my vision. I was sitting at home one evening doing some schoolwork, when I caught something out of the corner of my eye. At first I thought I was seeing floaters (little black spots that were always in my visual field) from the damage done to my retina in the car accident. I sat back, closed my eyes, and there, in my mind's eye, were three symbols. I didn't recognize them from anywhere, yet there was something so familiar about them.

The first thing that came to mind was Egyptian hieroglyphics. I had limited knowledge of Egyptology, and yet they didn't look like any hieroglyphics I had ever seen. The symbols appeared, one by one, and were flaming orange in color.

Flaming orange symbols? You've got to be joking!

Either the Universe was once again showing its never-ending sense of humor, or someone out there simply thought I was so dense that only something as dramatic as flaming symbols would get my attention!

The same three symbols flashed over and over, as if waiting for me to memorize them, or write them down. I studied each one in my mind, and then drew pictures of all three. Once I had noted each of them, the visions stopped.

For the next month or so, I continued to see symbols, only with each encounter a different set of three would appear. Each time I recorded them, and still, I had absolutely no idea what they meant. After seven lots of symbols, I was left with what looked like some sort of an alphabet.

*

I still had no idea why they had turned up, why they were in groups of three, why there were twenty-one in total, or what in the world was going to happen next. There was, however, a vague memory from my distant past.*

After Ben had moved out, I wanted a housemate, for a bit of company, as well as to help with the expenses. In walked Jo. He was such a character, tall and lanky, with wispy blond hair and thick glasses. His wacky sense of humor made coming home in the evening something to look forward to. We got along famously, and his energy, as well as his interest in the metaphysical, was a welcome addition to my home. We had such a blast! I couldn't have asked for a better living arrangement. He was always bringing unique and

---

* More information on the origins of these symbols is available in *The Gnosis Onward Series* (Volumes 1–4, fourth edition, 2013) by Lewis E. Graham, PhD, DD.

interesting personalities over to the house. He asked, one day, if I minded if he hosted an evening with a psychic for a few friends. I told him to knock himself out.

I had been working that night, so the event was well under way when I arrived home. People were waiting patiently in my sitting room to have their one-on-one session in the front room with Psychic Suzy. It looked like they were enjoying themselves, and as the evening was wrapping up, Jo knocked on my door and said, "Hey, she wants to see you."

"Me? Why does she want to see me? Tell her thanks, but I'm sure she's done enough for one night."

"You better go in there," he said. "I think she has something to tell you."

Curiosity got the best of me, and for the first time in my life, I found myself sitting toe-to-toe with a psychic. Ironically, I had never really felt the need. She was a lovely lady (no turbans or gold hoop earrings), just an average person you would pass no remarks on if you met her on the street. I was intrigued by her confidence to do readings on the spot for people. Up until this moment, most of my experiences had been sent to me, and I had never really "read" people, the way she was about to read me. She immediately acknowledged me as a colleague. She said that I was surrounded with help from the heavens, and not only was I clairvoyant, I was also here doing very special work that involved metaphysical healing. Not bad, but nothing that she couldn't have possibly said to anyone else. It wasn't that I doubted her, but nothing really seemed that specific. *That was, until she spoke again.*

"A light switch, I keep seeing a light switch turning on."

"Okay," I said, still unimpressed. "What does that mean?"

"When I see a light switch turning on, it means that you have been shown your destiny," she replied.

She sat quietly and closed her eyes for a moment, and then looked at me and smiled.

"You've been seeing something: symbols of some sort. These are your destiny, and they have something to do with someone you used to be, and somewhere you will be in the near future."

Now she had my attention. I had told no one, not Jo or even my confidant, Dan, about the visions.

"Eventually," she continued, "you will meet with a circle of twelve. These will be twelve who are from your distant past. You will *know* each one when you meet, and the work you will do together will move you one step closer to accomplishing your purpose here. This won't be here in America. It's definitely abroad."

When she had finished, I filed the experience away in the back of my mind, impressed that she knew about the symbols, but disappointed because I knew I was not going abroad anytime soon. I was flat broke, and I still had another year to go before I finished school.

*

My divorce came through in April 1997. I really had no interest in meeting anyone else because I was finally getting to know myself, independent of the dramas of having an intimate partner. Obviously, the Universe had different ideas for me *and* my independence and decided to shake things up a bit. A new guy was transferred into my class . . . and, well, I simply couldn't help myself!

Dave was a unique individual. He was originally from Philadelphia, and made the twelve-hour drive home nearly every weekend to work in his landscaping business. He had kept it running, even after moving to South Carolina, to help pay his way through school. I had never met anyone like him. He had the tough-guy Philly accent, was of Polish and Italian descent, and had a body that was as finely tuned as the great big pickup truck that he drove.

Dave was ten years my senior but looked younger and in better shape than most guys half his age. His energy was endless. The funniest part was that we were such an unlikely pair. I was Miss School Spirit, president of the student body, the real cheerleader type, and he was like something out of *Rebel Without a Cause*. I lived a very public life, always in the middle of everything, while he attended his classes, remaining detached from the social aspect of school and very private in his personal life. For whatever reason, it worked. We had a carefree, no-hassle relationship. We were in the gym working out together at five-thirty every morning, his routine, not mine. I can honestly think of nothing worse, but I just pretended that I was *so excited* to be there because I liked him so much!

Over the next few months my body, as well as my self-confidence, transformed. I was experiencing a level of physical and mental well-being that I had never achieved. Everyone noticed, and people got a real kick out of Dave and me. When we first began to date, I worked up the nerve and picked an opportune moment to tell him about *the real me*.

He laughed and said, "That's cool, MH, ya gotta do what ya gotta do."

That was it. No other response. It wasn't that he didn't care about my spiritual side, but he was a man with a rock-solid agenda for his own life, so in the grand scheme of things, as far as he figured, it really had very little to do with him. I actually found that very attractive. He said he liked his girls a little freaky, and freaky is exactly what he got! I felt free to do what I needed to do. This relationship had been handed to me by a Divine force that knew I simply needed to have some fun again. We really were great together, and each of us satisfied the other's need for lighthearted companionship, and good, old-fashioned moral support.

✳

One of the highlights of the school year was a celebration at school called Lyceum. This was a tradition that B. J. Palmer, developer of chiropractic, and son of its founder, D. D. Palmer, had originated at Palmer Chiropractic College, many years earlier. It was a time for alumni to reunite, for students to host and entertain, for philosophical debates, personal testimonies, music, and lectures from great international speakers. I had the privilege of meeting Dan Millman, author of *Way of the Peaceful Warrior*, the very first metaphysical novel I had read. As president of the student body, I was honored to mingle with some very influential doctors from the international circuit, and the highlight of the weekend was always the dinner banquet and dance.

Dave had decided not to stay around for Lyceum, because it was May, the busy season for landscaping. It was a shame, because I had an awesome little black dress, and the theme of the night was old New Orleans and jazz. I missed having him there, because he was such good fun, and I loved the way he danced! I managed to have a fabulous time anyway with all of my friends, and even had an encounter with the spirit world, quite unexpectedly.

When Ben and I had lived in Charleston, we lived off shrimp. His family would cast for shrimp every season and then freeze them to eat throughout the year. In the foothills of Virginia, this was a very expensive delicacy, so I was in heaven, eating it nearly every second day, for free! What I didn't know was that in the span of those few short years, I had eaten my lifetime quota of shellfish. It's much like being stung by bees at different stages in your life, with no reaction at all. Then one day, a bee stings you, and you nearly die.

On the night of the banquet, my body decided that in terms of shellfish consumption, enough was enough. Because the theme of the night was New Orleans, the main dish was crayfish, a much larger and uglier version of shrimp. I sat down at the table and began to dig in, when all of a sudden my head started to spin. My lips tingled, and at first my throat felt numb, before it began to swell shut. I ran into the bathroom, violently throwing up several times. Even after vomiting, it still felt as if I was breathing through a drinking straw. I knew I was going into anaphylactic shock.

One of the doctors staying in the hotel where the banquet was held offered for my friends to take me into his room while they rang for the ambulance. I remember lying on the floor, my eyes rolling back into my head, and I could feel *I really did not want to go!* Suddenly, I could hear a very familiar sound in the background as people were talking to me and to each other.

The buzz that comes before the whoosh, the Music of the Spheres that had carried me to the heavens twice before, was getting closer. This time, my head rolled to one side, and who did I see hovering in the corner? Two very familiar apparitions: the Guides who had accompanied me on this memorable journey before.

They seemed to be smiling, but oddly enough, it didn't feel like they were preparing to take me anywhere. It was as if they were only watching, overseeing the situation with their reassuring presence. The next thing I felt was a hand on my face, turning my head away from my spiritual spectators.

"Look at me, *do not* look at them. It's not time," a voice said.

Donald Epstein, a guru of sorts in the chiropractic world and the founder of Network Spinal Analysis, was kneeling down beside me. He made a few gentle impulses to strategic points on my body, and almost immediately, as if by magic, I could feel the swelling going down in my throat. I knew that I was now out of danger and was going to be fine. I was so fortunate that he had been there, and even luckier that his son had been a close friend and my own chiropractor throughout my time at Sherman. He had run to get his father when he heard that I was in serious trouble. After all of the drama had passed, I simply *had* to ask Dr. Epstein, "You could see the Beings in the corner of the room, couldn't you?"

He smiled, acknowledging that he had, going on to share some very beautiful anecdotes from his own life. His stories reassured me that I was not in this alone. His remarkable skill and kind reassurance made such an impact on me. Once again, I had faced a porthole of exit, an opportunity to check out of this world, and I definitively knew . . . *it just wasn't time.*

*

Dave and I spent a lot of our free time basking in the fabulous South Carolina sunshine even though I had given up sunbathing a few years earlier, in an attempt to save myself a few wrinkles. Dave was a bronzed god. He loved to stretch out in the sun, and because I loved spending time with him, I started to tan my skin again, every spare moment I could get. Many were the days that I went to see patients, covered in oil, with a bikini on underneath my clinic jacket. Whenever we could, we would hop in his truck and drive the three and a half hours to Charleston to soak up the sun on the beach.

Skipping school one day, we took a day trip to the low country. There we were, sprawled out on the beach, Dave with his earphones and music on while I dozed in and out of consciousness in the glorious heat, under a bright, blue sky.

"HELP, HELP!" broke my sun-filled daze.

I sat up and took a good look around. Nobody seemed to be rushing, or responding, to cries for help. I looked out to the sea, and at the end of a concrete jetty, I could see a child bobbing up and down in the waves, clearly struggling to stay above water. I thought it strange that no one else seemed to hear or see her, because I could hear her as if she were right next to me. I went running into the water and swam out to the girl. She was being bashed by the incoming tide. I wrapped my arms around her, only to discover that she wasn't budging. She had somehow wedged her foot into the rocks at the base of the jetty. I knew her foot would shred if I pulled it out, but it certainly beat the alternative. I gave a good hard yank and tore her away from the sharp stones.

As anyone who has ever been a lifeguard knows, at this point, you are nearly in more danger than the victim as their panic sets in, the sinking swimmer grabbing onto you for dear life. She was no more than ten, and I was a robust twenty-seven years old, but at that moment, the tables turned, and I found myself submerged, struggling to get to the surface again. In an eerie moment of calm, I remember saying to myself, " I'm going to drown *again!*"

I spent several seconds in this oddly tranquil space. A flash of perfect understanding threatened to lull me under. I gathered my senses, sprung to the top, grabbed her around the waist, and dragged her back to the shore.

People were gathering as they could now see that something was amiss. Her parents rushed over—they hadn't even noticed her gone—and Dave had just discovered that I was no longer by his side. The little girl was fine, bar needing stitches in her foot. I was on an adrenaline rush that lasted for the rest of the day. I find it very interesting that I love the water and have absolutely no fear of it, or of drowning, only memories of having been there before but under very different circumstances. The theme of drowning had followed me since childhood, always reminding me that this wasn't my first time on this planet.

\*

I had met some future doctors from a college in Bournemouth, England, during an international conference for chiropractic students earlier in the year. As president of the student body, I was invited to Bournemouth to visit the school and to speak to the students about the philosophy upon which Sherman College had been built. I had never been overseas before, and I had to come up with a crafty way to get the school to fund the trip.

Dr. Koch, my former teacher and always my friend, was now the president of the college. I went to him to plead my case, and he lovingly laughed at my desperate attempt to convince him of why my trip to England was essential to the growth and forward advancement of the college. I felt like I was thirteen again, trying every trick in the book to persuade my parents to let me go to my first concert. I was very convincing that the band Chicago was calm and decent, a positive influence on the youth of the day. It certainly wasn't going to be a wild rock gig. My parents will attest to the fact that my negotiating skills were a force to be reckoned with, so Chicago *was*, in fact, my first live band, and fourteen years later, *I was going abroad*! It seemed that Psychic Suzy was right, after all.

# Chapter 19

AT THIS point in my life I wasn't an experienced flyer (at least not in an airplane!). I wasn't afraid of dying, but the thoughts of going down in a plane, and dying with a bunch of *other people*, really unnerved me. I had always seen my death as a sort of "one-woman show." I had taken a flight to Florida once on a small plane with the propellers on the wings. Toward the end of the trip, one of the propellers began to slow down, and then stop, causing the plane to dip to one side. I was squashed into the seat next to a very large, very nervous, and very sweaty Southern belle.

"Oh my God!" she yelled out. "We're going down!"

The flight attendant immediately rushed down the aisle to keep her from panicking the other passengers, assuring her that we could make it just fine on one engine. She squirmed, fidgeted, whimpered, and moaned the rest of the way, and quite frankly, *I've never been right since*! One of the pitfalls of being so sensitive to energies and people's feelings is that when I find myself in confined spaces with a lot of people, I really feel anxious. Their excitement and their fears seem to stick to me like a magnet, and I feel as if I am being taken over by emotions that don't even belong to me. Meditation and concentration have helped over the years, but my first overseas flight was tough; I had white knuckles all the way from New York to London.

My only distraction was my friend Lee, a girl from Spartanburg, who was traveling with me en route to Amsterdam. I was introduced to her by my housemate Jo, and when she heard that I was heading to the British Isles, she asked if she could tag along. I welcomed her constant chatter, as it kept me from ripping the arms off my seat when we had turbulence.

The doctor who had invited me to come to the UK was originally from Dublin. We met him in London first and then flew over to Ireland for a week. Just before I headed back to England to visit the school, Lee took off for Amsterdam.

Fifty-seven viewings of my father's favorite classic film, *The Quiet Man*, had prepared me for stone walls, rolling green fields, and lots and lots of sheep. I was very surprised when I arrived in the cosmopolitan city of Dublin, with its fantastic character and a buzz comparable to that of any major city I had ever visited.

Our host's sister was kind enough to loan her car to us, so we could go explore the country on our own. The doc had business to attend to, and would meet up with us when we returned to Dublin. We were amazed by all of the beautiful little villages, and the fact that there seemed to be a pub on every corner. We stopped about an hour and a half outside of Dublin, in the midlands town of Athlone, because we saw a sign for a chiropractor. I wanted to pop in to see what an Irish practice was like.

We were greeted by a very friendly receptionist named Maureen. We clicked immediately; she had a twinkle in her eye that I loved straightaway. She seemed very familiar in some way. She introduced us to the doctor, a Canadian by origin. I liked the feel of the office and began to visualize what it would be like if it were mine. The doctor spoke of how difficult he found it to live in Ireland because it lacked many of the "creature comforts" of home. I immediately thought to myself, that it should be me, not him, running that office. At that moment, I had the funniest feeling, a certainty nearly, that one day *I would be*.

We expressed our thanks and said our good-byes, then walked

into town, across the river Shannon and into the most beautiful cathedral. Across the road was a *real* castle, something the average American doesn't see every day. It was perched on the bank of the river, like an ancient centurion, and down the hill, just behind it, was Sean's Bar, Ireland's oldest pub. We laughed, because in our few short days in Ireland, we had been told about ten different pubs that were meant to be the oldest in the country. When we walked in, it was like stepping back in time, with sawdust on the floors and low ceilings covered in paraphernalia from all around the world. This turned out to be the real McCoy. Sean's Bar did, in fact, proudly hold the record as Ireland's oldest public house. There were musicians playing that night, so we decided we would stay and check it out. By the next morning, I was in love with this town. During our travels, people would laugh at me when I said that my favorite place had been Athlone.

"There are so many beautiful places along the coast and in the majestic hills, why an old garrison town like Athlone?"

There was magic and music in the air of that old town, and something about it had captured my heart. If ever I had been somewhere that I felt I had been before, this place made me feel as if I was the prodigal child returning home.

We woke the next morning, not too bright and early, because the session from the night before had gone into the wee hours of the morning. My ears were still ringing with the sounds of guitars, pipes, and the bodhran (the native Irish drum). Real Irish music, in a real Irish pub, played by people who looked as if they were having the time of their lives; this was a sight that I had never seen in any bar at home. The people were there to enjoy each other, to share their talent, and I felt so at home in that environment.

Being fresh off the boat from America, I was unaccustomed to the *colorful* Irish slang that I was introduced to that night. The "F" bomb was featured at least twice in every sentence, by young and old, alike. Even those who looked like the sweet, little Granny types used the word to describe everything from the f\*\*\*ing horrible weather, to the f\*\*\*ing brilliant day they had with the grandkids! I nearly fainted when I was asked if I had enjoyed the crack! I soon learned that, in Ireland, crack (spelled craic) refers to fun. I also found it funny that, in Ireland, I was constantly referred to as a Yank—me, a girl from the South. Obviously, they had never seen *Gone with the Wind*!

✳

We hit the road, heading west for Galway, clueless to the fact that things were about to get *very interesting*. We got to Eyre Square, in the center of Galway, and wandered through the side streets, meandering through all of the quaint little shops. We went into an antique jewelry store and had a look around. My stomach began to turn flips when I picked up a necklace with a marking that was now very familiar. It was etched with one of the twenty-one symbols that had been haunting me for the last three months. Pulse racing, I took the necklace to the shopkeeper and asked if he knew anything about the symbol. He said that it was a character from an ancient Celtic script, which was found thousands of years ago in Ireland. I was thrilled as I called Lee over to have a look; I had told her about the symbols on the flight over. I couldn't believe I was now holding a replica of one in my hands.

I was starting to get that feeling; the sense that something incredible was about to unfold. We walked across the square and into a pub called Fibber McGees. We were making ourselves at home, sitting at a table, Guinness in hand, talking to an Irish couple. A friend of theirs sat down to join us. His name was Brian, and he was fantastically, authentically, stereotypically Irish, with his red hair and freckles: "Ginger," as the Irish called it. He was a good-looking guy, really friendly as well, and when his friends told him that we were touring around the country, he offered to show us a few of the sights. We were grateful to be shown around by someone who knew where he was going, and by someone who knew how to drive on the left side of the road. We had been lucky to make it as far as we had without completely destroying the passenger side of our friend's car.

Brian met us the next morning, and we drove through the rocky landscape of the Burren, and then the rolling, green hillsides of Connemara. Two days later, we arrived in the town of Lisdoon-varna, famous for its matchmaking festival for eager young bucks and beautiful Irish lasses. It was early evening. We stopped to have a bite to eat in a classic old pub and while Lee and I finished up, Brian disappeared for a few minutes. When he returned, he pulled me aside, and said that he wanted to give me something in thanks for bringing him along. He handed me a silver ring, with a twisted Celtic design. I was delighted and told him how much we appreci-ated him taking the time to show two complete strangers around his homeland. I put the ring on my finger, and that's when I noticed it. Inscribed in a tiny marking, within the design, *was another one of the symbols.*

"Where did you get this?" I quizzed him.

"Just over there, in the shop; if you don't like it . . ."

"No, no! I love it! But I need to see where you got this!"

He took me across the road and showed me a tray of rings that were all of similar design. There must have been over thirty of them. I frantically started looking through each and every one to see if they were all the same. Brian was looking at me like I was some sort of lunatic, but at the time, he knew nothing about the symbols or me. Of all of the rings, the one that he had picked for me was the only one in the tray that was marked with one of the twenty-one symbols.

After my strange behavior, Brian demanded to know what was going on. We sat down, and I told him a condensed version of my life story, ending up with flaming symbols that now appeared to be of Irish origins. He grinned from ear to ear, taking me by the hand, saying, "Get in the car; I know where we're heading next."

It was already late, but Ireland in the summer was much different from home. The nighttime sky didn't get dark until almost midnight, and the sunset seemed to last for hours. Brian drove like mad, heading east, but would not tell us where we were going. Eventually, as we approached our destination, I felt the hair stand up on the back of my neck. The sensation that something incredible was about to happen had stayed with me since we had arrived in Galway. But now it had escalated to a frenzied sense that I was about to uncover a great secret, the essence of my true self, something my Guides had assured me would happen, in the not-so-distant future. We pulled up to Newgrange, a Neolithic passage tomb in the Boyne Valley, built some five thousand years earlier. The historical monument had closed hours earlier, as it was now after ten-thirty. I didn't care though, because there, on the entrance gates, were replicas of the symbols inside, cast in wrought iron. I couldn't believe what I was seeing, even if it was only the padlocked gates leading into the grounds.

Brian said that there were curbstones all around the tomb, covered in symbols that had been found to predate the Celts by 2,500 years. This was my light switch: a connection so powerful that I knew in an instant I had found my way home. I didn't even need to see the quartz-covered burial mound to know that this was the beacon that had so boldly sent its signal to guide me to the next phase of my journey. I stood in tears, so totally united with my surroundings that I got a fright when Brian grabbed me, saying, "Come on, you're leaving tomorrow, you may never get this chance again!"

Before I knew what was happening, we were running across a field, trespassing on a farmer's private property, so that we could hop the fence and get a look at the tomb, close up. I wasn't intending to break the law that night, but when I touched the stones, so deeply carved by ancient hands, I just lived for the moment; it was only a moment, though, as I was snapped back to reality by the sound of barking dogs and the lights of an approaching vehicle. We ran through the fields and emerged on the other side, covered in cow poop and God knows what else! The evening light was fading into the royal blue of midnight, and the three of us laughed heartily, celebrating as if we had just discovered the Holy Grail.

The following day, Lee and I said our good-byes and promised to catch up when we were back in the States. I flew to England, where I was to encounter a way of life entirely different from what I had just experienced in Ireland. I had felt so at home there, and my time had been spent just getting to know the people and the places, ending with the momentous occasion of finding the ancient symbols. England was an entirely different kettle of fish, a melting pot of diverse cultures. I quickly discovered what a sheltered life I had led. My lack of knowledge about the rest of the world was not only embarrassing, it also made me feel a little on the ignorant side. The people that I encountered were so different from any others I had ever met, and the lifestyle was completely new to me. Everything in London seemed so crowded and stuck together. The houses were terraced, the cars were tiny, and nothing was "all you can eat." I hadn't seemed to notice these things in Ireland, because my focus had been on something altogether different.

Thinking of home, it seemed so strange now, and I began to understand the worldwide perception of America as a gluttonous society. Our cars were big, our houses were huge by comparison, our food consumption was off the charts, and our knowledge of the way the rest of the world lives now seemed very, very limited. Don't get me wrong. I loved my home, and its people, but my eyes were opening to the possibility that the land of the free and the home of the brave was sorely lacking in a few crucial areas, at least in my neck of the woods. I was challenged by complete strangers about my views on America's involvement in world politics and its contribution to resource consumption and the energy crisis. I was asked for my opinion on Third World debt and how I felt about the formation of the European Union. For a girl who had been well educated in the American school systems, through a university and now about to become a doctor, I suddenly became aware that I knew very little about the rest of the world, knowing for certain, *I wasn't alone.*

I had a lot to learn, and I would make it my business to remove my blinders, to become a citizen of the world, not just my own country. The mess this planet is in was now making a whole lot of sense to me, and my personal ignorance to the ways of the rest of the world was not a good enough excuse. If nothing else had happened, this epiphany would have made the whole trip worthwhile.

The difference between the energy in England and Ireland was palpable. Ireland was so relaxed and easygoing, while the UK felt much faster paced and hectic. I hadn't made it out of London yet, so when I headed down country, I began to see what made the English countryside so famous. I felt like I was traveling back through time, minus the superhighways that made getting from A to B a whole lot easier than traveling the potholed boreens of Ireland. The land was majestic, and the pace of life began to slow down the closer we got to the shore.

The chiropractic college in Bournemouth was outstanding. It was located in a quaint seaside town that reeked of history. The grounds were beautiful, and I couldn't believe my eyes when I was given a tour of the school that ended in the college bar! They had a bar . . . right there in the school! Dorothy was no longer in Kansas, and Toto was in the school bar having a pint of lager! I'd never witnessed anything like it! Where I come from, there's a church on every corner. In this lovely town, and in most others I had seen, there were churches *and* pubs, everywhere you turned.

The students were friendly and hailed from all over the globe. I had never really had the opportunity to mingle with so many people, from so many different cultures. I found myself gravitating toward the Irish students, because I seemed to feel more at home with the way they spoke, as well as their fantastic sense of humor. I also had a lot to talk about, having just returned from Ireland a few days earlier. Everyone was very nice, but they all got a big kick out of the fact that I had short hair and wore overalls, or dungarees, as they called them. I explained that they were very fashionable at home. My new friends were quick to point out that I wasn't in the South anymore! They said I had better not expect any men to approach me because in England, a *straight* girl did not, under any circumstances, dress like that!

I hate to say it, but they were right. I didn't heed the advice, and when I was taken to a nightclub, the only people who even looked at me, much less spoke to me, were the ones I had come with. The fashion was so dramatically different than what I was accustomed to. The girls were dressed to the nines just to go out for a few drinks, and everyone looked as if they had just walked out of the hairdressers. It was very impressive, but one thing that really shocked me was how the girls were wearing tiny little skirts, sleeveless tops and very high heels with no stockings in the bitterly cold English air. No one seemed to mind, and no one was willing to cover up a fabulous outfit for the sake of a bit of warmth.

The students found me comical. I had a heavy twang when I spoke, and I dressed even funnier than I talked, and when I danced . . . oh, the laughs of them all. The techno beat of European dance music was a far cry from Lynyrd Skynyrd or Guns N' Roses. I think they enjoyed having me around, though, because they felt as if I fit every American stereotype known to man. I was nearly too humorous to be true. Regardless of their motives, the students were very welcoming, and included me in all of their activities, both in school, and out.

I went to a house party one weekend just off campus, where I met a girl called Maryellen, from Canada. We became fast friends, for life. She introduced me around, and on that same night, I met a man who was to become a major feature in my life the following

year, and for all the years to follow. John was from Ireland and had
a personality the size of Texas. It was friendship at first sight, and
I think both of us would agree that we knew that we had known
one another before. Remember, soul mates come in many forms,
and one of mine had just appeared with a pint of Guinness in hand
and a head full of Southern rock trivia. John had lived in America,
traveling the country extensively, and he was as knowledgeable
about my country, *and* my favorite bands, as any other good South-
ern-fried soul. He shook his head in disbelief as I told him about
sneaking into the burial tomb at Newgrange, but seemed to totally
understand and admire the reasoning behind my actions. I think
he appreciated my genuine awe and respect for his country, and
being one who followed his intuition as well, he appreciated the
mission that I was on. I didn't get to spend a lot of time with John
on that trip but knew in my heart that the fun with him had only
just begun. He would be returning to Ireland to set up practices in
Dublin and Galway after graduation that year. There was absolutely
no doubt in my mind that he would somehow be an integral part
of my life in the not-so-distant future.

I gave a few talks to several of the classes at the college, and
my gratitude and appreciation for the chance to be educated with
Sherman's solid philosophical foundation were immense. These
students knew the anatomy of the body and they owned the scientific approach to chiropractic, but most were completely lacking
in its philosophy. If we had been taught one thing at Sherman, it
was that chiropractic is a science, an art, *and* a philosophy: each as
important as the other two. These students had been told stories
of the strange practitioners in America who viewed chiropractic
as a religion and prayed to the God of innate intelligence. After
hearing the truth, many of the future doctors found themselves
wanting to know more. Some just laughed and rubbished the idea
that owning a personal philosophy would make any difference to
running a successful practice.

Unfortunately, it seemed chiropractic would become just a job to those people, until they grasped the fundamentals of owning its philosophy. It takes all three sides to complete the triad, and thank goodness, there were some very motivated students, particularly my friends John and Maryellen, who were interested in stepping outside of the box. I had done my fair share of public speaking at Sherman, but when I got the opportunity to stand in front of new faces, sharing concepts that were new to them, I knew that somewhere down the line, I would be called to teach. I loved the challenge of being challenged, because when it came to chiropractic philosophy, I knew my stuff.

My Irish host in England was like no one I have ever met. Richard had the tenacity of a bulldog when it came to taking on the system, with a confidence and attitude that would see him become one of the greats in this field. After we spent a couple of days at the school, he took me to see a few of the sights around London, and I was particularly excited when he suggested that we go to Stonehenge. I wasn't sure what to think, as I had fallen prey to my own imagination of what I thought this enigmatic treasure that had baffled the world for so many years would look like. It was much smaller than I had pictured it to be, and it was also roped off, so that you couldn't actually walk through it. After my experience at Newgrange in Ireland, it didn't really stand a chance. The *layout* of the stones, however, sparked a memory, more like a familiar feeling, the details of which I had forgotten. I had seen these stones before, through different eyes. There definitely was magic in the air surrounding this mysterious site, and I was grateful for the opportunity to be there . . . again.

My trip came to an end, all too soon, and I hated the thoughts of returning to the grind of classes and exams. I left my new mates, vowing to see them again, very soon, even though I knew that the likelihood of a return trip any time in the near future was basically nonexistent. I had two more terms of school to complete and would spend the next year sitting state and national board exams. Still, I hoped that I would find my way back, because now I was hooked, and I could easily see myself returning to this part of the world, to live there.

*

In the last quarter of school, students were given the chance to do an externship (work experience) in the practice of a doctor who was sanctioned by the school board. If a student opted not to do this, the last term was spent continuing to practice in the school's health center. I introduced the idea of externing abroad to the school board, and found out that several of the school's alumni were practicing in Ireland. I worked hard to come up with contacts, and ultimately I would become the first student to do an international externship. I had never met the doctor with whom I would be working, but my friend Maryellen in England knew someone who knew someone, and it all came together.

When I made the decision, I ran it past Dave, and we came to the conclusion that because I would be leaving at Christmas, we would stop seeing each other for the remaining months before I left. I guess we all love a little drama in our lives. That idea lasted a whole week, before we admitted how stupid it was! We made up our minds to have the time of our lives, and when it was time to say good-bye, we'd leave it at that. Those next few months were amazing and probably some of the best times I have ever had. Those memories are precious to me, and we lived every moment *in* the moment.

Christmas break in 1997 came like a tidal wave. I had to pack up my home of the last four years, leave the security of college life and its friends, bid farewell to a remarkable man, and squeeze in a visit to my family, all before heading to England, then ultimately Ireland. My flight was to leave on Christmas Eve, and I would arrive bright and early on Christmas Day in London. On the day before I was to fly out, we got the news that Grandmother Clark had passed away. She and I had both known it was coming, which is why she had threatened to haunt me from beyond if I changed my plans. The very first thing that my Aunt Joyce said to me was that I had made a promise to Grandmother a year earlier. I was supposed to sing at my grandmother's funeral whenever she died, but I had also given her my word that I would not allow singing at her funeral to interfere with school commitments. Promise? What promise? I had never had any intention of keeping it in the first place. Of course, I would delay the trip and stay for the funeral. Even in her failing health, Grandmother was well aware that I was to make the trip abroad. She had been so excited for me to have this opportunity; it was *her* parents who were from England and Wales and her grandparents who were from Northern Ireland. For me to make this journey meant the world to her, the chance to visit my roots, to follow my destiny, and I was now faced with a serious dilemma. I wanted to be there for my mother, but she insisted that I take the trip, without delay. I ended up going to the church and recording the song that was played at her funeral. I made the flight to the UK the following day. I was never sure about the decision, but in the end, I did what she asked me to do and had to be content with my choice.

# Chapter 20

I ARRIVED in London on Christmas morning, feeling a little worse for wear from the all-night flight and due to the fact that I was missing my Grandmother's funeral. My fog lifted the second I saw my friend, Maryellen, waiting for me in arrivals. She was so happy to see me, and was to be my hostess for the next two weeks, while I awaited instructions from the doctor I would be working with in Ireland. We quickly caught up on events from the last six months on the drive back to Bournemouth. Maryellen was a couple of years behind me in school but had a real grasp of the fundamentals of chiropractic, and its philosophy. She couldn't wait to hear all of my news about board exams, the last two terms of school, and how I had left things with my boyfriend, Dave. We looked like two old hens, clucking down the road, in her little purple banger of a car, affectionately known as Barney.

The next week was wonderful as we spent time looking around the countryside, further developing our friendship. None of the other students were around, since most had gone home for the holidays. Maryellen was on a student's budget and going home to Canada for Christmas had not been a realistic prospect for her that year. We had a great time, topped off by a quick trip to Ireland for New Year's Eve. I thought I had died and gone to heaven (pun intended)! I met up with my new old friend, John, from Ireland. After initially meeting in England the summer before, I was now seeing him in action on his home turf. What a character and what an introduction to the Irish way of life! The weekend trip ended much too soon, and we headed back to Bournemouth, to wait for word from the doctor I would be working with in Dublin.

Things weren't going exactly as planned, and I was having difficulty getting in touch with my new boss in Ireland. I spent a lot longer time in England than I was supposed to, but as with all things, I trusted that there must be a purpose behind it all. The time was well spent, living it up, unwinding after the last five years of study. I also cultivated my relationship with John, enjoying every second spent in his company. I was enamored by his wit, wisdom, and amazing approach to life. I adored John, because he was the kind of guy who would see a girl walk by, maybe a little overweight, *not* Barbie-doll attractive, and he would pick out her greatest feature, then comment on how fabulous she was! His ability to see the beauty in everyone was incredible. I had come from a culture that was far too hung up on a perfect body image.

When the time came for my long-awaited stay in Ireland, the initial plan had changed a bit. The doctor I was working for had some unforeseen issues arise, and it meant that I would have to spend some of my time elsewhere. I was enthusiastic about the prospect of getting to live and work in more than one area, so it suited me just fine! He was a lovely, gentle sort of man, and I learned more than just chiropractic while in his company. He taught me a thing or two about attitude, outlook, and maturity as well.

With a stroke of luck, I was taken under the wing of a man I still consider to be one of the most extraordinary individuals I have ever met. Dr. Owens was larger than life, lived to the max, knew the most incredible people, and had traveled to places that I had never even heard of. He had graduated from my chiropractic school over fifteen years earlier and had returned to Ireland to practice, enjoying success at a very young age. He immediately put me to work in a clinic that he owned in Limerick. I was a little nervous at first, but I can honestly say, that to this day, I loved the people there, and found it to be one of the most wonderful places I have ever lived.

There were two American doctors, both of whom had recently relocated to Ireland, working to build the new practice. I moved in with them, and in between nights on the town, sightseeing, and a lot of laughter, I helped them in any way that I could with the practice. They were well used to the Irish lingo and one day when they sent me to buy some office supplies, I realized that I was not!

I was dressed in a miniskirt and high boots (I had long since ditched the dungarees) and was walking out of the shop with my arms full of supplies. Two policemen (or Gardai, as they are called in Ireland) were walking toward me. I must have had the look of confusion that only a blonde can get, when they asked me if I was all right. In my thick Southern accent, sporting my short skirt and long boots, I replied, "No, thanks, I'm just waiting for a ride."

Well, they buckled in two, unable to contain their laughter and explained to me that in Ireland, a ride meant a shag.

"Shag, you mean like the dance?" (The shag is South Carolina's state dance.)

One of them had now been brought to tears from laughter as he again tried to explain a ride and shag. Finally, I turned bright red as the lightbulb clicked. I was standing on a street corner dressed like someone out of *Pretty Woman* and had just told two policemen that I was waiting for sex! From that day forward I made it my business to learn all the Irish slang I could.

The experience was unforgettable, and the friendships, I treasured. What had appeared to be a possible hiccup in my training was turning out to be the most valuable practical experience I could have asked for.

When my time in Ireland came to an end in March, I had a meeting with Dr. Owens, in a place called the K Club, just outside of Dublin. I had never heard of it before, but most of the world has now heard of it, as it hosted the world famous Ryder Cup golf tournament in 2007. It was an incredible facility, stunningly beautiful and host to many famous faces. I went to the bathroom shortly after we had arrived, walking down the plush, ornate carpets and right past a member of the famous Spice Girls band. The stars residing at the K Club didn't faze me for long, though, because I was on a mission, trying to negotiate my future in Ireland. We went into a private room, and as Dr. Owens sipped champagne, I told him that I would do whatever it took to return to his country to live. He was very sympathetic to my plea, but the reality was that even with all of the offices he owned, there were no positions available. It wasn't as simple as hopping on a plane and setting up shop. There were visas and sponsorships that had to be obtained; then there was the little matter of three hundred and fifty thousand pounds (if you wanted to set up on your own practice) without getting hired under a working visa. I was three hundred and forty-nine thousand short, so that wasn't an option. Distraught but determined, I packed my bags and headed home, only two days before another big landmark in my life—graduating from student to doctor.

✳

Dave picked me up from the airport, and he laughed when he saw my additional baggage. Not the suitcases but the fifteen extra pounds I had packed on while overseas! Graduation was an amazing time, and I was so glad to be spending it with Dave. I really had missed him, but could see that our lives were beginning to separate and move in different directions.

Dave and I had a frank discussion about what we were going to do. As pragmatic as ever, Dave said that he knew that my ultimate goal was to go and work with "the leprechauns." But wouldn't it make much more sense to stay for the year, complete my final board exam the following November, and then look into moving over? He suggested that I move up to Philadelphia: to help him for the summer with the landscaping business while preparing to

sit the most difficult of the board exams. We had also both wanted
to take the South Carolina exam, for nostalgia's sake, as well as for
the experience. I said that it sounded like a good plan and prepared
myself to become a Yankee!

That summer, the fifteen pounds that I had gained in Ireland
melted off during the fourteen-hour workdays that Dave and I
were putting in. It was in the upper nineties every day, and let
me tell you, pushing a lawn mower around gigantic apartment
complexes was anything but glamorous. To make matters worse,
money was really tight that year. We were working hard, but between trying to set up a place to practice and paying for the exams
we were taking (and retaking, in my case), we were broke. I can still
remember the day that Dave said I was going to have to find a way
to contribute more to the fledgling practice than the wages he was
paying me. With great reluctance, I took the wedding ring that I
had invested so much time and energy into, seven years earlier, and
handed it over to what can only be described as a jewelry shark. I
sold the ring for so much less than it was worth, but I was under a
lot of pressure, and honestly, it was time to let it go. We purchased
our first chiropractic table for adjusting the spine, and, temporarily,
this contribution was enough.

Behind the scenes, I was constantly researching ways to get
back to Ireland. It had gone from mission to obsession. I was in
touch with my friends on the Emerald Isle, hoping that something
would give. Nothing was turning up, and my enthusiasm was turning to frustration.

The time came for Dave and me to sit the South Carolina board
exam. Heading back to our alma mater, we enjoyed reconnecting
with some of our old friends at our favorite haunts. The exam was
going smoothly, until I got into a room with a couple of doctors
who were going to ask me to diagnose some hideous neurological
disorder. True to form, my subconscious ability to summon injury,
or illness, during times of stress reared its ugly little head. I was

struggling to come up with the appropriate words, when one of the doctors went to move a very heavy wooden chair. The chair toppled over. Direct hit to the top of my foot! We could nearly hear each of the *three* fractures, as my bones cracked under the weight of the chair. Needless to say, not only did I give a very explicit answer to their question, I was whizzed through the rest of the exam.

During that summer of 1998 I had the opportunity to work with a legendary chiropractic couple, Drs. Reggie and Irene Gold, who were also based in Philly. I helped Reggie out with a couple of projects he was involved in regarding chiropractic philosophy, but it ended up being his wife who really put me to work! She was the leading authority and queen of the National Board Exam Reviews. Hers was a service that most students availed themselves of, taking them through rigorous preparation courses for the exams. I think I actually learned more in the short time that I taught for her, than I did my entire time in school. The information was condensed, taught with rhymes, songs, pictures, and endless repetition. Her system was incredible, and highly successful, and she was a genius at her work. I enjoyed the time I spent traveling and teaching at chiropractic schools around the country, further convincing me that eventually, I would wind up as some sort of a teacher. She knew a little about my curious history and would laugh every time we went through a security check in the airport. I would have to be searched because my *unusual* energetic constitution never failed to set the alarms off.

One of her requirements was that I sit as many board exams as I could, to further increase my knowledge of what her customers could expect. What a nightmare! In essence, I had spent the last twenty-four years of my life in school, and now I was willingly subjecting myself to one state exam after another in order to become a more proficient teacher. Dave thought I was nuts. Most days, so did I. When all was said and done, I could have held licenses in most states of the East Coast.

# Chapter 21

I WAS enjoying my time in Philadelphia, but quietly my heart was breaking, as Ireland seemed to be getting further out of reach. It had also been quite some time since my last encounter with my Guides, "the voice," or with being called to heal anyone. I seemed to be losing my focus, and in my despair, I was no longer listening. I had developed tunnel vision, and the more upset I became about not being in Ireland, the less I looked for solutions.

I was still doing a good bit of public speaking as former student body president of Sherman College and it was at a philosophy event that I embraced one of the most disturbing and powerful lessons I have ever learned in my life. I had prepared what I was going to say; standard material, nothing out of the ordinary. I was speaking last, and while I was waiting in the back of the room, a doctor pulled me aside and showed me an article in some health journal, written by another chiropractor.

The doctor in the editorial was what we would have called a "mixer." A chiropractor who not only adjusted the spine, but used a host of other modalities to treat the symptoms associated with spinal misalignments. The chiropractor who had brought this article to my attention pointed out that this guy thought he was practicing *real* chiropractic but was really just a "wannabe." In a moment of weakness, I let this man's opinions influence me, and when it was my turn to speak, I used the man who had written this piece as a blaring example of what we were fighting against in our profession. At one point, I even think I called him a loser. Before I could make it to the end of the speech, my internal "truth meter" had set off alarm bells and I began to feel physically ill, as I had just compromised my character, my moral standards, and my reputation to make a guy who was simply trying a different approach an embarrassment and an example.

It was I who was embarrassed, in shock at my complete lack of sensitivity. I couldn't even finish the rest of my talk and promptly announced to the audience that it would be a very long time before they would hear me speak publicly again. It was that day, which had caused me to see why the last year, and my attempts to get to Ireland, had been such a struggle. I was paddling upstream, against the natural flow of life. I had been such an *expert* in my field, so sure that I knew what was right and true. In reality, the philosophy that I thought I had owned, now owned me. That afternoon, I sat in a park, by myself, and wrote a letter of apology to the man I had slandered, *a man I didn't even know*. I made up my mind, then and there, that I would reclaim my power, never allowing apathy or disappointment in my circumstances to dictate my life ever again. I was solid in this decision and I was about to experience just how quickly the Universe responds when we make a real commitment to change.

The very next day, I got a phone call from my dear friend John, asking if it would be possible to give him a hand with opening his new office in Galway, Ireland. It was only temporary, but it was a start.

*"Ask and ye shall receive."* It was so simple, it was scary.

*

I could hardly wait to get to Ireland, and Dave and I both knew that our relationship had run its course. We finished as friends, remaining that way to this day. When two lives are congruent with their purpose, this is the way that *any* partnership can finish up: with joy, and gratitude for the time shared in each other's lives. Dave took me to the airport; we kissed, and hugged good-bye, not sure when we would see one another again. I was unsure how long I would be in Galway; it could be weeks, or months. There was one thing I was certain of, I would invoke all that I knew to ensure that, this time, I was staying in Ireland for good.

The time I spent in Galway in the spring and early summer of 1999 was amazing. I learned so much about the actual practice of chiropractic and what it meant to see a high volume of people. John was in Dublin, so I didn't see him often. I spent a tremendous amount of time on my own, walking the streets of Galway, sitting at the edge of the sea, so grateful to be on the Irish side of the Atlantic. There was something so soothing about dwelling among the castles, the ancient architecture, the evergreen fields, and the endless stone walls. I was deeply connecting to my Celtic roots, and never in my life had I been so at home. I was centering my soul, rediscovering my path, and understanding that just because we follow our calling, it doesn't mean we are exempt from life's toughest lessons.

When my time in Galway was finished in June, I still was no closer to finding a way to live there permanently. I refused to crumble this time, and kept sending out signals to the Universe that I trusted the process and knew that my prayers would be heard. I got a phone call from my friend Maryellen, in England, inviting me to join some friends and her, on a sailing trip around the islands of the west coast of Scotland. I could think of nothing I would rather do, so I packed up and flew over to England, where I met up with Maryellen. We drove up to Scotland to meet the rest of the group that would be on the yacht. I was ticking off another lifetime goal, because as much as I loved and longed to be in Ireland, I had always wanted to spend time in the highlands of Scotland. I guess it was because Dad always reminded us that he was a descendent of Rob

Roy, the famous Scottish warrior, and he had the birthmark to prove it! Both of my parents were also of Scottish descent, as well as having ancestors from England, Wales, and the north of Ireland. I was thrilled to finally get the chance to be there.

The trip around the islands was incredible. The scenery and the wildlife were breathtaking! The experience of being on the crew of this yacht was also a first. The most important part of this trip, however, was the phone call I received two days before we finished the journey. Dr. Owens, the doc who had come through for me during my externship in Ireland, was about to do it again!

"MH, when are you back?" asked Dr. Owens.

"The day after tomorrow. Why?" I replied.

"I have an office I need you to cover. The doctor has gone for good. I need you to stay there until I figure out what I'm going to do."

I could barely speak but tried not to sound overeager, when in actual fact, I was ready to burst. "Of course, I can help you out," I said calmly.

"Good," he said. "I'll see you in two days."

Then I asked him where I was going.

"The town of Athlone. I'll chat to you later," he replied, and promptly hung up the phone.

I couldn't believe my ears! I was going to be working in the office that I had stopped in a year and a half earlier. This was the office that I had visualized as my own: the one that was located in my very favorite town in Ireland, the one with the secretary with the special gleam in her eye. I screamed to the heavens, "YOU ROCK!"

As clear as day, I heard: *"We know, and so do you!"*

Just as I knew it would, everything had fallen into place, and suddenly, there was magic all around me. I had to return back to Philadelphia to pack my belongings. Dave was genuinely happy for me and never did or said anything that made me feel anything but supported. I would miss him, but now it was my turn to shine!

Baking in the early July heat, so heavy you could see it rising from the tarmac in the short-term parking lot of Philadelphia International Airport, Dave and I shared one last kiss. While we would both feel the loss of a genuine companionship, we were also both extremely excited to move to the next level. I represented the levity of school, the anxiety of exams, the financial struggle of opening a new practice, and Dave was ready to experience success. I had nearly been rendered useless in my longing, my obsession to get back to Ireland. The feeling was right for us both, and the time had returned to move on. A plane ride across the Atlantic, to the mysterious shores of Eire, was now the last page to be turned before starting the next chapter in the book of my life.

# PART II

## Circles of Light

A wishbone ain't as likely to get you
someplace as a backbone.
—*Unknown*

# Chapter 22

"I WANT YOU!" a deep voice with a painfully fake American accent boomed through the arrivals hall as I turned around to find myself face-to-waist with Uncle Sam on stilts, decked out in red, white, and blue, complete with star-spangled top hat. The bearded icon was pointing at me, just as he had looked in the US military recruitment posters of years gone by. Lady Liberty, a woman badly spray-painted from head to toe in a strange combination of silver-and-puke green, was sporting a spiky headpiece that looked as if it had been made from the insides of a few paper towel rolls. Both American idols were entertaining the masses for the Fourth of July celebrations. Old Glory was proudly on display, patriotic tunes wafted through the air, and the festive buzz around the airport was spine tingling. And yet it was Dublin, Ireland, I had just landed in, not the capital city of the land of the free and the home of the brave!

It had been a long, strange trip. I had left my practice and boy-friend behind in Philadelphia to chase the meaning of twenty-one ancient symbols. Ireland, though I didn't know it at the time, was to become more than just my new home. This was the place where I would discover the purpose behind my capacity to facilitate heal-ing, my innate ability to commune with those in Spirit, and most importantly, to dispel the mysteries surrounding who we are as human beings and the legends regarding the origins and the very future of our planet.

Work began July 7, in a town along the river Shannon. Athlone had been my favorite place on my first excursion through Ireland because it had something . . . a vibe that is difficult to explain unless you've experienced it. Although not known for what one would think of when dreaming of classically quaint Irish towns, its charm and mystique were palpable. I had picked this spot nearly a year and a half earlier; or rather, *it* had picked me.

I was going to take over a chiropractic practice until my friend Dr. Owens could find someone to work there permanently. I had made it no secret that I wanted that someone to be *me*, so in I went, with guns blazing, ready to show him the stuff I was made of. There was no way I was going to let this opportunity slip through my fingers, and the thoughts of going back to America to live anytime in the foreseeable future were simply unthinkable. I had held up my end of the deal with my Spirit Guides by releasing everything and relocating to this strange and wonderful new place. I fully expected them to see me through it, making sure that at all costs I was home to stay.

*

Dr. John Fay had been instrumental in my move to Ireland by providing temporary work in Galway prior to my opportunity to practice in Athlone. We'd just "clicked" when we first met in England, while he was still a student at the chiropractic college in Bournemouth. We shared an amazing chemistry. Our mutual passions for chiropractic, rock bands, and commanding an audience made us a force to be reckoned with. We began to reconnect with our past, building the foundation for an unshakable friendship in the future. John understood me and accepted my gifts for what they were. He, in fact, was no stranger to psychic experiences himself. He had set up practices in Dublin and Galway and I was now working in Athlone. My few belongings resided at Maureen's house; she was my marvelous new office manager and the same special lady with the gleam in her eye I had met the previous year while traveling. I should have bought stock in Irish Rail, as I spent so much time on the train back and forth between Dublin and Athlone. It was truly an amazing summer spent gallivanting all over Ireland with John, but before long, staying in my office manager's spare room was no longer suitable and I had to find a home of my own.

I had always cringed at the concept of permanent residence, particularly the thoughts of owning things like a washing machine and dryer. Somewhere in my twisted perception, owning these devices equated with my being stuck. Finding a place to live in Athlone *should* have been first on the agenda, considering I had recently relocated to another continent. I *should* have wanted to choose a place where I could finally plant some roots. I had moved so many times in my twenties that my vagabond soul *should* have been craving some stability. But I *hated* the idea of being stuck.

I moved into the neighborhood of Retreat Heights on a Friday and, even though it wasn't winter yet, the house had no oil and it was freezing. I had started moving my things in and a few hours later, took a little trip to the shop to get a drink. I came back to the house and set my large Sprite on the coffee table and began to unpack more bags. A few minutes later, I walked back into the sitting room to take a sip of my drink. When I lifted the cup it was completely empty, ice and all. I knew I hadn't finished it off, as it was nearly full when I put it on the table. I looked around to see if it had spilled, but the lid was secure and there wasn't a drop to be found anywhere. Peculiar. So far, I hadn't really sensed anything unusual in the house, but then again, it was my first time in it other than the twenty-minute viewing I'd had earlier in the week.

That night, I built a fire using turf briquettes. It was such a proud moment because it was my first night in the new house and my very first fire. The fire wasn't for ambience; it was the only source of heat I had until I could get oil ordered and placed in the tank. Being a naive girl from America, any house I had ever lived in just required the flick of a switch and the temperature remained constant. I had never had to think about purchasing my own fuel. Very quickly, I came to understand the value of a roaring fire. With flames blazing, I pulled out a mattress and two duvets to the sitting room because if I hadn't, my frozen, dead body would have been discovered days later in the back bedroom. I parked myself right in front of the hearth, wearing a sweat suit and hat, and prepared to go to sleep. Oh, did I mention that there was no fireguard? Sparks?? It never even crossed my novice mind.

At about four o'clock in the morning I awakened, feeling as if I had been left naked in the frozen tundras of the Antarctic. I looked through sleepy eyes at the dwindling fire and discovered that I was so cold because I had obviously pushed the duvets off the side of the mattress. I looked around—no duvets. I was wide awake by then and got up to turn on the lights. Still no duvets. The setup in this house was quite unusual in that there was a sitting room in the front of the house and two adjoining living rooms in the middle and to the back of the house. The rooms were both large and were conjoined by an arched open doorway. There were couches in the room where I had made my bed and another set of couches in the adjoining room to the back. I was absolutely perplexed by the fact that the duvets were nowhere to be found. I was on my hands and knees looking under one of the couches when I looked up and across into the other sitting room. There, perfectly folded on one of the couches, sat both of my duvets (cue in creepy music). Even more disturbing, there was a perfectly circular hole the size of a grapefruit, where a spark had jumped out of the fire and on to the duvet. Not only was I dealing with the reality that my ignorance could have caused me to burn alive, but "something" had taken the duvets off me, folded them up, and left them out of harm's way in the next room. Suddenly, I wasn't so upset that my drink had disappeared earlier that night. The presence in my new home had just saved my hide in a big way. I graciously expressed my thanks to the ether and vowed never to be so stupid again. While my "housemate" never made a physical appearance, it often made its presence known. That protective force and I cohabited peacefully from that day forward.

Secure in my new abode, acquiring the practice was now top of the list. My temporary stay had become more permanent as the practice began to flourish, and I wanted nothing more than to make it mine. On December 1, out of the blue, I got a phone call from Dr. Owens asking if I wanted to buy the practice in Athlone. My secret prayers had been answered, as I had yet to mention my interest to buy to him. By December 6, I had secured a loan and the office was mine! It was a fantastic time in the business, but personally I had made a poor choice on the dating front and found myself in the most volatile relationship. Distance, time, and the focus on building our practices meant that I hadn't seen John in quite some time. We weren't really dating, I suppose . . . or were we? I had begun to go out with a guy from town. Pure mayhem ensued right from the start. Ooohhhmmm. . . . Growth and understanding, growth and understanding, growth and understanding. I know from experience that if we listened to the clues that our bodies give us, our lives could go so much more smoothly. During that time, I had grown a small tumor on my right tear duct. Right side—male issues. Tumor—stagnation. Eye—not wanting to see what was in front of me. At a routine eye exam, my glaucoma readings were off the chart, purely due to stress. I felt I knew better and did it anyway. Doesn't that always seem to be the way? One area of your life is aces and another is ripping your soul in two! A whole lot of growth and understanding was going on from winter to spring and into the summer months.

My office manager and I were preparing to throw a party on July 7 to mark my first year in the practice. The day was beautiful and someone from the local newspaper had come by to take a photo of me in front of the office. Maureen was dashing around buying bits and pieces for the evening while we kept our fingers crossed that people would turn up. It was morning time and there was still a day's work to be done before the festivities commenced. July 7 . . . the birthday of several of my past romantic interests, the day I started work in Athlone, and the day my world was turned on its proverbial ear.

I was standing behind the desk, chatting to Maureen, when the front door opened. I saw a guy bent sideways (not an unusual sight in a chiropractic office), struggling to get to the desk. "G'day mate!" was the last thing I heard as my attention shot immediately past the guy who looked like the Leaning Tower of Pisa, and focused on the smiling face behind him. Shoulder-length blond hair, savage tan, built like a god, with a childlike grin from ear to ear. I locked eyes with this Adonis and then, instantly, my mind flashed back. I saw a covered wagon train in the western plains of America. I clearly saw the image of a terrified woman holding a screaming infant. Then, suddenly, the woman and all in her party were brutally killed by Indians. The baby's life was spared, and he was taken away to be raised by this tribe.

I blinked. Back in the office, still staring at the perfect body behind my new patient, I tried to snap back to reality as the injured man explained his problem. Simon and Jake were marine engineers from New Zealand, just off a long stint at sea. A friend with whom they had sailed was from Athlone, so they decided to come home with him for a visit. An old injury had flared up when Simon donned his backpack, so he was in real trouble with his lower back. They were staying up the road in the same B&B I had stayed in when I made my first visit to Athlone. Simon had hobbled down to the office to get himself sorted out. The entire time I was working on him I could not take my mind off the hottie in the waiting room who had triggered this most bizarre mind movie of what I was sure was a glimpse of our collective past. I was instantly drawn to him; the fact that he was gorgeous was a bonus. As soon as they left the office, Maureen looked me in the eyes and uttered the fateful command I'll never forget.

"If you don't 'pull' that one, girl, I'll kill you meself!"

Oh, Maureen, the power of your words . . .

*

As soon as work finished that evening, Maureen and I rearranged the office and set up for the party. People began to arrive shortly after, including my former boyfriend, the master of mayhem, who refused to acknowledge the term "former." All I needed was Adonis to arrive to make things awkward. Sure enough, in walked Jake and Simon. Simon was looking much taller, I might add, and, well, that's where it got interesting. The party was a wonderful success, so when the last of Maureen's famous finger foods had been eaten and the last drop of wine had been supped, we made a move into town to continue the celebrations by dancing the night away. When I say "we," I mean a few of my friends, Jake and Simon, and the glaring face of the prior boyfriend, who had no intention of seeing me with another man. I had stated on numerous occasions that I could no longer remain in the relationship and retain any semblance of sanity, but he refused to shake hands, call it a day, and walk away in peace.

I spent the night on the dance floor laughing with Jake. I was besotted and really felt as if I had known him all of my life.

As we walked home that night (the former boyfriend was furious and long gone at this stage), Jake took my hand as we headed toward his B&B. He stopped in his tracks, pulled me close, and kissed me. Bells, whistles, sparks flyin', you name it! *Kaboom!!!* The physical touch from a soul mate is like no other and from that kiss forward, our judgment became shrouded with clouds created by the smoke from our own fireworks.

Because I had no real commitments at this time in my life, I was a perfect balance of work and play. I worked hard and took frequent minibreaks to keep the equilibrium in check. One of my favorite things to do was to go to my travel agent, give her a short list of requirements of what I would like to experience, and then collect the tickets to my unknown destination just before leaving for the airport. Oh, to be so free again! It just so happened that the weekend after Jake burst on to the scene, I had placed my order with my travel agent for the following weekend. I was to collect my mystery tickets on the Friday morning and fly out that afternoon. Jake had taken a Paddywagon Tour around Ireland that finished in the seaside city of Galway. He had been in touch every day he was away, and the thoughts of not seeing each other for another week were killing us both. Also unencumbered by any real responsibilities and loaded with cash from his last trip at sea, Jake had decided he would ring my travel agent and book himself on the same flight to my unknown destination. Thursday night after work, I drove the hour and a half to Galway to meet Jake. The following day we made our way across the country to Dublin Airport and boarded a plane to our mystery destination, which turned out to be Portugal. The week in the sun was enchanting, enhanced by the deep lust and, as of yet, unexplained love that Jake and I were feeling for one another. We sat by the pool one day and I figured that it was time to fill Jake in on who I really was, and what I was all about. This had been an uncomfortable crossroads in the past, because I was never sure how someone would react after being told that I talked to spirits, had died and come back with an uncanny ability to facilitate healing, and that supernatural events were an almost daily part of my unusual way of life. Not to mention, we hadn't yet discussed this deep connection that we'd felt when we first met. As I launched into my story, I had just gotten to the "died and come back" bit, when Jake said, in his thick Kiwi accent, "Ah yeah, I had this freaky picture in my head when I first saw your face. I remembered being a baby and you were my mother. There were covered wagons and all I know is that you abandoned me."

I couldn't even hear the subtle accusation of his memory. He was glistening with sweat, legs crossed, and hands tucked behind his long, wet blond locks, as every toned muscle in his beautiful surfer's build bulged to my delight. I sat up from my lounge chair. "Are you serious? That's exactly what I remembered when I saw you!!!!"

"Ah yeah," he laughed. "It's destiny I suppose." And he sat back, as cool as a cucumber, and took a mouthful of his ice-cold beer. I smiled, blissful yet aware that I was treading in very dangerous waters.

When we returned to Ireland, Jake and I said our good-byes, with the promise that he would return after his next trip to sea and explore what work options would be available to him if he were to base himself in Europe. It was one of those pivotal decisions in life. Should we have simply relished the fact that we had met up again, had the time of our lives, and left it at that? Or would we attempt to work against all that was rational, ignoring the deafening alarm bells that were frantically warning us that our life paths had taken us in two entirely different directions, knowing that any attempt to bring them together would end in complete and utter chaos? Well, I've always loved a good challenge, so it was Option B or nothing at all!

Thus began our incredibly insensible courtship. The whole idea of having a relationship without having the person actually in my space really appealed to that peculiar aspect of my personality that seemed to habitually duck the commitment issue. I was laying the foundations for a disastrous outcome, and the worst part was . . . I knew it!

*Chapter 23*

IN THE spring of 2000, I got a phone call from America that turned my carefree life of self-indulgence upside down. Mom was her usual upbeat and positive self when gently telling me that my dad had experienced not one but three heart attacks. Impossible! A giant had fallen: My indestructible hero, the first man I had ever loved, was in the midst of his greatest challenge. This man had held the world title for bench press from 1993–1995 in the forty-nine-years-old-and-up category when he was in his late sixties! But it seemed that this was the very reason that he now found himself in crisis. Although he had lived an immaculate lifestyle, never taking a drink or a smoke and eating a vitamin-enhanced, healthy diet, Dad's heart had gradually enlarged from all the heavy weight lifting, resulting in a condition known as congestive heart failure. The doctors believed that he had probably suffered several heart attacks while weight lifting without even knowing it.

What now faced him was an unthinkable quintuple bypass surgery. My father and I were cut from the same cloth. Despite an unwavering faith in the safety of our souls, neither one of us was exactly chomping at the bit to meet our maker just yet. In my case, I already had met my maker, so to speak, and I'm not really the homesick type. I knew my Dad well enough to know that if I walked through the hospital door from Ireland, he would think they had cashed in his chips and he was a goner. On the other hand, I really felt like I needed to be there. How right I was, when I arrived just in time to have a little conversation with Dad's doctor.

When taking the Hippocratic oath, which, incidentally, was originally sworn before the gods and goddesses in days of old, most physicians do so from the viewpoint that they will treat the patient to the best of their ability. Unfortunately, over the years, the Westernization of modern medicine has seen the simple art of living broken down into a mechanistic, pieces-and-parts type of industry that has long since forgotten the emotional needs of the patient at hand. Of course, I know that not all doctors are this way, as I have met many compassionate souls practicing well-rounded, decent medicine that considers all aspects of the patient's needs. However, a growing number of traditional health care practitioners have desensitized themselves from "knowing" the patient in exchange for delivering the cold, hard facts—the statistical probabilities, underwritten by a moral obligation to tell it like it is. If the patient is left-brain dominant, the very fiber of his or her being depends on factual evidence.

Therefore, this method of practice can be quite satisfactory. However, if the patient is a right-brainer, a creative sort who is more inclined to manifesting possibilities as opposed to probabilities, this type of care can often be detrimental to their outcome. Mechanistic medicine for creative thinkers is as if the Grim Reaper himself was handing over the death warrant with his icy-cold fingers.

Dad's doctor was about to deliver the news of probabilities when I arrived at the hospital in Roanoke, Virginia. We had a very serious conversation about the way in which my father needed to be dealt with. My dad's mind was a powerful thing, and I believed that if the momentum was directed in such a way, he would defy the odds and live well into old age with vigor and vitality. I have to hand it to the doctor; he took it all on board and approached Dad from a different angle. I am convinced that this saw him through with flying colors.

This man cared for my father with impeccable regard for his physical and emotional needs from that day forward. Dad was facing what I refer to as a portal of exit—an escape clause put in place before incarnation, allowing him the opportunity to leave this world if his soul felt that it had accomplished all that it wanted to in this particular lifetime. Portals of exit are the opportunities to leave this Earth during the course of a lifetime. We all have them, the near misses, the illnesses that have the potential to snuff out our life force, or the so-called "accidents" we encounter along life's journey. Each of us has several portals of exit that are ironclad, written into the outline of the life we have chosen. This does not mean that every illness or accident is a portal of exit and it also does not mean that on a soul level, we are not in control of what direction our lives can take. Portals of exit are like rest stops along the highway of life, giving us the chance to get off the road if we feel we have finished our journey or the choice to continue on to the final port of call. I knew that Dad had a window of opportunity to leave this life, but I also knew that he would be choosing not to take it. Why, one might ask, would anyone choose to leave before they reached a ripe old age?

Because not everyone can quantify the quality of a life well lived by its quantity.

I tend to think of the many outstanding members of the human race who left their mark on humanity in what would be considered a "short life." Portals of exit can still be quite daunting, even for those with a working knowledge of the afterlife. I must admit, on the night before I flew home to be with Dad, I checked in with the other side to see if there had been some sort of mistake. I was quickly reminded and reassured that this was a portal of exit, a time of great growth and understanding for his soul, and that his very essence was well aware of what was before him. The decision to remain on had already been made. I was well prepared to let him go if he had altered his path and decided to leave early, but being

human and here to experience the emotions that go with the terri-
tory, I found myself confronting the pain and fear that go with the
loss of a loved one.

Just because we "know" doesn't make us immune. . . .

One of the strange yet comforting aspects of my psychic ability
is the knowledge of when both of my parents are going to cross
over and when I myself will be making the trip home again. Some
people might find this type of foresight terribly frightening, or
at the least, totally creepy, but I have known the exact time and
circumstances of all three of our deaths since I was a child. I have
always just accepted this as a fact of my life. The concept of portals
of exit can be a bit difficult to swallow, especially for those who
may never have considered that we existed prior to incarnating in
this lifetime. It can also be a challenge to grasp the concept that we
may have "called in" or set up an illness in order to create learning
opportunities for our own souls and for those around us.* And, of
course, I suppose there are some of you who wonder why I, the
healer, couldn't simply fix my father with the wave of a hand. If
only it were that simple.

Just because a person comes to you looking for help with a
physical, emotional, or spiritual problem, doesn't always mean
that you are the most appropriate person to deliver the type of
care that will best meet their needs. My gift allows me to tap into
a person's past, discover exactly what incident or thought process
triggered the current health crisis that they are dealing with, and
then connect the two. The individual is then able to clearly see
the purpose of the illness, or what next step would create a more
congruent path with his or her soul purpose. Healing often takes
place instantly if that is what best serves that soul, particularly if

---

* For the reader to gain a greater insight of this life-changing concept, I would highly
recommend a book written by prebirth researcher Robert Schwartz, *Your Soul's Plan:
Discovering the Real Meaning of the Life You Planned Before You Were Born.*

they are able to remember that they, in fact, custom-ordered the scenario prior to incarnation. In my father's situation, his heart was on the blink. Connecting him to the reasons behind this was not going to keep him alive. He needed a heart mechanic—I'm a spine specialist, and a metaphysician. On that day, he was exactly where he needed to be. There would be plenty of time for my kind of care in the future.

# Chapter 24

I RETURNED to Ireland, secure in the knowledge that Dad had safely made it through this portal of exit. On the flight home, I sat back and closed my eyes, asking the powers that be to give me a heads-up if he had any more portals looming around the corner before the time that I had been told his life would end. I was given the whole scenario this time. Come on, fair is fair. It was the least "they" could do, knowing that I had lived my entire life with the knowledge of when my parents were going to cross over. Happy with the answer, I relaxed and prepared to land in my home away from home.

The summer was full of practice-building, earning more money than I had ever seen in my working life. Don't get excited, I had never made any real money to speak of, so I had nowhere to go but up! All was well in my world. Jake had been in constant contact and as the summer came to a close, I moved into a new house that we would share when he made Ireland his home. The separation while he was at sea had left me in two minds. One of those minds didn't want to live without him; the other mind (the one that didn't get my attention) was having second thoughts as to how this would all pan out. On several occasions, Jake had alluded to the fact that he wanted to return someday to New Zealand to live. "Someday" just wasn't in my live-for-the-moment lifestyle, so I simply refused to acknowledge how this would affect us as a couple. As far as I was concerned, I was in Ireland to stay and I just knew Jake would come to love it as much as I did!

I know, I can hear you all groaning from here . . . Remember when I said I knew in the beginning that our life paths had taken us in two entirely different directions, despite having known each other in the past? Well, I kept on going anyway. The first few months were blissful as they are in most new romances, but then came the dark and stormy night. The Irish winter came like the hammers of hell, cold and wet, wet and cold, and I learned an interesting fact: Kiwi birds don't like the cold. More interesting than that, Kiwi boys don't like it either! It's hard to wear flip-flops and shorts when it's zero degrees and blowing a gale. Surfing in a wet suit? Blasphemy!

Adding insult to injury, Jake and I woke up one morning in early December feeling a bit worse for wear. It felt like the flu, but the tiredness was reminiscent of when I had glandular fever, or mono, as we call it back home. I went into the bathroom and stripped down for my shower, when suddenly I noticed that I looked like I had been slapped all over my arms and legs, hence the name (slap rash). My mind went immediately into doctor mode as I flipped through my mental files. "No freakin' way," I said out loud. "What's wrong?" said a weary Jake. Not wanting to alarm him, I got dressed and told him I was calling in sick and going to the doctor. He knew something was up because I never missed work, certainly never because of illness in those days. I drove straight over to my doctor, told her how I felt, and then showed her my rash. "Tell me that is not what I think it is!"

"What do you think it is?" She couldn't help but giggle.

"Well, it looks like scarlet fever to me, but didn't that go out with the last plague or something?"

"Not in this country, my dear. You and a whole lot of school-children have made it very popular this week!" *Oh, good God!* cried my inner hypochondriac. *My heart! Crap, I'm already deaf in one ear. What if I lose the other one?* But the doctor reassured me and suggested I look at it as a well-deserved break.

As Christmas approached, I got a bit of news that cheered me up. My friend Maryellen, my soul sister, was coming from England for a visit. Jake and I were still a bit on the weak side, but after three weeks in each other's continuous company, we were both ready to get back to work. Jake was a marine engineer on the ferries, and Maryellen and I decided that it would be fun to take a trip over to Wales and back, spending time on the ship with Jake. On New Year's Eve, we boarded the impressive ferry and headed off on our adventure. We were holding court for the night, entertaining Jake's workmates while he was down in the engine room keeping us afloat. When it was time to start the countdown to 2001, some members of the staff were in the cabin next to mine. Now, I had never been seasick in my life, and even though the water was a bit choppy, I couldn't figure out why I suddenly felt so ill. It must have been the last of the scarlet fever purging itself from my body.

*"Three . . . two . . . one . . . Happy New Year!"* they all shouted with glee as I hit the floor and hugged the toilet. I threw up for the next hour, listening to "Auld Lang Sync" through the paper-thin cabin walls. If I could hear them, there was no doubt they could hear me, too, as I power-puked my way into the New Year.

I was still feeling a bit rough for the next week or two. I had lost a lot of weight and my appetite along with it. My friend Greta came over from America for a visit and we had planned to meet in Galway for a couple of days with another friend, named Sheila. Greta, who had gone to chiropractic school with me in the States, was looking at work opportunities in Ireland. She had been a midwife in New Zealand for many years before becoming a chiropractor. Not only was she a virtual walking encyclopedia of knowledge about the human body, but she was a lovely human being as well.

Then there was Sheila. I had met her the year before at a seminar in Limerick. She was from New York, her parents were Irish, and she and I had lived an uncanny parallel existence. We were the same age, both born under the same star sign, had too many identical life experiences to count, including a few unpleasantries. We had both been married when we got to school and divorced when we left, attending chiropractic college at the same time in two different states, both student-body presidents at the same time before we both moved to Ireland after first working up North in the States, all within months of each other. We had instant kismet and remain tight to this day.

We booked in to a B&B, owned by my good friend, Sean, and my home away from home whenever I was in Galway. The following morning, I awakened with terrible stomach cramps. I was hot and sweaty and fed up with being ill. This must have been the longest case of scarlet fever on record. I made my way to the bathroom, feeling like I was going to pass out. Luckily, Greta and Sheila were right there. Greta immediately began to ask me questions while holding a cold cloth on my head. She was going through the meals I had eaten over the last twenty-four hours when suddenly she stopped. "When was your last period?" she asked with her doctor's hat firmly in place. I had been so ill for the last month that I really hadn't taken notice. When I took the time to think about it, I was actually a few weeks late. "No way," I emphatically replied. I was too sick to . . . Uh-oh. Do you know how baby booms tend to happen during times of recession when people are off work and home a lot more often? The same phenomenon also seems to apply to long-term illness! There was once, I began to recall . . . when I was stopped short by a terrible cramp followed by a deluge of blood. Holy cow! I was in the middle of a miscarriage and I hadn't even known I was pregnant! I had felt so horrible from the scarlet fever that I never noticed the signs. The nausea, the weight loss, the throwing up at sea; it was all coming together and going out at the same time!

As fate would have it, Greta was helping me through the loss of one child, and she would be there in the future to help bring two more into the world, as my birth coach and midwife. Amazing when I think about the serendipity of life and the good fortune I have had with my friendships.

In August of 2001, I awakened one morning and told Jake about the weirdest dream from the night before. In the dream, he had given me an engagement ring: a silver band with two antennae on it. The two antennae represented the two children that would stem from our union (I didn't tell him that part, as I was still not entertaining the idea of having children). Jake wanted a family and he wanted to be married but was convinced that it didn't mean as much to me because I had been married before. In one way, he was right, but there was also the small detail that I really did not want to move to New Zealand. Getting married was only going to complicate an already delicate subject.

I have since accepted that even though Jake and I both proclaimed having a very *go-with-the-flow* attitude toward life, we both had our own agendas, and the flow that we were going with had no room for them both. I knew that Jake was in my life for a very important purpose; for God's sake, *I remembered him!* And soon, I was to remember exactly why we had come together again.

\*

Tuesday, September 4, had started out like any other day. I got up and went to work as usual, but because Jake was on a week off, he came to meet me for lunch. Instead of driving into town, he headed out to Moydrum, a place I loved to visit, because there, in the peaceful fields of sheep and cattle, were the ruins of Moydrum Castle. The castle had an interesting history. It had been owned by Protestant aristocrats, and in the wee hours of July 2, 1921, the lady of the house was escorted out, allowed to bring one possession with her. The story goes that Lady Castlemaine was given the wardrobe that held her wedding dress just before the IRA torched the house to the ground. The front pillars of the home were left standing and this was the backdrop for the album cover of the band U2's "Unforgettable Fire." Not only was I captivated by the twisted, romantic aspect of the story, but anyone who knows me is well aware that I am a massive fan of U2.

Jake was acting more peculiar than normal. He disappeared as I walked up to the imposing remains. I went through the space that used to hold an impressive front door, only to see Jake wearing a Scottish tam with fake red hair, my red minikilt that we had gotten on our trip to Scotland, and a pair of flip-flops. There was a blanket on the ground with two glasses and a bottle of champagne. All I kept thinking to myself was, *On a Tuesday? He's doing this on a Tuesday?* It's really hard to get one over on me, but Jake had managed to pull off the impossible. On bended knee, he professed his undying love and produced a ring. Now, this wasn't just any ring. Remember the dream I had a month earlier about the silver band with the two antennae?

Oh yes, he had gone and made the ring exactly as I had described it, antennae and all, and slipped it on the ring finger of my left hand. I laughed out loud; shocked, elated, horrified, and, well, impressed by the thought that had gone into the moment. And for the moment, none of my other concerns seemed to matter.

Jake had decided that he wanted me to pick out my own engagement ring. Because I am always working with my hands, he wanted me to find something that I would be comfortable wearing every day. The time that should have been spent contemplating the ramifications of this commitment was replaced by a mad hunt to find the perfect ring. For a girl who is not materialistic in most ways, this peculiar behavior was, for the second time, making an appearance in my life. I was like a magpie or a wild coyote, hypnotized by shiny things, and the day finally came that this bird swooped down and found her prey.

A few days later, Jake and I were walking up Grafton Street in

Dublin, when suddenly I saw *the one*. It didn't look much like an engagement ring, as it was primarily sapphires (and I don't even like
blue!). It was shaped something like a rugby ball or the Egyptian
Eye of Horus, and it was flat. An unusual choice, to say the least,
but hey, it wasn't a usual set of circumstances. As we walked out
of the shop, Jake's wallet much lighter, buskers in the street were
playing "All I Want Is You," one of my all-time favorite U2 songs. I
know, I know, but the signs all *seemed* to be there at the time!

*

Jake's birthday was on October 2 and we had been engaged barely a
month when he came up with a great idea to honor both occasions.
If he couldn't be in New Zealand to celebrate, he was going to bring
New Zealand to Ireland. A traditional hangi was what he wanted
and what Jake wanted, he created. Raw meat and vegetables would
have ordinarily been wrapped in palm leaves and placed in metal
baskets, lowered into a pit, covered in red-hot stones, and left to
slow cook all day long. In our case, it was food wrapped in tin foil,
placed in a pit *in our back garden* (in a housing estate), in the middle of town. If our neighbors hadn't figured out that we were nuts
before this, beyond a shadow of a doubt, they knew it now!

I got up that morning and prepared myself for work, as I did
every Saturday morning. I started at eleven a.m., working for two
hours, but seeing nearly as many people as I would see in a four or
five hour shift because it was Saturday. My head was focused on
growing my new business, so that in the years to come, I would be
able to take more time off, fine-tuning my office hours to suit my
needs. I really wasn't a workaholic in the classic sense of the word, I
simply accepted that it was time to knuckle down and start making
a future for myself. Jake didn't quite see it that way. To him, work
appeared to be the center of my universe. In some ways, I suppose
he was right, because on the day of his hangi, I got up and went to
work, business as usual. You see, in my mind, I would be at work

for two hours, make all of the money to pay for the party, and be home to help for the rest of the day before the guests arrived that night. In my mind, I was paying my dues. I think, in Jake's mind, I had abandoned ship.

"Screw the money!" he said, not impressed with my decision to work. At the time, I had no idea why he was getting so upset. He said that I was missing the entire point of the hangi. He explained that it was a family affair, all hands on deck, everyone pitching in and enjoying the art of the preparation. Ahhh, therein lies our problem. It took me a while to figure this one out, but I finally got it, *many years later mind you*, but I did eventually "get it."

Jake and I were miles apart culturally—Jake came from the tropical climate of the North Island of New Zealand, raised on the ocean, eating fresh fish from the sea and vegetables and fruit produced on his own land. If they didn't catch it, they grew it. I, on the other hand, hailed from the Blue Ridge Mountains of Virginia. While I'm sure there were people growing things in gardens and catching things in the lakes and rivers, I never saw it, and I certainly never saw it prepared. I *could* tell you that my mother was quite the cook because I have heard legends of the oven being used in the years prior to my birth. But when Helen Hensley was told in her early forties that baby number four was on the way, she made a firm decision and, true to form, she stuck with it. Mom decided that life would be much easier if she just didn't cook anymore. Now, I always remember her making banana bread and chocolate turtles at Christmas for us to give to our friends and schoolteachers as gifts, but other than the odd carrot cake for the church and covered dish dinners, that was it.

It suddenly dawned on me that Jake's value system surrounding food was totally different from mine. He struggled with the idea that I could go to work and miss out on a few hours of the fun and camaraderie of cooking the food. What he couldn't digest was that I placed absolutely no value on the art of food preparation, simply because it had not ever been a part of my life. I relished eating the food and showering adoration on the people who made it for me. To this day, I still only "assemble" food, like making wraps or pouring the soup from the carton into the bowl—I don't create it. At the time, I placed more value on going out and making a living, blind to the fact that he wanted me to participate in something that was important to him, something that he *did* place great value on. Not speaking to me for the rest of the day of our engagement party could have been handled a little differently, but I get the thought process behind it. The party was amazing, the food came out of the ground that night perfectly cooked, to my sheer amazement and to that of our friends, who had never seen nor tasted anything like it in their lives! The kegs flowed and the traditional music kicked off with a most clever engagement song written in tribute to Jake and me, by our friend and very talented musician Tony Dunne.

When the attention was focused on us, Jake was forced to act as if he wasn't mad at me. When we pretend long enough, sometimes it can become reality. Later that night, when the last partygoer had gone, Jake and I went to bed for the last time as two. In a moment of perfection, we both knew that despite all of the odds that were against us, somebody was knocking at the door and this little soul was not going to take no for an answer. Less than three weeks later, I was attending the birthday party of my friend, Healy, at a restaurant in town. Jake had been at sea for the last two weeks and was coming in later that night. I had eaten my starter, when suddenly I didn't feel so well. I took a sip of my drink to wash it down and took off in a mad dash down the stairs. I just made it to the toilet in time to get sick. *I must have eaten something funny.* I then thought back to Jake's birthday and the reality of what I had known to be true began to sink in. I didn't say anything to Jake when I picked him up that night. I stopped by the pharmacy on the way from the restaurant and picked up a pregnancy test, *just in case.*

The following morning I was still in shock; even though I was still a few days away from my period being due, I knew the test would be positive. I sat in disbelief for a good half hour before telling Jake. I had bought a little pair of hand-knitted baby booties on a trip to the Aran Islands to give as a gift to a friend. I took the positive test, stuck it in one of the booties, and gave them to Jake. It took a few minutes for the penny to drop and I can truly say, Jake was the happiest man on Earth at that moment. I, on the other hand, went from shock to excitement to panic stations.

*

From the moment I conceived, I knew this pregnancy was going to be anything but easy. Almost instantly, a nausea like none other that I had ever experienced set in. I was lucky in one way, because this baby was already expressing its antipodean genes and was on a time schedule completely opposite to mine. My baby decided to wait until eleven p.m. each night before causing me to violently throw up. Like clockwork, I would begin to gag and hurl from eleven p.m. until exactly one a.m. every single day of the pregnancy. My unbelievably heightened sense of smell created a challenge all of its own. The fact that I worked in the Midlands and many of my patients came to me straight off the farm added a whole new angle to my olfactory nightmare. I would catch a single whiff of slurry or sheep and go running for the toilet. I only gagged severely during the day and saved the projectile vomiting for late at night. I could tell what someone had eaten for dinner before they even walked into the adjusting room and my love for coffee soon became my greatest enemy, as the smell of it brewing, or the smell from anybody's breath, would cause me to retch. I also developed a very strong relationship with chicken during those days. After work I would run down the block to the shop where they sold whole roasted chickens. The women would crack up when they saw me coming because I carried out the same ritual for months on end. I would buy a whole chicken, tear off the greasy skin, inhale it right there in the store, and then throw away the chicken before I left. The sight and smell of the carcass made me terribly ill, but I craved the skin as if my very life depended on it. Early on I began looking for ways to help lessen the hardship of the pregnancy.

In May of 2001, a woman had walked into my office looking to rent space. While I had no room available in the practice, I quickly made space in my life for someone who was to become a very dear friend. Aidean Ryan was beautiful, bubbly, and highly intuitive. She was a Reiki practitioner from the town of Ferbane. When I became pregnant, I regularly attended Aidean's practice, which she had set up in the cutest little crooked stone house by the river. My intention was to help myself integrate with the soul who was coming into my life. I found her work so beneficial, as it helped to soothe my body while it transitioned and changed shape, and calmed my mind as it adjusted to the idea of becoming caretaker of another human being. The physical strain was already beginning to show. I had been told after my accident that due to my mangled pelvis and the fact that my entire spine was so misshapen, I would probably never be able to conceive. The "experts" also threw in that if I did manage to get pregnant, my body would most likely not be able to sustain the new life. This was probably the reason that I had never really craved children or developed much of a maternal instinct. Aidean lovingly took me through all of these emotions and helped me to release any fear or negativity surrounding the baby, while reconnecting me with memories from past lives that were important in dealing with my current circumstances.

Throughout the pregnancy, in addition to regular Reiki, I also attended a brilliant massage therapist and acupuncturist named Amy Moore. Amy practiced from home in the peaceful surroundings of Glasson, Athlone. I loved her energy and her work was brilliant for helping my contorted body deal with the new life inside of it. She also coached me through relaxation techniques that were invaluable during the pregnancy and in labor.

In January of 2002, at the end of my first trimester, Aidean invited me to a weekend workshop in Galway that she thought I would really enjoy. Aidean had met Dr. Lew Graham at a previous seminar he had given and they had remained friends ever since. She briefly explained that he was a Huna master and that I might resonate with his presentation of Gnostic ideas (an alternative history of the world) in an intimate group setting in Galway. Of course I agreed, even though I didn't know what a Huna master was and barely had a grasp on Gnosticism. But, I reasoned, if she liked it, then it was a given that I would, too, as we were so similar in our belief systems and esoteric views on life in general. I had an incredible sense of anticipation, the kind I would get before any of my premonitions. I invited my friend Sheila to come along. She was so open-minded and had a real thirst for new knowledge that she was an ideal companion for the weekend away.

Meeting Lew marked a turning point in my journey. He had made the courageous choice to share information from years of research, which could potentially undermine everything that he had accomplished as a traditional academic. I learned that *Huna* was a Hawaiian word created by the New Age author Max Freedom Long and that it referred to the metaphysics of ancient Hawaiian philosophers. I listened eagerly as he described an incredible alternative to history as it is traditionally taught. Dr. Graham suggested that the Earth died less than 15,000 years ago in a series of catastrophies and outlined something called the Fourth Age epoch that represented the society of Atlantis. He spoke of the world's oldest language, called *Gotte*—of three simple symbols. I was immediately reminded of a vision I had seen as a child, where I was standing at the ocean's edge in a flowing purple grown and saw meteorites flaming through the sky. There were symbols, too, in my vision, of holograms containing vital records.

When Dr. Lew Graham started talking about those symbols, that rainy Saturday morning in Galway, he described me as having a "deer in the headlights" look, when in reality, my chubby, pregnant body nearly fell off the chair when he showed the group the first three symbols. Not only had he referred to them as iconographs used in a meditation by the Pythagorean school of "Ancient World Mysteries," but as the first form of communication used to catalogue the wisdom of an ancient people, whom most only think of as characters of fable.

I could barely stay focused while he described a past sequence of events that were as real to me as the current life I was experiencing. My heart began to pound as I relived the catastrophic memories he described with such detail, scarcely able to digest what he was saying. For the first time in this life, someone was recounting a tale that had played over and over in my mind from the time I had been lost at the beach as a child so many years before.

Imagine my shock as I heard this stranger, Dr. Graham, describing an event that had been burned into my mind since I was five years old. Never had I met anyone who had knowledge of, or experienced, anything similar. Suddenly, I was hearing a description of my own death, thousands of years ago, with details that no one could have known unless they had been there themselves or had heard it from someone who had.

I couldn't wait to ask Lew if he knew about the rest of the symbols, as he had only shared three with the group. I was dying to know if he was actually aware of what they meant and how they had been used.

When I approached him at the break, it was he who now looked like the deer in the headlights, as I questioned him about where he had found these symbols and whether he was cognizant of the fact that there were eighteen more? He was like a child on Christmas morning as he relayed his fervent efforts to recover the remaining symbols and his anticipation that I might, in fact, have possessed what he so desperately sought. He was more than receptive when I explained that each of these ancient markings had literally burned itself into my mind, acting as a beacon that preceded my move to Ireland.

Things were starting to click as we both acknowledged the importance of what was happening. As I continued to talk with Lew, this stranger began to become very familiar. Things were still a bit fuzzy, but his work, my work, our shared knowledge of something so far-fetched that neither of us could have made the exact same story up independent of one another, all began to weave together the loose ends of the tapestries of both of our lives. There was a deep respect and love, manifested as friendship in this lifetime but recognizable as having been in many other forms throughout our shared lifetimes together. It would take some time to uncover it all, but things were going to get unbelievably interesting for both Lew and me.

As a point of interest, Lew and I discovered that we had grown up only twenty miles away from each other in Virginia. More than a decade my senior, Lew had gone to the high school that was the big rival of the school where Dad had been head coach. He knew exactly who my father was. We laughed at the serendipitous nature of it all and the humor of the Universe as we were now meeting years later for the "first" time, at a seminar in a rented flat on a backstreet in Galway, Ireland.

When Lew returned to America, I sent him a scanned copy of the remaining symbols, and he set out on the difficult task of authenticating them as the original Gotte "alphabet." This would take some time, as to date, there are only three people that Lew has come across who knew anything of the lost language. We remained in touch sporadically, as he was deeply involved with research for his many scientific projects and I was equally busy with watching my pregnant belly stretch like a beach ball.

*

In April of 2002, Lew and I met again to celebrate the wedding of Aidean, the beautiful soul who had "reintroduced" us the previous year. Lew and I had the chance to visit and catch up on all of the news from his research. So far, he and his team had still been unable to authenticate the Gotte symbols, but all of the feelers were out, and a positive outcome was just around the corner. He filled me in on an interesting project that involved healing, using the sounds generated by the various planets throughout our solar system—frequencies above and beyond the earthly plane of existence, also known as the *Music of the Spheres*. Lew invited Jake and me to come visit his home in L.A. on our next jaunt to New Zealand. With the birth of our baby close at hand, we graciously accepted and promised to make the trip as soon as we were able.

# Chapter 25

ON SATURDAY, June 8, 2002, I awakened after a very restless sleep and went to shower before heading to work. As I reached to turn the water on, I looked down, noticing that my legs and feet were already soaking wet. Groggy and in a complete fog, it took a few minutes before I surmised that at thirty-seven weeks, my water had just broken. I can visualize myself now, standing behind the glass, bodily fluids running down my legs, shower water blasting down my back, looking out into the bedroom where Jake slept. I was feeling very alone—a frightened little girl about to embark on parenthood with a man, that truth be told, I might have known from the past, but barely even knew this time around.

Angst quickly turned to excitement as I awakened Jake and held up a handwritten sign that said, "We're in labor!" He sprung out of bed, running around like a headless chicken, talking out loud to himself as to what he needed to do next.

"Okay. Get the bag. Why aren't you dressed? Where are the car keys? Do you want a cup of tea?"

I laughed and told him to relax; I didn't even have any labor pains. This was going to be a breeze. I couldn't figure out what everyone had been going on about. This wasn't painful at all. . . . I had heard that I would start cleaning like mad days before I went into labor, the nesting phenomenon. Well, I had somehow missed that memo and now began to panic. Suddenly, I decided that my bedroom furniture was all wrong and needed to be moved . . . right then! Jake came up the stairs with two mugs of tea only to find me in my underwear, pushing the bed from one side of the room to the other. "What are you doing?!" he yelled! "You're going to have the kid in the middle of the floor if you don't stop!"

Of course I ignored him and proceeded to rearrange the bedroom, right before pulling out the cleaning products to scrub down the bathrooms. I was on autopilot and there was no stopping me. For several hours I cleaned, all the time thinking to myself how brilliant I was in dealing with the labor pains—because at that point, I didn't really have any! I went to the kitchen next, and as it was now a decent hour of the morning, the doorbell rang. My good friend and physiotherapist, Jack Mannion, had stopped by to drop something off, unaware of the events of the morning. We sat down for a chat, had another cup of tea, and he was amazed at how well I was handling labor. It had been hours since my water had broken and I was full of energy and feeling mighty.

My contractions were mild at the start and so far apart I couldn't even keep track of how frequent they were. Around midday, Aidean arrived to lend a helping hand. My friend Greta, the chiropractor/midwife, had been called in Sligo, the town where she lived, about two hours away. She would make her way down that afternoon, as we didn't seem to be in much of a panic in the contractions department. I spent the afternoon on the sitting room floor with Aidean behind me, hands around my belly, giving me Reiki love. It was during this time that things got a little strange.

I have found, through talking to a multitude of pregnant patients and friends, that an extraordinarily high percentage of women think that their first baby is a boy. Guessing? Wishful thinking? Who knows, but I have seen this as a common occurrence for years. I was front row on that bandwagon, and until the afternoon of June 8, 2002, in my mind, a baby boy was on the way. So convinced was I that I had a list of boys' names as long as my arm and only one name for a girl . . . just in case. I couldn't wait to meet baby Blaise, Fabian, Jayden, or whatever name we decided on, after looking him in the eyes and choosing a moniker that suited his own individual personality.

Aidean and I sat chatting and laughing in between darts of pain that were mysteriously a bit more severe than what I had experienced while redecorating my house that morning. During a "pregnant pause" in the conversation, I looked across the room, and standing there in front of me, as clear as day, was my grandmother Clark. Grandmother had died just before Christmas in 1998, yet there she stood, in a form so solid that I would have sworn she had never been dead at all. I said nothing and waited to see if Aidean picked up on her. Seconds later, she exclaimed, "The hairs on my arms are standing on end! Somebody is in the room!"

A gifted seer, Aidean had detected Grandmother Clark and both of us sat, mouths agape, as she proceeded to deliver the news. "I know you think that you are having a boy, and while the energy is quite male-dominant, you are about to give birth to a very special baby girl. She will have your abilities tenfold and you will need to guide her as her gifts reveal themselves."

"Oh my gosh, Aidean, did you hear that?"

I was blown away with the apparition's prediction.

"A girl?" shrieked Aidean. "You're feckin' kidding me!"

Totally unfazed at the fact that my mother's dead mother was right there in front of us, Aidean was aghast that we had both been so convinced that the new arrival was a boy. We fell around the place laughing, only to be stopped by a whopper of a contraction.

Aidean and Jake walked with me around the neighborhood as the pains became more intense, but the contractions still weren't close enough to make a break for the hospital. It had now been nearly ten hours since my water had broken and a few of the ladies from the "hood" who saw me waddling around the block were kind enough to interject that there was a time limit before infection could set in. Ah yes, God love them, they simply couldn't resist the urge to create a bit of drama. Little did they know that my dead Grandmother had already sealed the deal and we knew that all would be okay.

Dr. Greta arrived in from Sligo that evening, homeopathic birth kit in hand, and made the call at around ten p.m. that we should make our way to the hospital. We arrived in the maternity ward in Ballinasloe at around ten-thirty, and from then on, things got a little ugly. They had their own ideas on how I was to bring my child into this world, hooked to a monitor and on the flat of my back, not to mention the talk of giving me medication to bring on the birth because that dirty ol' infection might set in. I calmly explained that like a good little Girl Scout, I had left my birth plan with the attending doctor and had every intention of following it, bar any unforeseen emergencies. "Well," sneered the nurse on duty, "it just so happens that your doctor is on his holidays so we'll be doing things my way. This is my ward and, birth plan or not, you'll do as I say."

I'm a fairly levelheaded girl by nature, but as I lay on the bed and a wave of crazy pain gripped my lower back, I looked the nurse in the eye and, without raising my tone, I calmly said, "When I get off of this table, lady, I'm going to kill you stone dead." We were off to a great start! The nurse said not only was I not allowed my homeopathic remedies, but my friend, midwife Greta, would not be allowed in with me. Red rag to a bull. . . .

Again, without the slightest inflection in my tone but through clenched teeth, I explained to my nurse that I had a signed copy of my birth plan from my doctor and if she didn't back off, she would be hearing from my attorney.

In a huff, she stormed out of the room and left me to my own devices. Greta had to quickly shift gears from being absolutely appalled at the attempt to change the approved game plan on a woman in the horrors of labor, to the loving doctor and labor companion who would see me through the most difficult night of my life.

My contractions were strong and close together, but I wasn't dilating the way I should have been. Greta deduced that the lip of the cervix needed to be gently readjusted so that the baby's head could make its way down. Now, you can only imagine how that went down when Greta made the suggestion to Nurse Nightmare. "You may do that where you come from," she bellowed, "but we certainly don't do that here! I'm calling down to theater to prepare for a section."

"I won't consent!" I screamed at her, in absolute agony. The sun was rising and it was nearly four a.m. I had hemorrhoids the size of golf balls and because I had so many allergies, I refused the chance of finding out if I was allergic to the pain relief, while in advanced labor. Greta stayed by my side, pushing into my lower back until the muscles in her forearms finally tired out from the all-night workout. I swayed back and forth, standing at the end of the bed as I would periodically run to the sink to throw up. That morning sickness stuck with me to the bitter end.

Did I hear someone ask where Jake was? Poor thing was just so exhausted that he slept peacefully on the floor, in the corner for most of the night. He woke up not long before the baby popped out. Greta explained to me once again that it was absolutely standard procedure in a birth such as this to simply reach in and lip the cervix over the baby's head. On my thirty-seventh trip to the toilet, exhausted from endless hours of fruitless labor, Greta snatched a pair of surgical gloves and decided to take matters into her own hands, putting me out of my misery. Out of the watchful eye of my worst Nurse Nightmare, I straddled the toilet and leaned back, as Greta reached up, and in a matter of seconds had the baby headin' down the highway. The relief was unbelievable and with a new burst of energy, I went back into the room and climbed on to the bed on all fours. As luck would have it, the shift changed at breakfast time and a new nurse came on duty.

Young, new at her job, and eager to listen to Greta's infinite wisdom, the novice nurse stepped back and let the pro get to work. Literally fifteen minutes after the Nightmare had gone off duty and Greta had rearranged my bits, I went from having completely unproductive contractions into experiencing a normal progression. With a seemingly endless night of horrific pain behind me, the simple readjustment began several hours of what would be considered a normal labor. Now, just after one p.m., over thirty hours into the drama, the new midwife held my tearing bottom together with a towel and prepared herself to catch my baby girl. A few screams, one last push, and out came the most beautiful little head I had ever seen, followed by two perfect shoulders, all ten fingers, a round belly, a pair of lanky, long legs, and . . . "It's a boy!!!" shouted Jake, fresh as a daisy from his bedside slumber. "A what?" Totally confused, I looked at Greta in disbelief. She was laughing out loud as she lifted my baby GIRL and showed me the umbilical cord hanging between her legs. I looked at Jake with pure disgust, as only a woman who has been in labor for the last thirtysomething hours can look at the father of her child, the man who will NEVER touch her again, the man who thought that the child's umbilical cord was the world's biggest willy.

At 1:08 p.m. on Sunday, June 9, 2002, my gorgeous little girl came into this curious world. Jemma Skye, the only girl's name I had chosen, was named for the precious gem that she is, and for the Scottish Isle of Skye where her father and I first said, "I love you." She was twenty-one inches and seven-and-a-half pounds of joy, and the fun was only beginning as my very unique baby girl drew her first breath and let out an unmerciful scream, making sure that all within a ten-mile radius knew that she had arrived!

If the nurses in the labor ward had thought I was being a difficult patient during the labor, you should have seen them when I announced that as soon as the attending physician had checked my baby out, I was heading home. "But she hasn't had her injection of vitamin K yet!" a nurse protested.

I smartly told them if they had read the mysterious disappearing birth plan that I had given them, we wouldn't be getting that, or any other injections. My babe was going au naturel from day one. Greta had already checked her spine and given Jemma her first chiropractic adjustment after the long and difficult birthing process. I would be feeding her, no one was in any danger of hemorrhaging, and the last time I had checked, the need to put drops in her brand-new eyes, just in case I had gonorrhea, was an unfounded fear.

I had to sign all sorts of paperwork releasing the hospital from any responsibility. I was fine, my baby was fine, and I much preferred the comfort of my own home as opposed to the single toilet and the rust-stained bathtub that they proposed I share with the thirteen other new mothers on the ward. Four hours on the planet, and Jemma Skye and I were outta there!

# Chapter 26

I HAVE to say that after having worked nonstop for the last few years and throughout my entire pregnancy, I was relieved to have a bit of a break. I settled into motherhood more smoothly than I had anticipated and the fact that I was feeding Jemma myself made for a demanding but healthy baby with no bottles to wash. Jake returned to work soon after the birth and I began to foresee that more often than not, I would be going it alone. I returned to work just before Jemma was three months old (an unfortunate necessity when running your own business), leaving her with a babysitter during the day.

I was in a good space, tired yet productive, and I was experiencing a phenomenon that was becoming more frequent with each passing day. I had always had the ability to see things before they happened. I don't know if it was the hormones, the sleep deprivation, or the fact that I was switched into overdrive, but I was now tapping into global events before they took place, as if I was downloading the details from a press release on the Internet.

Before two months had even passed since my return to work, I found out that Jemma's babysitter was moving away from Athlone. She barely gave me a heads-up, leaving me only a few days to find someone new. Enter serendipity.

I was working away one afternoon when I came into the waiting room to call in the next patient. I interrupted a conversation that Maureen was having with my new patient, a striking and happy-faced guy named Keith. In a matter of moments, Maureen had completely figured Keith out and found out that his mother had babysat children for years. This was the start of what continues to be a most fortunate and beautiful relationship.

Lily and Tommy Henry can only be described as salt of the Earth. They have three adult children, Gordon, Keith, and Anne, and this family took our child and immediately loved her as one of their own. Having no relatives in Ireland, this new family dynamic created a security that gave me the freedom to work with peace of mind, regaining a portion of my pre-baby lifestyle. I have never doubted that they were lovingly placed in our lives to watch over us. Our daughter thrived in the Henry household, and I couldn't wait to collect her in the evenings to hear the latest "Jemma story." She was a funny little kid right from the start, with a headful of white-blond hair that stood straight up like a fuzzy wee chicken. Always smiling, she had a peculiar glint in her eye that was captivating, leaving us with the feeling that fascinating times were ahead.

Soon after we met the Henrys, Jake and I decided to take a trip to New Zealand to introduce his parents to their newest grandchild. Jemma was going on eight months and it was the chance to celebrate my thirty-third birthday in a different country and culture. Frankly, I really wanted to find out for myself the reason Jake had driven himself demented about the Irish climate. I wanted to see firsthand if New Zealand was as fabulous as he made it out to be. After the longest flight I had ever been on in my life, pure torture for a kinesthetic, empathetic psychic trapped in a flying cigar tube, we touched down in Auckland, NZ, in the pouring rain. I laughed heartily as I couldn't resist the temptation to rub the lack of sunshine in Jake's face. He assured me that it was only temporary, and while I would agree that the scenery was magnificent, the temporary rain continued for the next three weeks of our stay. Far be it for me to gloat. . . .

The trip was lovely, but I could see Jake becoming more and more homesick as the days passed. My hope that a visit home would satisfy his needs instead backfired, making his not-so-subtle push to get us out of Ireland even stronger than before.

On the way home, we made good on our promise to visit Lew Graham in Los Angeles. It was exciting for me because this was my first time in L.A. and I had always wanted to see Hollywood. Although much smaller than I had imagined, the glitz and glam did not disappoint. We did all of the touristy things, the Walk of Fame, the restaurants, and the live spectacle that is Venice Beach. This place blew my mind. I'm sorry, but those who say that all the bodies photographed in magazines are airbrushed have obviously not seen the likes of the people at Venice Beach. I felt like a beached whale as girls in teeny bikinis whizzed by on Rollerblades and the bodybuilders all looked as if they had walked off the pages of a Mr. America calendar. There was one guy posing for photographs, flexing his enormous pecs for a crowd of astonished spectators. For a laugh, I hopped on stage next to him, pulled off my tank top, revealing my enormous milk-engorged boobs, cradled in an ill-fitting bikini top. I then struck a pose for the audience. They erupted with laughter and applause and I could now claim that I, too, had been a poser on Venice Beach. Nothing like a good laugh to divert attention from one's insecurities.

Early one morning, I left Jemma with Jake while Lew and I drove to San Diego to check out one of his "projects." We walked into what appeared to be a normal office, with several adjoining rooms. In the back was housed the wildest-looking research room I have ever laid eyes on. There were wall-to-wall keyboards, each one wired to what looked like a massage table in the middle of the room. This was an experiment in the use of tone to match the innate tone of the individual who would lie on the table. The general premise was that, by realigning the tone of a person who was out of synch and matching it with one of the thousands of tones hardwired into the modified keyboards, illness could be resolved within the body. Recreating the Music of the Spheres, the vibrations connecting physical mass with the etheric aspects of sound, would simply be impossible; however, delving into the prospect of extracting frequencies that could realign and help an individual to heal was something I could see coming to fruition. We are at a time in history where archaic technology is the only way to express the memories of our past and the promise of our future. I trivialize this inspiring concept with my description, but this is an utterly amazing subject, in which I hold a deep, intuitive interest.

I was asked to put on a set of headphones while Lew prompted me to describe the sounds that I could hear. One I would liken to a deep bagpiper's drone and another, when sped up slightly, was a carbon copy of the squeaks and clicks dolphins use to communicate. He explained that these tones were recordings of the frequencies emitted by the planets of our solar system—the Music of the Spheres. This was serious stuff, folks, and I resonated with it! The thought of using tone and vibration to heal were not only familiar to me but ingrained in my memory from a time when this technology was commonplace.

That evening, Lew took me to meet a most intriguing friend of his—incredibly gifted, in this world but not of it. I was discussing topics with this man that I had never been able to address with anyone, prior to meeting Lew. I felt heard, understood, and respected in regard to my memories of a time when life on this planet was extremely different from the world we know today. I went to bed that night, only to be awakened by what looked like a holographic image of the man I had met earlier in the evening. Unbeknownst to me, this man was testing me, checking out if I was genuine in my ancient memories and professed abilities. Early the next morning, he rang Lew to tell him that he had paid me a visit during the night. He advised Lew to say nothing, to wait and see if I mentioned anything. When I sat down to breakfast, I told Lew that his friend, or some form of him, had come to visit while I slept. Lew laughed, gave me a big hug, and welcomed me to "the team."

We said our good-byes, as it was time to return to our life in Ireland. Jake made it no secret that he wanted me to pursue moving to L.A. to work with Lew and his team on a permanent basis. Although he had no idea what this work would entail, he saw my connection with Lew as a potential ticket out of Leprechaun Land. The idea was appealing, but timing is everything and nothing, all at once. I knew that my time in Ireland was not finished, but I could not explain this "knowing" to Jake in any way that he found acceptable. Upon our return, I dug my heels in and proceeded to participate in a series of events that would make and eventually break us as a couple.

## Chapter 27

BECAUSE I simply did not have enough on my plate, with a full-time practice, a bouncing baby girl, and a relationship headed for the rocks, I decided that I would try my hand at opening a new business, just to liven things up a bit. I convinced Jake that this would be a great move for us, that opening a business in Sligo, by the sea in the northwest border region of Ireland where we could work together and build something that belonged to us both, would make us happier. I easily took out the loan required, because in those days the banks were handing money out to eager entrepreneurs.

A women's fitness center was a really "bright idea" idea in a country where a six-week course in anything related to fitness was the most to which people were willing to commit themselves. Initially, things were off to a fantastic start. Jake's attention was diverted from the fact that he wanted to leave Ireland because he was working with his hands, building and painting, spending more time away from Athlone. The potential for a thriving business was there and all it required was someone's full attention. Yes, *full-time* attention. In between working part-time in my office (I had hired a doctor to cover the days I was away), we made trips to Sligo nearly every other day with Jemma in tow. She had a ball and played on the building site that would eventually house our new business venture.

In the summer of 2003, we opened the doors of our new gym with a host of customers who were sure to make it a success. We had a manager in place and we were headed for financial freedom. Jake, Jemma, and I would have more disposable income, be able to travel more, and this would, hopefully, relieve Jake's need to move out of Ireland. Well, it sounded good at the time. . . .

"Out of the mouths of babes" took on a whole new meaning in our house. Forever present in the back of my mind were the prophetic words my grandmother Clark had spoken on the day I went into labor with Jemma. I had kept a casual lookout for any signs of "the gift," but as of yet, nothing strange or unusual had come to pass. In the autumn, we caught the first glimpse of what was to come.

Aidean had called by the house for a cup of tea and a chat. She was heavily pregnant with her first child and she delighted in Jemma's antics as she ran around the place like a lunatic. When I say lunatic, I mean stark, raving mad. She was acting like a child possessed, running in circles, shrieking with excitement. The next thing we knew, Jemma had taken a big gulp of water from her sippy cup. She stood right between Aidean and me, pushed her cheeks together with her two hands, and spat the water out all over the floor. She started running in circles again, this time screaming, "The water, the water, the water is broke!" Aidean and I stared at her, each of us as puzzled as the other, until Aidean's phone rang. "I don't believe it!" Her mouth hanging open as so often it did when we were in one another's company. "It's Niamh," she whispered. Niamh was Aidean's sister, who also happened to be pregnant with her first child.

"Her waters have just broken, just this minute! Oh my God, her waters have just broken." Now, two mouths wide open, Aidean and I looked at Jemma, squealing with delight as she clapped her hands.

And so it began. Jemma's journey into the paranormal had

started with a big, wet bang. So innocent, so sweet, and so incredibly tuned in to a higher dimension.

Jemma wasn't the only one learning to integrate her psychic abilities. I was dealing with my own personal struggle on the work front. Maybe it was because the volume of people I was interacting with had increased dramatically, or because the Universe was trying to show me that the nature of my work was eventually going to change. For whatever the reason, the line between my work as a doctor of chiropractic and a girl with the ability to "see, feel, and heal" suddenly started to blur. Increasingly, I began to find myself in situations where messages or spirits were coming through during my working hours. It's not that they hadn't ever done this in the past, but I had always acknowledged, and then looked the other way, when dealing with my patients. It's like going to a car lot with the intention of buying one type of car and the salesman then attempts to sell you something entirely different from what you were looking for. It's not that the other car wasn't nice or wouldn't fulfill your needs, but it's not what you had intended to purchase. When someone would come in to have their spinal needs addressed, I was always very careful that no matter what messages were coming through, I would keep these to myself. Now, I can't say that I didn't use my abilities to "cheat" every now and again, already knowing a person's problem, feigning the standard protocol for coming up with a diagnosis, and then sharing the information with the patient with details and clarity that often resulted in a puzzled look of "how on earth did you know that?" I would often scan people's bodies and immediately refer them to their general practitioner if I saw something in the aura or energy field that was outside my scope of practice.

In those days I had no X-ray, and due to the fact that illness is literally written all over the energetic field, I knew when someone was dealing with a malady. However, these people hadn't come to see me for metaphysical healing, to connect with past emotional issues that were creating their current physical state, or to talk with their dead relatives, for that matter. For whatever the reason, someone up there decided that what I was doing, *or not doing*, just wasn't good enough.

I began to get uncomfortable withholding knowledge that could possibly help someone. I was starting to feel like I was holding out on people, when things outside of the realm of chiropractic were happening during their visits. It's a touchy subject; there is a legal responsibility, and moral obligation to one's patients. But I could no longer brush aside information relevant to the person on my table. The need to express "metaphysical me" outweighed any risks to my reputation as a doctor. At home, I was watching my daughter develop her intuition with childlike wonder. I began to reconnect with my own faith and my innate metaphysical abilities, the way I had before my educated mind got in the way.

*

As Jemma developed her language skills, her little personality really began to shine through. She loved to make people smile and her own contagious laughter was a tonic. She talked nonstop (wonder where she got that from), and she was already starting to show signs that she was going to have similar sleep issues, like those I experienced as a child. The night had always been a busy time for me. My mind would rev up and the hours of darkness were strange, exciting, and full of anticipation. I had regular visits from my mother's father, Judge. I was twenty-seven when I discovered the real story behind the legacy of healing that had been passed on to me by my ever-present spiritual companion. Luckily, my daughter wouldn't have to wait so long.

One evening, after putting Jemma, not yet two, in her cot for the umpteenth time, her relentless cries for Mommy were replaced with giggles and lots of chatter. I crept up the stairs and sat on the landing, trying to decipher what sounded like a full-blown conversation. Jemma would say something, then laugh hysterically, and there were a lot of *uh-huhs* and *yeses*, as if she was responding to someone's questions. I tiptoed down the hallway to see if I could catch a peek. There she was, standing at the end of the cot, reaching out as if touching something or someone in front of her. She turned suddenly and squealed with delight when she saw me. "Mommy, Mommy, look!" She was pointing into thin air. My heart began to beat a little faster with the anticipation of her answer to my next question: "Who were you talking to, sweetie?" I was secretly hoping and only delighted when she cooed, "Judge, Mommy! Judge and Grigs!"

I lifted her out of the cot, tears streaming down my face as I bonded with my baby in a moment so full of joy that the tears are making a repeat performance as I write this. My little girl had been visiting with my grandparents. My grandmother's nickname had been Grigs throughout her lifetime, but our side of the family had always called her Grandmother Clark. Jemma would have never heard the name Grigs because I had never used it myself. It looked as if my baby was going to be on the receiving end of the same incredible visits that I remembered with such fondness, only this time, she got my grandmother as well.

As things were beginning to spice up in the spooky-baby department, I started to contemplate how I would share this unusual little tidbit of info with Lily and Tommy, Jemma's caregivers. It was only fair that they be told, and even though nothing had happened on their watch yet, it was bound to happen sooner or later. Well, procrastination got the best of me and on one fine autumn evening, Jemma beat me to the punch. Just after work, I drove over to Lily and Tommy's to pick up my little sweetheart. I pulled up in front of the house and started walking toward the back door. I looked left and there sat Lily, outside on the windowsill. She was holding Jemma on her lap with a face so pale it looked as if she had seen a ghost. And as the story goes, she had. . . .

According to Lily, they were in the kitchen, Jemma playing and Lily cleaning up after dinner. Jemma began chatting away, as if someone was standing there listening to her playful banter. "Ah, who are you talking to, love?" Lily innocently asked, not realizing what was coming next. "Alice! Alice is here, Lily!"

With hands shaking, Lily tried to compose herself before going to her purse and taking out a card. She showed it to Jemma, who looked at the card and squealed, "Dat's her, Lily, dat's Alice!"

Alice was Lily's sister. At fifty-two, she had died of a brain tumor in 1991. The card was her memorial and had a photo and verse of remembrance. Lily wasn't quite sure what to do or say, so she grabbed Jemma and took off out the back door. This had been an hour earlier. There they sat, waiting for me to turn up, so consequently, on that day, we finally had "the chat." "I always knew there was something about her," said Lily, kind of proud yet totally freaked out at the same time.

Good thing she thought so, because my sweet baby was only getting started!

In October of 2003, I went into hospital to have repair work done to the tear in my anal sphincter, as a result of the thirty-plus hours of labor while bringing Jemma into the world. This was my second procedure, and the tear had become increasingly more painful as the months passed. It was then that I discovered that my body, growing more sensitive with each passing year, could no longer take anesthetic. From the moment after my car accident in 1991, not only had my system been rewired with new capabilities, but my body had become intolerant to a number of items, ranging from MSG in foods, to shellfish resulting in anaphylaxis, to washing myself with ordinary soap or my clothing with soap powder. The list was endless and every day it grew longer, with products that most people take for granted. From perfumes to household cleaners, these had all become potential threats to my well-being.

The only thing I could really remember following the surgery was being on all fours in the recovery room screaming, and then, yes, barking like a dog. This was an allergic reaction to the drug that had been used as sedation. I know, even I think it's funny— can't you just picture it? The nurses were ready to ship me off to the psych ward as I wailed like a woman possessed. Let's just say that the weeks to follow weren't very pleasant and I spent most of my free time immersed in a hot bath, to help ease the pain in my nether regions.

Less than two weeks after the surgery, I was having my morning soak when Jemma stripped off her jammies and climbed into the tub with me. She splashed around as I lay back and relaxed, when suddenly I heard her gasp. "Mommy!" she shrieked, pointing her chubby little finger at my belly. "A baby! I see a baby in your tummy!" "No, no, honey, Mommy's just fat." I laughed nervously.

"No, Mommy, a baby girl is in your tummy!" Sore butt and all, I shot out of that bathtub like flash lightning. In light of Jemma's recent extrasensory escapades, I was freaking out! I quickly dressed us both, rang Lily, and asked if she could watch Jemma for a few hours. I said nothing about the bath when I got to Lily's, only that I had a few things to do in town. I threw Jemma at her and sped over to my doctor's office. When I finally got in to see her, my doctor, Patricia, laughed when I asked her to do a pregnancy test.

"Calm down," she said in a soothing voice. I had always loved her accent, as it had a beautiful lilt, unlike the flat Midlands accent of Athlone. "When was your last period?"

"I'm not due for another week." She told me that it was too early to do a test, but she would agree to it if it would make me feel better. Try peeing in a little cup when your very future is hanging in the balance. Let's just say it's not an easy task. Eventually I managed and handed it over to my confident doctor and friend. A few moments later she was congratulating me.

The room started to spin and I began to feel hot all over. I couldn't catch my breath and then suddenly, I erupted into tears. I explained to Patricia the series of events that morning, and instead of prescribing me the latest dose of anti-psychotics, she listened intently. After some much needed reassurance and a big hug, she eventually sent me on my way to deal with the fact that Jake and I had just seriously complicated an already unbelievably complicated situation.

I went to my car, turned on the radio, and cried for the next two hours. Yes, I sat for two hours trying to figure out how this could have happened. I had just had surgery, there was no way, there was . . . Jake's birthday, October 2. For the second time in a row, in the midst of an ailing relationship, the second of October had sealed my fate. I got myself together, took out my phone, and rang Jake on the ship. I could not believe this was happening.

# Chapter 28

WITHIN DAYS of discovering that I was pregnant, I began to get sick. This was nothing like the first time, where at least I could hold out for my late-night puking extravaganza. This was morning, noon, and night. The heartburn was relentless and this time I immediately developed carpal tunnel syndrome in both of my wrists. This is not a good thing for a chiropractor. I would retch at the thought of most food, except for the peculiar combination of cranberry sauce, brie, and bacon on a bagel. Every day that I was in town, I ate at Poppyfields, a fab little bistro run by my friends Terry and Alec. The girls working in the café would crack up at the fact that I ordered the same dish throughout my entire pregnancy, but it was seriously the only thing I could keep down.

Unlike the first time, I was finding work extremely difficult. My body ached, my back was not coping, my wrists were killing me, and if someone looked at me the wrong way I would throw up. Before I was even halfway through, I decided to call in a relief doctor and go on maternity leave.

*

On the outside, the gym in Sligo appeared to be moving along nicely. In actual fact, it was being completely mismanaged. My exhaustion and apathy toward my current life meant that I turned a blind eye to the fact that money wasn't being handled properly. I was falling into a quagmire that would be most difficult to recover from if something didn't give. So what would any sensible businessperson do? I bought another gym. I was physically and emotionally worn out, up to my eyes in debt, and oh yes, did I mention that we were now building a house in the country?

Jake had grown up in a beautiful yet isolated part of New Zealand and didn't place the same value on living in a close-knit community that I did. His disdain for Ireland was growing stronger with each cold, wet day that passed, so rather than address the core problem, we decided to move. It would take a while to build this home, an amazing American-style split-level, out in the lovely community of Drum.

So there I was, pregnant, with a partner who was dying to get out of Ireland; someone else was running my office; our gym in Sligo looked good from the outside but was in total disarray on the inside; we'd just bought another gym and now we were building a house. This became the new definition of insanity. I was bubbly and positive on the outside, but the very fiber of my being was crumbling right before my eyes. I needed a break, a bit of peace, somewhere that I could escape to and get back to the things that were actually important to me.

Autumn turned to winter, my belly expanded, and my need for an escape before the baby arrived consumed me. I had seen a leaflet advertising a program that was taking place in the tranquil setting of Clonmacnoise. This was an ancient monastic site that I had enjoyed on numerous occasions. When I had visitors over from America, this was where I took them because this historical landmark was just about as Irish as it gets. With timeworn stone, Celtic crosses, and ancient church ruins, it sat perched above the mysterious banks of the river Shannon. Its haunting beauty made it a regular stop for the tourists who were lucky enough to get off the beaten track and discover the Midlands. Nearly 1,500 years old, a staggering concept for an American, Clonmacnoise was established by Saint Ciarán and went on to become a seat of higher learning for scholars from across Europe. What an ample setting in which to reconnect with one's spirituality.

And so, in the spring of 2004, I had the good fortune of making my first visit to a spiritual retreat near Clonmacnoise. I was instantly at ease when I entered its gates and was warmly welcomed. As we settled into the program, we were each asked by our instructor, Gertie, what had brought us to the workshop. When it was my turn, I had explained that it was the leaflet advertising the event that had captured my interest. I was a chiropractor and, while spiritual in nature, the scientist in me was intrigued by the concept of Healing with Angles. Note the spelling. Angles, as in lines, mathematical equations, the geometry of the human body. I was fascinated. Everyone started to chuckle as Gertie broke the news to me.

"Well, that was actually a misprint, Doctor. The title of this course is 'Healing with Angels.'"

And there I sat, the laughing butt of another Universal joke. I didn't mind, though. I was in a peaceful setting; no Jake, no Jemma, no patients, no gym, no false sense of financial security, just me and the Angled Angels.

When we broke for lunch, I noticed a woman in the kitchen who was busily working at preparing the wholesome lunch we were about to eat. Margaret had a lovely smile, was quick with a joke, and something special just radiated from her. I was immediately reminded that the Creator is present in all forms. There, glowing from the center of her being, God was in the kitchen making my lunch. I fell in love with this place and the way it made me feel. The construction of labyrinths and pyramids, which was taking place around the gardens, gave a sense of forward momentum, growth, and evolution of the spirit.

I had the opportunity to sit in the intimate setting of Clonmacnoise while absorbing the quick wit and vast spiritual knowledge of one of my favorite authors. Caroline Myss, a medical intuitive and author of best sellers *Anatomy of the Spirit, Why People Don't Heal* (a life changer for me), and *Sacred Contracts*, had been engaged to speak.

A former journalist, she'd had an overnight induction into the world of medical intuition. Her straightforward and humorous approach to her work made her an icon in my mind of what it meant to be a regular gal with an unusual gift. I sat in the audience of fifty eager listeners, so grateful to be the student of such a down-to-earth teacher. I was nearly eight months pregnant, living in chaos and she was just what the doctor ordered.

During the afternoon break, people were taken on a tour around the gardens, while given an explanation of the detailed thought process behind each structure, which had been specifically placed on a certain energy vortex, based on the human chakras. I was walking toward the labyrinth when Caroline Myss joined me, putting her arm around my shoulder.

"How are you doing there, Mom?" I was so excited by the one-on-one interaction that I hardly knew what to say.

"Let me ask you a question," Caroline said in her distinct Chicago accent. "Who is Judge?" Well, I stopped dead in my tracks, heart racing, and looked at her as if she had just handed over a million-dollar lottery check. She patted me on the belly, and said, "Watch this space." It wouldn't take long to discover exactly what she meant.

\*

Resting on the couch one Saturday afternoon in mid-June, miserable, fed up, and very upset by the fact that I was only weeks away from my due date and had developed a chest infection that was so severe, my doctor had given me two options: one was antibiotics with complete bed rest, and the other was to spend the remainder of the pregnancy in the hospital. The hospital was out of the question and I didn't like the idea of taking antibiotics when I wasn't pregnant, let alone over eight months into it. I lay on my side, watching television while Jake played outside with Jemma. I stared at the bottles of unopened prescription pills, mocking me as if they were my mortal enemies, all the while clutching my chest with each cough, feeling as if daggers were piercing through my lungs. In the same sitting room where almost two years to the day my grandmother Clark had appeared, heralding the news of my "gifted" baby girl, my grandfather Judge materialized. Not completely a solid form, he was wearing a topcoat and holding an old-fashioned doctor's bag. This apparition looked different from the way he would come to me as a child. He was ready for business, my loving grandfather, now with doctor's hat on and dressed for work. As he moved closer, I closed my eyes and waited for what was to come next.

My body felt as if it was vibrating from the inside out. I began to sweat profusely, and my eyes filled with tears as the pain that was ripping through my lungs began to ease. I coughed and spluttered and ran for the toilet, this time not vomiting the usual contents of my stomach, but buckets of mucus, laced with blood. I thought I would start puking up organs if I didn't stop the retching. I staggered back to the sitting room, looked around, but no Judge. I lay back down on the couch, fatigued and completely washed out. Just as I closed my eyes, I looked over at the door and there he stood. He smiled, tipped his hat, and with bag in hand, vanished into thin air. Hallucination? Dream? With my track record, I had no reason not to believe that Judge had healed me for a reason. Little did I know that reason would wake me at four-thirty in the morning the following day. In fairly severe pain right from the start, the muscles of my stomach contracted and released hard enough to awaken me from my sleep. I got out of bed and went downstairs to make myself a cup of tea. I switched on the television and was delighted to see that some Irish cable network played reruns of *Happy Days*, my all-time favorite show when I was a kid. I stood there in the living room, content to spend this time on my own, reliving my childhood. I was feeling much better after the previous day's house call from my own Spirit doc. I rang Greta at around five to tell her to start making her way down from Sligo. This labor was different and time was of the essence.

The pace of my contractions became more frequent and much more painful than I had remembered. I had waited as long as I could before waking Jake and Jemma. Then I rang Lily and Tommy and although it was so early, Lily's excitement over the phone set me aflutter. In a souped-up, bright purple ancient Mercedes with the name of our gym plastered on the side, we hit every bump and pothole on the forty-minute drive to Mullingar Hospital in County Westmeath. I actually thought I would have the child in the front seat of the car. All that kept going through my mind were visions of the nurse who had plagued me from the moment of my arrival when I was in labor with Jemma. I was in no fit state to argue with anyone; I was mentally exhausted, recovering from a serious illness, and desperately in need of an easy birth. My prayers were answered. I waddled into the labor ward and not only did I have the entire place to myself, I was greeted by a fresh, open-minded, smiley midwife. Greta had arrived from Sligo and I briefly explained to the nurse the drama of my last delivery. Her words were like honey as she replied, "I don't care if you hang from the chandelier, love. You do whatever you want. I just have to be present when it's time to catch the baby."

Greta was a star and once again she took charge, creating a calm atmosphere, getting me through this very different labor. My water hadn't broken until I arrived at the hospital, just before seven in the morning. With three or four guttural screams and even fewer pushes, at 8:34 a.m., just over four hours after my first signs of labor, out flew "The Bird." And I mean out she flew. If

Greta and the nurse hadn't been right there, I would have shot that child out with such force that she would have flown across the room! Perfect in every way, Jada Pacifica arrived in at seven pounds, six ounces, with a head full of jet-black hair. Jada, meaning precious jewel, and Pacifica, in honor of her South Pacific heritage.

# Chapter 29

SOMEONE HAD forgotten to mention to this new mother that taking it easy following the birth of a new baby was essential. After Jemma, I had returned to my prepregnancy state rather quickly. With Jada, the fact that I had thrown up morning, noon, and night had left me tired and very, very hungry. I made a pact with myself that for as long as I breast-fed, I could and would eat whatever I wanted to. Big mistake. Although I was running around like a lunatic the pounds began creeping up and not only was I dog-tired, I was getting really fat. To make matters worse, although we had remained in the hospital for a total of less than six hours from labor to birth to discharge, Jada had managed to pick up a nasty staph infection. Her poor little bottom looked as if someone had poured scalding hot water all over it and her wounds were so severe that she could wear no nappy (diaper) and had to be left lying on a blanket "free style" for the first six weeks of her life.

Remember that I mentioned that we took on another gym? It was scheduled to open in July, only three weeks after Jada was born. So there I was, in the car making the forty-five minute drive to Longford every day, to oversee the completion of our new fitness center and my second chiropractic office. Oh . . . did I forget to mention that? Another office. It was as if some entity had possessed my body, causing me to make every stupid choice there was to make. I intended to put another doctor in there, not handle it myself, but honestly, did I really need to take on anything else?

After being forced to reconstruct the management of the businesses, I was left to oversee both the Sligo and Longford facilities myself. This was not working out the way I had visualized it. I must say though, I was beginning to learn a very important lesson about a tendency that I had. None of these business ventures had ever been about the money or becoming wealthy beyond my wildest dreams. Sure, I wanted to be comfortable and master of my own schedule, yet I really loved the thought of being in a position to supply not only jobs, but opportunities for my employees to excel and grow. I loved giving bonuses out of the blue and I was always hiring people (with what some people might consider to be fairly complicated life situations) to give them a chance when nobody else would. Sounds noble, right?

What I came to discover about myself was that my generosity was conditional. Hard thing to say about yourself but sometimes the truth hurts. I gave and gave and in return expected people to perform at my standard. I discounted where they were on their own journeys, not taking into account the fact that they might not have acquired the tools yet for a work ethic beyond doing a mediocre job. I realized that with some of my employees, I had given so much that I had literally incapacitated them, cutting them off at the knees, giving no incentive to work hard for rewards, because I just gave the rewards anyway.

A worker bee I was, a beekeeper I was not. I was up to my neck in the reality that I had bitten off way more than I could chew. At three weeks old, Jada was being dragged to work with me every day, lying in the middle of the floor on a beach towel, when she should have been at home, curled up in my arms, receiving my undivided attention.

✳

My parents came for a visit to Ireland that summer to meet and greet the new baby. I was so proud to be able to take them over to Scotland, their favorite destination abroad, with Jake and their granddaughters, treating them to a Highland fling. We packed up the Jeep and took the ferry across for a week's holiday. From Inverness to Iona, we had a wonderful adventure. Jada was only tiny, and Jemma was just at that age, a precocious two and a bit, that she was a constant source of entertainment.

Things took an interesting twist as we headed out of Fort William and into the Highlands. We were driving past a majestic hillside covered in a blanket of heather that was postcard perfect, when Jemma yelled, "Stop!!!" I pulled the car over to see what had her in such a state. She pointed and banged on the window with pure excitement exclaiming, "Look, Mommy, look! Don't you remember? We used to play there! Remember, when we were sisters? Right there, right there!" Well, my mom nearly fell out of the Jeep. She looked at me with utter astonishment as we both watched my daughter have a past-life recall that was as vivid to her as my first one had been to me. I had always had an unusual affinity for Scotland. So much so that it would have been my first choice of places to live if the powers that be hadn't firmly steered me in the direction of Ireland. We caught our breath, drove on, and listened to Jemma chat away about her life in a Scotland, with me as her sister, a very long time ago.

Scotland was beautiful and I treasured the time that we spent with Mom and Dad, but the trip solved nothing for Jake and me. In retrospect, being trapped together in the same vehicle for hours on end probably doesn't rank up there as one of our wisest moves. In the autumn of 2004, I was wearing very thin, figuratively I might add, as I was now a whopping thirteen stone (that's 182 pounds, guys!). My "eat what I want" pact with myself had packed on close to fifty extra pounds! Still, I knew the day would come when I would simply make up my mind and stop. Subconsciously,

I think it was an advertising ploy to beef up and then use my own fitness center to get back into shape. I was a walking, talking billboard! Just when I had to come up with a new way to juggle all of my self-inflicted responsibilities, none of them at which I was doing an exceptional job, Jake injured himself at work and ended up having to have knee surgery right around Halloween. He was trapped at home, wearing circulation stockings due to a subsequent blood clot, it was raining in Ireland, and he was now in his own, personal hell.

# Chapter 30

WITH JAKE'S current state of health and frame of mind, and my feeble attempts to rule the empire, our relationship was heading down the tubes. He was in such a bad space that I refused his attempts to get involved with running the gyms. It was a double-edged sword, and the darker he became, the more I turned him away, deepening an already festering wound. He didn't want to sit around, he wanted to help, but his moods were unpredictable and the more I shut him out, the more he shut down. I had put my foot down: I didn't want to hear another word about moving to New Zealand. I was tired, working nonstop, raising two small children, and unable to tolerate another complaint. He was frustrated, unable to work or travel, terribly homesick, and disgusted with the fact that I had completely disinvolved him with the businesses. It was truly a mess, an ugly, disappointing and terrible mess that we were both responsible for in our own ways.

At one point I suggested that we employ the services of a counselor to whom I referred many of my patients for relationship and other personal issues. Brian was down to earth, compassionate, and had a brilliant sense of humor. Jake didn't want to go, so I began couples counseling on my own, spending an hour each week pouring my heart out. Brian was open, honest, and a real blessing at a time when I needed unbiased advice. I wasn't interested in a pity party or someone who reinforced the idea that I was the only one who had been hard done by. I wanted to find out exactly where I had screwed up, learn the lessons, vow to avoid repeating them, and get on with my life. His insights were invaluable.

There simply weren't enough hours in the day to get everything done. Every minute was accounted for and the normal activities, such as going to the grocery store, were done after the day's work and the girls were in bed. One evening, I made a late-night trip to the supermarket to get groceries for the week. There, walking through the aisles, was Kate, the wife of a former patient of mine, named Barra. He had been diagnosed with secondary melanoma and, soon after, developed double pneumonia. Barra passed away in June, two weeks after Jada was born. He had come to my office a year earlier, when he'd been initially diagnosed, asking that I not tell Kate yet, indicating two very interesting facts: one, that he'd like me to help her down the road after he passed, and two, somehow in his state of illness he had become acutely aware that I had the capacity to assist her in some "out of this world" kind of way. I had always liked Barra; he had a wonderful sense of humor and a gentle heart. And so here we were. I had not seen Kate since the funeral, and immediately thought back to the prophetic words her husband had spoken in my office. I greeted her with a big hug, engaging in a dialogue that was not typical for us, as we had only been casual acquaintances up until that day. Much to my surprise, Kate started with, "You knew, didn't you?"

I suddenly found myself entering that awkward space of disclosing information to a person I hardly knew. I explained to Kate that I had known that Barra was going to die by the nature of his auric field. I went on to tell her about a request he had made, that I help him execute changes that he would later instigate from the other side. At the time, neither of us had a clue what this meant. Still, rather than pushing me into the bin with the rest of the fruits, Kate was fascinated and began to ask questions about how my gift worked. She wanted to know what it sounded like when I "heard" her husband speak from Spirit, and how I had known he was going to die, simply by looking at him.

So I used the tomatoes in the supermarket as an example, explaining that I assumed that she and I could both see them, red in color and of a certain size, that when I was younger I thought everyone could see the way I could, including the live energy field around all things, and so I never bothered to question them. She understood. I was attempting to explain the whole "seeing the aura" thing, not very well I might add, but Kate listened patiently. I explained to her that I had been able to communicate with the dead since I was a child and she immediately asked if I had heard from Barra. I would have loved to have been able to say yes, but at that point, I was still in the dark regarding his promise of communication. Having piqued Kate's curiosity and rediscovering mine by sharing what Barra had said at my last meeting with him, I told her that I would keep in touch if I heard any news. Oh, that Universal sense of humor. . . .

No sooner than I had walked away, I heard a voice so clear that I actually turned around to see if someone (alive) was speaking to me. You guessed it! *Barra.* Talk about timing. I had just told this man's poor widow that I hadn't heard a word when he made a complete ass of me right in the middle of the frozen-vegetable aisle. Now, come on, how staged was it going to look if I walked over to Kate and said,"Ooo, ooo, I just got a message from Barra!" Give me a break, that's so lame.

I immediately responded back, in my head, of course, that he better give me something good if I was going to march back to this grieving woman and tell her that her dead hubby had just decided to open the lines of communication in aisle nine. As it was, this was to be the first of numerous encounters with Barra, who was obviously clever enough to discern that the whirlwind of madness that my life had become would mean that he would have to grab whatever opportune moment he could, in order to communicate.

And so I walked over to Kate, reluctantly whispering her name as she stood at the checkout.

"I know you're probably not going to believe this, but I just heard from Barra."

Not the slightest bit freaked out by my words, Kate stepped out of the line and smiled as if she knew. I told her Barra wanted her to remember the discussion about the shoes just before he had died. The actual line he requested I say was, "Hellooo! Paddy here, ringin' from Ireland, and I'd like to order meself one shoe please." *This* was what he gave me to offer her. About a week before he had died, he told Kate that he had lost one of his shoes, and it wasn't any shoe. It was a shoe belonging to a pair that Kate had bought for him in Churchill's of London. From his sickbed, Barra had suggested that he ring Churchill's and order himself a single shoe. Kate and Barra had a great laugh about how that phone call might sound. They both imagined what they might say to the salesperson, how they might go about purchasing just one shoe. It had been a priceless joke between them, intimately shared from his sickbed.

Kate had tears in her eyes, not of sadness but of joy, as she recounted this, one of their last moments together. A key was turned, a door unlocked, and a journey that I'd dare say neither of us expected had just begun. There, in the checkout line of our local supermarket, a magical friendship had just grown wings.

# Chapter 31

WITH THINGS being as hectic in our lives as they were, Lily and Tommy were unable to look after the girls full-time. On the days that they did have the girls, they would go on little adventures to the lakeside, or out to the graveyard to "tidy up" around Lily's parents, Granny and Grandad Mullally. Jemma loved to visit the graveyard and one afternoon, she squatted down on her hunkers on top of Granny's grave. She started to push the stones aside, when Lily asked her what she was doing. "I'm going to sing a song for Granny Mullally!" And away she went.

When she finished, Lily told her how beautiful it was and asked if Granny Mullally liked the song. "Oh yes, she kept kicking one leg out and saying "Woo-hoo!" Tommy, who was standing to the side of the grave holding Jada in his arms, nearly dropped the baby as he looked at his wife in disbelief. Lily quickly brushed the stones back over the grave and they took off for the car.

Later that evening, when I came to collect the girls, Lily met me at the door and launched into the story of their visit to the graveyard. "How cute!" I laughed, until Lily stopped me and said, "Mary, when the lads used to play music in our house, Mammy would stop what she was doing and listen because she just loved the music. She used to sit, kicking one leg out and say, 'Woo-hoo,' as they played! It was this thing we all used to laugh about because it was so particular, the way she did it. Jemma described it exactly the same way! How on earth would she know that unless . . . ?"

I wasn't quite sure how to respond. Tommy sat by the fire, shaking his head with an all-knowing grin. "Mary, where did we get this child a'tall?"

While Lily and Tommy were always on the scene, I eventually had to employ the services of another babysitter to help out a few days of the week because of the very long hours I was keeping with work. First there was Josephine, a lovely girl who eventually went on to become a Christian minister. The girls loved Jo-Jo and she loved them. Jo was a good sport about our paranormal encounters, but at the end of the day, I'm sure it must have been a challenge for her. Then there was Elaine. Young and energetic, Elaine came with the added bonus of her boyfriend, Ian, whom the girls adored and loved to spend time with. Elaine was mesmerized when I filled her in on who we were and what we were all about. She waited patiently to witness something "out of this world" and it didn't take long for her patience to pay off.

She told me one story of Jemma "playing" with a friend at her house, a little boy. They were usually on all fours, chasing each other and playing "horses." Weeks passed, and she continued to watch, asking Jemma about her friend and where he came from. Jemma said that he always came in and left the house at the bottom of the stairs in an empty corner. This seemed to be some sort of "opening"' where he and Jemma could connect. Jemma explained that he missed his mummy and daddy and he liked playing with her. She also said he had died of leukemia and from what Elaine could gather from Jemma's description, he was around the age of four. This was the first of a few of Elaine's "out of this world" experiences with our family.

On February 15, 2005, Jemma, Elaine, and I were watching *Mulan*, one of Jem's favorite movies. In fact, she loved it so much that she knew nearly every line and every song word for word, often using them in her daily speech. Jake had once told her to sit down and eat her dinner, to which she replied, "Don't worry, Father, I won't dishonor you!" On this evening, we were snuggled in the bed, laughing at Jemma as she performed all of the actions in the movie. Suddenly she stopped what she was doing and looked into the hallway and as casually as you like said, "Hi, Freddie."

Elaine sat bolt upright and there standing at Jemma's door was my uncle Freddie, a light-filled apparition, but definitely him. A tremendous man, devoted husband, and loving father, Freddie had been battling cancer in America, and until that day, was still alive. He smiled and waved and Jemma waved back, returning to her film as if nothing out of the ordinary had just happened. I looked at Elaine and explained to her whom we had just seen, and although she was a little spooked, she was so excited to be a part of it.

Not long after, the phone rang. "Hi, Mom," I said before she had even said hello. "I have some sad news," she said, waiting for my usual response. "Freddie was just here, Mom. He's doing just fine." Mom was well used to ringing with news of a death, only to be told that I already knew. I asked her to pass on the news of Freddie's visit to my aunt Hope, but only when the time was right. She knew the drill, yet remained ever amazed, as did I, that we were so blessed to have this gift in our lives.

As spring set in, despite the growing turmoil between her father and me, Jemma had no problem expressing her metaphysical self. One day, Elaine was driving down the road with her younger twin brothers and the girls in the car. Jemma had mentioned a few times that they were going to crash. Never had she done this before, until this day. Elaine stopped the car in a single lane of traffic due to roadworks ahead. Jemma started to shout, "We're going to crash! We're going to crash!"

Knowing that the other kids were starting to get upset, Elaine pulled up the hand brake, and as she turned around to tell Jemma to stop . . . BANG! The driver of the car behind her had failed to notice the stopped traffic, and smashed into the back of the car. Jemma looked at Elaine, still shaking with shock, and with a big grin, she smirked, "I told you so!" Well used to Jemma by now, it was understandable why I came home one evening in May to find Elaine very upset. "Jemma keeps telling me there's a baby in my tummy and that there is black all around it. She also told me that it wouldn't grow bigger, it wouldn't be born, and that it was a girl. Oh my God! What does that mean?"

A few weeks later, after just discovering that she was pregnant, Elaine had a miscarriage. The first time that Jemma saw her after losing the baby, she told Elaine that it was gone from her tummy. They named her Sophie, and Jemma continued to speak about her for some time after.

## Chapter 32

AT THE end of May 2005, I decided to take a break from everything, on my own, and head over to South Carolina to attend Lyceum, the annual homecoming at my chiropractic college. It was great to catch up with friends and teachers and the blast of sunshine did the power of good for my ailing body and broken heart. I went home to Virginia to spend a week with my folks and landed myself in a situation that was unusual and uplifting for us all.

My father had just lost a friend, named Turner, to cancer and the one request that this man had made was that Dad help him write his own eulogy and then deliver their combined sentiments at his funeral. We sometimes take for granted that just because someone is accustomed to dealing with death as part of their job, it does not affect them emotionally or carry the same impact. Dad had participated in countless funeral services, and his presence and conviction of faith had seen many families through very difficult times over the years. This time it was different. Due to a sudden change in Turner's situation, Dad had been unable to sit with his friend and make good on his request to coauthor the final musings about his life. Dad was really struggling, as the onus was now on him to say what Turner would have wished to say about his time on Earth. The day before the funeral, I walked into the kitchen to find Dad sitting in his seat at the head of the table, staring at the yellow legal pad that he had been staring at when I had gone to bed the night before. It wasn't that he didn't know what to say; it was the fact that his friend had so much wanted to be a part of this process and had been unable to last long enough to do it. Dad wanted to honor the way in which Turner had hoped his public life review would play out. He had wanted it to be personal, humorous, and in keeping with the way in which he had lived. Standard sentiment was not an option and Dad was humbly attempting to find just the right words to pay tribute to this man's life.

I sat down at the other end of the table with a bowl of oatmeal. Before I got the first spoon into my mouth I heard a voice. I looked to my right, where Mom was puttering around the kitchen, listening to Radio WMVA. Dad was in the same position, pen in hand, across the table. I took a bite of my breakfast when I heard it again: *Remind him of when I used to swap him milk shakes for Coca-Cola.*

I put my spoon down and looked again to my mother, who was now aware that something strange was going on.

"What is it?" she whispered from across the kitchen counter. I shrugged my shoulders, looking back at my dad, who had not yet looked up from his partially written notes. I went back to my breakfast when I heard the same voice, now laughing: *Be sure to say the milk shakes were strawberry. Dick loved his strawberry milk shakes!*

I got up from the table and walked into the living room. Mom followed me in, knowing by the look on my face that I needed to talk.

"Mom, I think Dad's friend is speaking to me!"

"Really! What did he say?" She was excited and a little weirded out simultaneously. She wasn't the only one. . . .

I relayed the first two messages when suddenly the voice started again, this time going into a full history of when he and Dad had played on the old gravel field at Brown Street.

He went on to discuss their circle of friends in detail, even calling one of them by a nickname that only those in this close group would have known. By this time, Mom had gone in and told Dad what was happening, as the messages continued to flow. His friend was fulfilling his own wish: to participate in the writing of his eulogy with my dad. A bit stunned, but unable to deny the accuracy with which the memories were being relived, Dad was given the details that would complete this undertaking, only instead of doing it from this side, his old buddy had shed his broken body and spoken from Spirit. He went as far as to direct Dad to use something from his prayer book entitled "It's Never Too Late to Start Over." I must say that I enjoyed hearing the tales from my Dad's youth, and the method of communication gave a whole new meaning to "ghost stories"! My father and his friend reminisced one last time. We all got a little emotional when Turner finished up by exclaiming, "Oh boy, oh boy, Dick, just wait 'til you see it here!"

The following day, I stood in the back corner of a packed-out church and watched as people nodded their heads, shed a few tears, but mostly smiled and laughed as they, too, got to reminisce with Turner, as Dad delivered the most beautiful and uplifting eulogy. Everyone left with a feeling of celebration of this man's life. Oh, if only they knew what had really happened that day: a most astounding confirmation of how the Spirit lives on. Well, I suppose . . . now they do. After the service, a very dear friend of Dad's, an elderly but very lively character, joked with Dad in private that when he died, he would send him a message. Only Dad knew the quirky line that this man pledged to repeat. When he passed away less than a year later, I was sitting in bed one night when I heard this man's unmistakable voice. I rang home immediately and told my folks that I had just gotten the strangest request from their departed friend. It didn't make any sense to me but maybe it would to Dad.

*Tell Dick that I'm playing cowboys and Indians!*

The phone was silent on the other side. It seemed as if an eternity had passed when Dad quietly replied, "That's exactly what Jack told me he would say."

Following Turner's burial, I went out to the cemetery on my own. I noticed that some of the flowers on his grave had blown over. As I went to set them upright, I had the sudden urge to visit the grave of a woman who had been very dear to me when I was younger. We called her Granny and she had, funnily enough, been a part of the same circle of friends as Turner and my Dad in their youth. In my childhood, she and her husband, Tom, had opened their home and hearts to the children and youth groups at our church. They would throw barbecues and parties and were always on hand to help out in any way they could. She and her husband were madly in love and when she passed away, Tom was never the same again. As I walked up to her grave, I distinctly heard Granny's voice say, *Tell Tommy that I'm sending him a postcard.*

I smiled and in my mind told her that I promised to deliver the message. That Sunday, our church was having its annual Ice Cream Social, my favorite church event since childhood. Each year, there was a different theme, and people would dress accordingly. There was music and fellowship, all topped off by homemade ice cream of practically every flavor known to man. That year had been a country theme, including a contest to see who could whistle the best rendition of *The Andy Griffith Show* theme tune. There was a pound of barbecue on the line, so yours truly got up, brought the house down, and walked out with the pork! After making a complete show of myself, I wandered around, sampling everything from my mom's peach delight to Mrs. Abbott's strawberry surprise. As I delicately shoveled in another mouthful of creamy goodness, I looked across the parking lot and spotted Tom Leath (Granny's husband) chatting to someone. I waited for him to finish and ran up, giving him a huge hug like I used to when I was a kid.

"Hey, gal!" He had always called me "gal." "Eleanor would have loved this so much."

"Well, don't worry; I don't think she's missing a thing, Tom."

He smiled and asked what I meant. I explained to him the

message I had received from her and he immediately broke down in tears. I was worried that I had upset him terribly, but when he took his hands away from his face, he wiped his eyes, and laughed as he sobbed. "Oh, thank you, my darling, thank you, thank you!"

He shouted up to heaven. Tom then explained to me that he had genuinely believed that because he and his Eleanor were so very close, he was sure that she would have sent him some kind of message, letting him know that she was okay. Until that day, he had heard nothing. He then went on to explain that in a moment of grief, only a few days earlier, he had cried out loud, "A postcard, Eleanor, all I need is a postcard, honey!"

Now I understood.

That trip home had been very special. At a time when my own life was falling down around me, I was reminded that this gift that I had been given had the power to lift more than just the spirits of those it was helping to heal. It was lifting me. I had a brief respite on my old stomping ground, surrounded by people who loved me . . . just because. I was able to catch my breath, see things more clearly, as I came to understand that the very reason I had been given this gift in the first place was for my own benefit. When I got to Charlotte, North Carolina, to catch my connecting flight to New York, I was in a good space. I was feeling less stressed, ready to face what was ahead of me at home, and at peace with the path I had chosen for myself. It was a good thing that I was feeling so perky, because a terrible storm had appeared out of nowhere, and at 4:30 p.m. that's exactly where I was going . . . nowhere! The 5:30 p.m. flight was canceled, followed by the 7:30 p.m. and the 9:30 p.m. flights. I had already missed my connection to Ireland so there was nothing to do, only wait. At 12:30 a.m., they loaded up the small prop plane with the remaining twenty people who had waited around the airport to get to New York. I stayed around, in hopes that I could catch the early morning flight back to Ireland and get home to my babies.

As we took off into the dark night, I felt certain that all would be fine, because surely they wouldn't let us fly into a terrible storm. When the friendly pilot's voice came over the intercom, I eagerly awaited his certain reassurance that smooth skies were ahead. Instead, with a thick Southern drawl that reminded me of a cattle rancher anticipating the adrenaline rush of heading into a stampede, he chuckled and said, "Buckle up and hang on folks! I can't fly over or under this lightning, so we're gonna have to fly right through it!" Palpitations, sweating palms, pounding heart, and sick stomach all came rolling in on top of me. By now, I think we all know how I feel about flying, particularly the difficulty I have as an empathic intuitive, feeling everybody's "stuff" in a confined space from which I cannot escape.

An airplane is the one place where my faith cannot override this horrible sensation, and that's on a good day, with clear skies and NO thunderstorms.

With the armrests nearly torn off my seats, we bounced and pounded our way to New York. After completing my zillionth list of what I would do with my life if I made it to the ground in one piece, I saw the bright lights of the Big Apple ahead in the distance. *We made it!* I thought to myself, still not willing to unpry my white-knuckled hands from the armrests. And then it happened.

*Kabooom!!!* It was like a war movie—like when the fighter plane has just been bombarded by enemy fire. I had the sudden urge to scream, *We're hit, we're hit!!!*

But before I could get the words out of my mouth, the Vietnam vet a few rows up beat me to it. As the lights went out and one of the engines made an unnerving humming noise, the pilot came on to inform us that the sudden jolt had been from the bolt of lightning that had *just struck our plane!* As he was attempting to assure us that there was nothing to worry about, and that we would be perfectly safe to land, his voice was muffled out by the screams of the elderly Southern gentleman in the seat next to me.

"Oh, help me, Lord! Help me, Jesus!" Over and over and over again. . . .

If I hadn't have been so scared I would have actually found the whole thing hysterical, but my sense of humor was stifled by my attempts to prevent myself from having a freaking heart attack right there in seat 9B. All of a sudden, I was overcome by a calmness that was nothing short of the sensation I had when I was dying in my car accident and when I had a severe allergic reaction to shellfish. "Uh-oh." I cringed.

I naturally associated this sudden peace with my imminent demise. At that moment, the image of a good friend of my mother came into my mind. Nancy was a gifted clairvoyant and it was as if, right then, she knew that I was in danger. I could sense that she was sending me a message that I was going to be okay. (As I later found out, she had, in fact, prayed for me at that precise moment.) This lasted for only a few seconds, though, because my attention was promptly drawn to the window on my left. I could not believe my eyes!

Now, for me to say I could not believe my eyes was a big statement. I've seen some pretty weird stuff in my time. But there, on the wing of the plane, stood a figure. Male, as far as I could tell, at least eight to ten feet tall, with a big smile on his beautiful face. He appeared to be surfing on the wing of the plane, arms out to either side, knees bent, having a ball! I looked to my right and saw a similar but different guy doing the same thing on the other wing. Blissful delirium just before the crash? I could hear the names Michael and Stephen dancing through my mind as these two beings were hangin' ten on the wings of our wounded plane. Were they angels? Who knows! I couldn't have cared less who or what they were. All I know was that when we made it to the runway safely, I got down on my hands and knees and literally kissed the ground!

The following morning I had the easiest flight I've ever taken.

The slight turbulence back to Ireland was nothing compared to being struck by lightning, then guided to safety by two giant wind-surfing angels. I lay back in my chair and slept the whole way back—a first for me, as I never sleep on planes (I generally choose to amuse myself by believing that as long as my eyes are open I can somehow control the plane). I was so grateful to see my children that day, and even Jake was a sight for sore eyes after the "flightmare" from hell.*

---

* It's important to note that just because I know when and how I am going to die, it doesn't mean that I won't be subject to injury or illness along the way. I experience pain, terror, and sometimes dread, the very same as the next person. There are many valuable lessons to be learned in the uncomfortable moments in life.

Chapter 33

FOLLOWING JADA'S birth more than a year earlier, strange things were happening to my body. My hair completely changed, something my friend and hairdresser, Rosaleen, could attest to. My once perfectly straight, blond tresses now had this bizarre curly patch, smack in the middle of the back of my head, dark and wiry like an old soot brush. Rosaleen would laugh each time she cut or highlighted my hair, at this unusual shift in my body's chemistry. I would sit in her chair and unload my life's events, as she listened patiently, like a barmaid tending to a babbling drunk. I have marked many seasons while sitting under her skilled hands, looking at my changing reflection in the large mirror before me. She has been a constant, from the very first time she washed my hair, watching me work in the chiropractic practice, purchasing it, coming to hear me play music, meeting Jake, getting glasses, opening more businesses, and having babies. Everyone needs a witness to his or her life. With steadfast support, there, in the hairdresser's chair, she has been mine.

The changes in my hair were only a superficial symptom of the changes in my entire constitution. From the first month after Jada was born, I had been getting excruciatingly painful migraines for exactly three days during ovulation and for three days during my period. For someone who had never experienced headaches, this was debilitating. Whatever changes had taken place, chemically, physically, and emotionally, they were now manifesting as a knife-like pain in the left side of my face, concentrated directly into my eye. For six of every twenty-eight days of the month, I was in absolute agony, only to be told by my doctor that this would probably continue until I hit menopause! Dealing with other people's pain during those six days of the month was more than challenging. I tried to accept the fact that maybe this was keeping me in check, ever mindful not to be flippant or unsympathetic to the suffering of others. I must be really dense in this department because this phenomenon persists to this day. Still, I would smile, never taking a break to sit with the pain; afraid that if I did, I would simply give up. I was no stranger to severe discomfort, as I can't recall a day since my accident, in 1991, that I have been without it.

This pain, however, was so draining. I would get angry and unable to understand why this could be necessary as a lesson. I had already agreed to lead a life less ordinary. Nothing I tried worked, so finally I had to schedule my life around these black days when possible. It was difficult to digest when some patients would callously remark at how easy I had it, unaware that on many days, I was experiencing symptoms so intense it was a wonder I was still standing. On these days, I just wanted to lie down and go to sleep, not caring if I ever woke again. I completely understood why the neuralgia I was experiencing was often referred to as a "suicide headache."

Instead, I persisted, pushing through the pain and hanging on until the three-day cycle would pass. Dealing with Jake, the children, and the insane mess that was my personal life was really getting to me. Oddly enough, the more chaotic my life was, the more skilled and focused I became at using my gifts. I found that when my energy levels were at their lowest, working with people on a spiritual level temporarily put me into a space of ease. The dynamic was paradoxical, and I was like a hamster in a wheel, exhausted yet elated, but getting nowhere fast.

I was also beginning to see the parallel between the state of my body and the state of my businesses. All of my businesses were in bad shape. For a long time, it appeared as if I had turned a blind eye, when in reality, I was now working in my office in Athlone and part-time in my office in Longford, using my own wages to pay the people who were working in the ailing gyms. The bright spot in my week was my time in Longford. I was renting the top floor of a building that housed the gym, my practice, a massage therapist, and a beauty salon. I had become good friends with Mary, the massage therapist and Reiki healer, and Tanya, the beautician who showed people their inner beauty as opposed to just what they saw in the mirror. I learned a lot about life from these dynamic ladies and treasured their friendship, as we waded through the proverbial muck together. They brought much needed laughter and shared a lot of tears, as we explored the mystical side of life in our paradise of the paranormal. Longford became my escape and it also became a place where I finally made the move into making office hours outside of chiropractic time, to practice metaphysics. I had always been doing it, at home, behind closed doors, but I decided to hang up a new shingle and open myself up officially to the public. Word spread like wildfire and I began to embrace the idea that one day, I would make the leap to full-time metaphysician.

*

In October of 2005, my dear friend Kate, Barra's wife, was diagnosed with breast cancer. Interesting to note, from the first time that Barra had "spoken" to me in the supermarket following his passing, he had never stopped talking! He persistently contacted Kate with messages of a very personal nature, right down to the suggestion that she get out of law and begin to explore her own gifts as a healer. Kate initially resisted this push, not out of fear, but out of deep commitment to the families and clients with whom she worked. A few years earlier Kate had told Barra that she instinctively knew that she should be doing something else.

There's nothing like someone else's trauma to take your mind off your own problems. In my experience, I have yet to meet a woman diagnosed with breast cancer who hasn't spent a huge portion of her time overnurturing others. Most women are nurturers by nature, yet when they move into the realms of taking on the responsibility of other people's difficulties, it gets messy. Kate is one of the kindest, most generous human beings I have ever had the privilege to know. Not only would she give you the shirt off her back, but the handbag and high heels to go with it. She would never see someone go without, and following her husband Barra's death the previous year, she had dealt with a lot of postmortem chaos of her own.

She worked tirelessly, coped with her husband's passing, and took care of her family until eventually, it all caught up with her. The week before she was to go in for a mastectomy, Kate came to the house for a healing session. Granny Brennan came through, her maternal grandmother who had passed thirty-five years earlier, now acting as one of Kate's spirit guides. We laughed and cried as the air in the room virtually tingled with energy. Her surgery went off without a hitch and if ever somebody "got it," Kate so got it! She changed her life in ways that most could barely comprehend and continues to thrive to this day, not in remission but free from a disease process that was, by her own admission and design, a true blessing in her life.

Barra continued to make regular appearances, often filling me in on his insights into his own journey from the other side. He would send me on excursions to pick up specific gifts to help Kate through the tough times. He would often tell me things that I didn't know about him, some deeply painful and others more lighthearted, like his love of collecting odd spoons. Each time he made contact, not only did it comfort Kate but it reaffirmed my belief in the fact that when the soul has left its body, the learning continues.

For quite some time Barra was an unlikely angel on my shoulder, guiding me from the other side, not just in matters of the spirit, but of the most practical ways to deal with the legal issues that I would be forced to confront in the near future. Talk about an attorney with spirit! I had my own legal advisor in Spirit! During this time, my bond with Kate grew deeper and stronger. Like observing a child as she first crawls, walks, and then takes off running, I watched Kate tap into and develop her own latent psychic abilities. Her ability to connect with angel energies was nothing short of incredible and I sat back and witnessed the manifestation of her gifts as a full-blown intuitive healer.

*

If you have ever had the challenge of living under the same roof as a partner or spouse from whom you have already separated, you'll relate well to the next six months that followed. Jake was still in the house, unable to work due to his injury, watching me come and go. We barely spoke, and that Christmas was a real treat all the way around. We did all of the things that other families do, except speak. We bought and decorated a tree, bought gifts for the girls, cooked the dinners, and throughout the festive season managed to live in the same space, sans communication. The tension was unnatural. The fact that I was a communicator by nature, living in the same house with someone who acted as if I wasn't even there, nearly finished me off.

*

Rapidly approaching my thirty-sixth year, the stress of it all finally got to me. One dark, wet morning that winter, as I was getting dressed, I suddenly turned green, and then doubled over in horrific pain. The symptoms were that of an acute gallbladder attack. I had two grandmothers and six aunties with diseased gallbladders; the fact that I had allowed myself to pile on weight, was fair-complexioned, and not miles off forty, meant that I fit the "fat, fair, fertile, and almost forty" profile to a tee. Jake put me in the car, as he was now forced to take care of me, and took me to the hospital. There, I spent three days undergoing tests, the worst being the camera down my neck with no anesthetic, due to allergy. It was like being choked alive, but at that point it beat the slow suffocation I was experiencing at home. Because I was so out of control of my own circumstances, I had now made myself ill in order to take a three-day breather from reality. And for three days, Jake was really nice to me. All of the tests came back negative, and I became a classic example of how the human body can be distorted and manipulated by the mind.

I would love to say it stopped there, but I don't do things by halves. My next trick became the manifestation of panic attacks. As soon as I would turn onto the road to my house, I was able to go from zero to full-on panic in less than two miles. At first, the attacks were mild enough. Eventually, though, they became so severe that on several occasions, I opened the car door, stepped out, then passed out. I became a regular at the local hospital, with chest pains so severe that I would have sworn it was "the big one." My body had spiraled out of control. Instead of my spirit driving the vehicle, the vehicle was now driving my spirit.

# Chapter 34

THAT SUMMER I spent a great deal of time at Clonmacnoise. The girls were now two and four, and everywhere that I went, they went, too. They loved nothing more than to play among the ancient ruins on the banks of the Shannon, also feeling a deep connection to the land and the people at the retreat where all three of us found solace. I was at peace there, and the speakers who were sharing their wisdom in this intimate setting gave me a lot of food for thought. I had mountains of enthusiasm, but what I lacked was structure. I had allowed the tornado that was now my life to uproot me from the core. Sure, the amazing supernatural events that were a regular occurrence kept things exciting, but what was I really doing with them? I certainly didn't seem to be applying any of these insights to my own experiences. I was helping others to heal while simultaneously not taking charge of the actions that were currently shaping my life. I was a walking contradiction and I knew it.

The next teacher to enter my life was Neale Donald Walsch, author of the *Conversations with God* series. I had enjoyed his wit and wisdom from the time my father had given me his first book back in 1995. I enjoyed this man's work, and hearing him share his thoughts about spirituality with such passion and humility was an honor. Besides, at the time I began his workshop, I had also started work on my book and felt I could use some insight and support from a successful author. I had wanted to write my book for some time, particularly because my girls were giving every indication that their lives were heading down the same path as mine, with regard to having the gift of clairvoyance and communicating with those in the world of Spirit. I desperately wanted them to have some kind of reference, a guidebook that would let them know that what they had was something special. I wanted to provide a glimpse of my own growth and development, making them aware that their abilities were tools that could greatly enhance their life experiences. I desperately didn't want them to grow up thinking they were weird or strange, only blessed and privileged to have the opportunity to help themselves and others with their extrasensory perceptiveness.

Neale's talk was full of powerful insights. I diligently took notes as he asked us to ask ourselves, "Who am I, and what am I doing here?" He spoke of cohesive awareness, the need to acknowledge the mind, body, and spirit on a personal level if we expected to do this on a global scale. Bells were going off in my mind as he described crisis, or great change, in life as the interruption of a pattern of monotony or meaningless cycles, offering us the opportunity to behave differently. "My friends, the world is hungry for another point of view."

And then it happened. My paper was covered in notes in my own handwriting, when suddenly, it was as if my pen had a mind of its own. It began to write, sentence after sentence, looking nothing like my previous lines, but in bold, capital letters.

WRITE YOUR DAMN BOOK AND QUIT TALKING ABOUT IT.

It went on and on, encouraging me to write, to love, to live my life fully. And then it stopped. My hand trembled from the sheer speed at which my pen had forced it to write. Unaware of what I had written, I went back and began to read. Tears flooded down my cheeks as I absorbed the words. Had my subconscious mind just spoken to me, an angel, or was it God? It made absolutely no difference, because wherever the message had come from . . . I got it.

That evening, I went home a very different person. Knowing that the road ahead would be anything but easy, I was beginning to feel my passion reignite and a stirring in the depths of my soul that had long since been forgotten. The workshop continued the following day, and after hours of mind-bending stimulation, I was looking forward to going home to eat! Although I had been easily talked into staying for dinner on numerous occasions, I hadn't planned on it this night. Convinced to stay, I helped Margaret, or "God in an apron," who was working away in the kitchen, preparing a nourishing meal. I helped to set the table in the conservatory. When the meal was on the table, I walked outside to call people in from the gardens. It was then that I noticed two guys talking by the newly planted willow vines.

There were less than fifty people in attendance at the workshop. I thought it was kind of strange that two days in, I hadn't come across either of these men. There was something very familiar about them both, yet I couldn't place them. When we sat down to eat, one of the guys sat next to me and the other across from us. I was immediately captivated by the accents. Steve and Rob were both from Enniskillen in Northern Ireland. A few years younger than me, with short, sandy-brown hair and a muscular physique, Steve had the classic Northern dialect. Looking the part of a sophisticated yet outdoorsy Englishman, Rob had an accent that gave away that he had been educated in England. Both were charming and full of chat and yet I still couldn't believe that this was the first time that I had come across them over the weekend. I felt nervous sitting next to Steve, so nervous that I was barely able to eat. I don't skip many meals, so I knew something was up! Under the table, my knee brushed against Steve's, and the most peculiar sensation shot through my body.

It was like that of a teenage girl having her hand held by a boy for the first time, mixed with a feeling of being reunited with a long-lost love. It felt exhilarating and confusing and I was anxious to see what was to follow. After dinner, it was suggested that we head to the nearby village of Shannonbridge. This was a place I was very familiar with, as I had played the bodhran in many sessions in the antiquated kitchen in the back of a sensational pub called Lukers. As fortune would have it, I was asked to give Neale a lift to the pub. From the moment he shut the car door, I took the opportunity to explain to him the difficulties I was having with the story line of the book I was writing. I gave him the basic gist and within minutes, he reconstructed what had been a consistent time line of events into a gripping tale by simply rearranging its contents. As I said earlier on, it was structure that I was lacking. By the time we arrived at Lukers, I nearly wanted to jump back in the car, head home, and write the remainder of the book that night. Instead, I went in for a friendly game of cards with the rest of the crew. Greeted by John, the most hospitable publican west of the Shannon, we settled down in front of a roaring turf fire and engaged in a lively conversation and game of Penniless Poker. Immediately, I found myself sitting next to Steve again, drawn to him like a magnet, feeling like a giddy, little schoolgirl. The night was magical in so many ways. My writer's block banished by a world-renowned author in mere minutes, as well as pangs of attraction to a man that left me feeling like there might just be hope for my heart, yet.

From that day forward, hardly a few hours went by in the day when I wasn't in contact with Steve, either by text, email, or on the phone. I felt safe in his company and there was an honesty between us that would soon reveal the compelling attraction I had for him.

He immediately began to champion my cause, pushing me to make the leap to speaking publicly about my life experiences and healing abilities.

Jake had finally moved out of the house, and on the weekends that he was with the girls, I would go to Steve's house, a beautiful cottage on the outskirts of Enniskillen that he had previously shared with his best friend, Corky. Although I never knew him in person, Steve described Corky as a true gentleman, a kind and loving soul who would do anything for anybody. He had passed away from cancer the previous year, leaving not just an empty room, but a vacant space in Steve's heart forever. They were the best of friends, and one night, as I lay in what had been Corky's bed, I finally got to meet him.

I was having trouble sleeping when the room filled with a soft, warm glow. In my mind's eye, I could see Corky and could clearly hear him as he spoke. He assured me that all was well and he wanted me to pass on a message to Steve and his own family about what his death had actually been like. As he spoke, it was as if I could feel my spirit rising out of my body, hovering just above it, then back in again. This happened several times as Corky explained to me how he had dealt with what appeared to be a very painful death in the end. He showed me how he had mastered the ability to detach his essence from his ailing body in peak times of pain, only appearing to suffer. It was a most extraordinary night, as it reminded me of when I had the power to remove myself from my body just prior to being smashed in my car accident. This was my first exposure to another spirit showing me the process of temporarily relieving itself from a body in distress. I felt so privileged to meet the man who had meant so much to Steve and couldn't wait to tell him the following morning.

As soon as I awakened, I went straight into Steve's room. He was elated to hear news of Corky's appearance and intrigued by the way in which he had described how he dealt with the pain of his illness. At some point I reached over and touched his hand and—well—I had a vision. I saw a stone-wall prison. I saw a dark, dank cell and inside the cell I saw Steve, or a version of him. I seemed to know that he had been unjustly tried, locked away for life. Outside of the prison wall stood a woman, and I knew that she, too, was to spend the rest of her days, miserable and alone. I knew that she loved this man. The woman was me.

Then the images left me and I was back, looking at Steve.

"Where were you just then?"

When I explained the vision to him, something he had said to me after we first met now made complete sense. The immediate attraction I had felt for him was the memory of love lost long ago. While he hadn't recalled the specific event, he instinctively knew that there was more to "us" than a fleeting romance. He had said that maybe we weren't seeing the big picture. Our love for one another was deeper than the rebound relationship that we both could have forged after first meeting at Clonmacnoise. It was all so clear now, allowing us to move forward with a beautiful friendship that I treasure to this day. We had come together again to lovingly nudge one another further down the path of self-discovery.

Before long, Steve arranged for me to give a talk in the Human Development Centre in Enniskillen, which belonged to a good friend of his named Matthew Armstrong. An eighth-degree-dan black belt in Budo Taijutsu, Matthew was the embodiment of health and fitness, not to mention an expert in the fields of human behavior and psychology.

Matthew and Victoria, his partner in business and in life, were fully supportive in providing me with the space to introduce myself for the first time as a metaphysical speaker. I had spoken to numerous crowds over the years as a teacher and as a chiropractor, but this day would mark my transition from talking about the physical body to teaching about the intertwining of the mind, body, and spirit.

I opened the discussion by reading the first chapter of the book I was working on. Before meeting Neale Donald Walsch, the story had begun with my birth, the complications with rubella during my mother's pregnancy, and the celestial visit my father had received telling him that all would be well. Neale, on the other hand, advised me to begin the book with my car accident, a fairly gripping rendition of an extraordinary death experience and the information I was given while out of body. How right he was. I sat in front of my audience, nervous, stunned, and inspired as they hung on my every word. This opportunity was a pivotal moment for me, as I connected with the concept that sharing my life story could really shake things up, possibly motivating people to reconnect with their own incredible histories, taking them down the path of personal healing and soul development. Steve had recognized this, knowing long before I did that his timely appearance was to be the catalyst for beginning my career as a professional metaphysical speaker.

# Chapter 35

WHAT WAS left of my relationship with Jake was now unrecognizable. Although we were no longer under the same roof, we had to interact with one another because of the children. The only time I wasn't completely on edge was when he was out of town. He had taken a job earlier in the summer on a superyacht in the Mediterranean. While he was away, I decided that if I carried on in my present state of disease, or incongruent behavior, I would quickly move into the space of the diseased. My body and mind were broken, no differently than Jake's, and in a gut-wrenching series of unmentionable events, our house, the girl's home, my dream location, was put on the market.

The fortunate thing about having such an unusual house was that it was on the market less than a week when several substantial offers came in. An elderly man had come in first, at our asking price, but I couldn't bear the thought of this guy living alone in the family home that we had designed and created from scratch, down to the last Scottish cobblestone in the two-story open fireplace. This wasn't just about the money. A piece of me was in that house and, literally, pieces of my children, their placentas, were buried under the palm trees in the front garden. So we turned it down.

When the house had just been a week on the market, I was getting out of the shower when the front doorbell rang. The auctioneer had arrived unexpectedly (I had actually forgotten), with a couple who were looking to relocate from Dublin. I locked eyes with Joe, a man I had never met, feeling as if an old friend had returned to my life with a new friend, his gorgeous wife, Mary. I threw on some clothes, towel still wrapped around my wet head, and showed them through what I knew was to become their new home. Mary was pregnant with their first child, and Jemma took her by the hand and escorted her down to her bedroom, an air-brushed fantasy with walls covered in fairies, angels, and other playful creatures.

"Your baby will love this room," she said, still not fully understanding what was actually happening.

My heart ached as I felt an incredible sadness, uprooting her from the home she loved. It all seemed so unfair, but at the same time, I was already able to visualize Joe and Mary and their new family as caretakers of this space. It felt right, they seemed so familiar, and I knew that the Universe was helping to make something so upsetting just a little bit easier. When we went into my bedroom, Jemma put her hand on Mary's stomach and said, "That's a baby girl. She'll really love that room!" (Many months later, Baby Mary Jo did, in fact, love her new home.)

The house sale took place in record time, leaving me very little time to downsize, pack up, and move to a tiny house not too far from where we had lived. With all of the disruptions in the girls' lives, I wanted to be sure that Jemma remained in the same school, St. Joseph's Primary, in Summerhill, to keep some sort of continuity. I also had a great respect and rapport with the school's principal, John O'Neil. Both Jemma and I agreed that he was something special. When I had first explained our unusual family circumstances and the likelihood that at some stage, one or more of Jemma's teachers would have to deal with the maturation of her special abilities, John was nothing but supportive. Like a Guardian Earth Angel, he always watched over us.

Jemma was very open about her memories of previous incarnations and generous with her comedic approach to life, its lessons, and the art of forgiveness. On a regular basis, when asked what she would like to be when she grew up, Jemma would reply, "When I grow up? Sure, I'm already a healer."

She once had been perched atop a horse, wanting to have her photo taken in her Disney princess ball gown. Another horse had come up behind her, and spooked the horse that she was sitting on, causing the animal to shoot off with my little girl screaming frantically for help. I'm horrified when I think of it. She bounced off, her head smacked off the ground, and she was unconscious. The rest of the evening was spent on a gurney in the hospital to monitor her for head injury. We were moved into the children's ward, where I slept on the floor beside her for the night. When she was released, I took her back to the same field, so that she could make peace with the horses. I didn't want her to imprint a lifelong fear into her psyche that would prevent her from enjoying these majestic creatures in the future if she was drawn to them. As we approached the field, she stopped me at the fence as we spotted the culprits, quietly grazing in the distance. She squeezed my hand, cleared her throat, and in her "big girl" voice shouted, "I forgive you horses, but I'm forgiving you from right here!"

During the madness of this transitional phase, the girl's babysitter, our beloved Elaine, had gotten a job working for kids with special needs. We missed her, but the children that she would now be working with would benefit from the same love and compassion that she had shown us. Eventually, I ended up hiring a friend of a friend named Malika. As serendipity struck again, it just so happened that Malika was a professional nanny from France.

This woman was different from anyone who had worked for us before. She was stern, by the book, and regimented in a manner that we weren't accustomed to. Her thick blond curls were always pulled back into a ponytail during working hours. After taking care of the girls each day, Malika taught yoga in the evenings, therefore she was into health and fitness, only feeding the girls good, wholesome foods, making sure that they were always physically active. When I think back, I don't know what we would have done without her during that terribly trying time. She loved the girls, and although she was strict, the girls thrived under her disciplined care. She was also not afraid to share a few home truths with me about my parenting. Sometimes it was hard to hear, as my inclination would be to justify my constant bending of the rules because I was now a single parent with a ridiculously demanding workload. In her own way, she prevented me from slipping into a space of self-pity, when in all honesty a little self-pity could have been excused. She annoyed me with her frankness at the end of a long, hard day of micromanaging the unbelievable mess the businesses had become. But it was that same honesty that fueled a determination that would see me through some of my most horrific moments.

She was an angel in disguise, and we were so fortunate to have her. She even jumped into the river Shannon fully clothed to save Jemma's life, when she accidentally slipped down a bank into its racing current. How do you thank someone for such an act of bravery? A bit like Nanny McPhee—when we did not want her but needed her she was there, and when we wanted her but no longer needed her she would move on. Luckily for us, we really needed her and it would be a while before she eventually left us.

Coupled with the grandparent-style love provided by Lily and Tommy, the girls were finally in the most stable and loving environment that I could possibly have afforded them. They were becoming more accustomed to seeing less and less of their father, who had taken a land-based engineering position that he seemed to be enjoying. Despite all of our belongings from an enormous space now caving in on top of us in a very cramped, semidetached house, I could breathe for the first time in a very long while. Having no intention of staying for too long in this "between space," or the halfway-to-sanity house, as I liked to call it, I set out on a search to find our next home. I was emotionally and physically exhausted by the move.

*

Just before Christmas, Jake made up his mind that he could no longer stay in Ireland. We couldn't be in the same room for more than five minutes before I would start talking him to death, trying to come to some form of a truce. My poorly timed attempts to make peace were met with seething anger that, in turn, would create a rage inside my body that frightened me. Different continents didn't seem like such a bad idea after all. With no concept of time, the girls had no idea that the move their dad was making was a permanent one, so they bade him farewell, fully expecting to see him in a few weeks. I know his heart was breaking because, regardless of our differences, he really loved the girls.

Not wanting to spend Christmas in the "halfway to sanity house," I packed up our bags and took the girls back to America for the holidays. It was great to get home and away from the illusion that was currently posing as my reality. Due to the five-hour time difference, I awakened at the crack of dawn my first morning home only to discover that while I had removed myself from the immediate stress back in Ireland, my body had taken the opportunity to release some of the pressure and anguish through my skin.

My face looked as if it had been scalded with boiling hot water and I was covered in painful rosacea, a stress-induced skin disorder. I was furious at myself and broke down in a sobbing heap on the bathroom floor. *What had happened to me? Had I really gotten it all so wrong?*

My mother came in, and helped me up from the floor, saying she knew just the woman to get me through this. Mom went into the kitchen and rang our good friend Judy. She explained that I looked like one of the shiny, red bobbles hanging on the Christmas tree and was in desperate need of her help. Judy had been our dermatologist from the time I had first visited her office to have a small wart removed from my hand when I was in seventh grade.

Judy had come to visit me in Ireland earlier in the year. A single mother and doctor, we shared a similar past, in terms of the types of relationships we attracted and the way we handled them, with our strong and independent natures. When I explained to her all that had been going on in Ireland, she completely understood how I had managed to manifest this awful skin condition the very moment I had removed myself from the stressful environment. A kiss on the forehead, a great big hug, and a jar of cream quickly put me on the road to recovery.

We spent Christmas day at my sister's house in Richmond, Virginia. It was festive and fun, especially because Beth's house looked like something out of a Dr. Seuss Christmas book. With her quirky, nontraditional pink-and-turquoise decorations, whimsical pigeon-toed angels, and unconventional Santa figurines, it was a child's paradise. The girls adored spending time with their cousin Max, who had the patience of a saint when dealing with his lively Irish cousins. It was a good trip home in so many ways, and I looked forward to returning to Ireland to start a new year that did not include the stress of dealing with Jake face-to-face.

My office in Athlone was now being covered by a good ol' boy from Kansas. Ty, his wife, Kelly, and their three children had relocated to Ireland to get a fresh start on their own lives. He did a good job, keeping the office ticking over while I set out to systematically deal with my New Year's resolution for 2007. The task of getting rid of the three gyms that were depleting my resources, right along with my life force, was going to be an enormous undertaking. The office in Longford had a loyal and stable patient base, so I would continue to work there two days a week and in the practice in Athlone on a part-time basis. I'm sure that some of my long-term patients thought that I had abandoned ship, but it was time to get going and start putting out fires. If I was going to survive, I had to cut my losses, take a few very hard knocks financially, and get back to basics.

*

I have often heard it said that moving is one of the most stressful events that can take place in life. For me, finding a place to call home would remove a significant amount of stress and was on top of a milelong list of things I wanted to accomplish in early 2007. I had everyone I knew on the lookout but was having no luck finding a place that felt right. Then someone suggested Brideswell, a classic village consisting of two pubs, an undertaker's, and a shop, just outside of Athlone. I had been playing music there for the last couple of years at O'Connell's pub, the home of the Thursday night session. The guitar player, Seamus, had been a close friend for years and had also been my neighbor when we lived in Drum. It was he who asked, why didn't I consider moving to Brideswell?

It was peaceful, in the country, yet close to town, and would be a great place to raise the girls. I told him that I had been looking for quite some time and nothing of interest had come up in Brideswell, or anywhere else for that matter. The very next week, there was a feature in the real estate section of the paper with the heading "Old World Charm." This immediately caught my attention, and the photographs of the stone fireplace and the old brick wall leading up the farmhouse stairs had me sold. I read on, only to find out that this two-story cottage, with apple trees in the front garden, was located in none other than the village of Brideswell.

I drove out to have a look the following morning. There had been a heavy frost the night before, so the rolling green fields and old stone walls were glistening white and looked like an old-fashioned Christmas card. I pulled into the driveway and peered through the frosty windows to see the room that had been in the newspaper. The huge open fire had been fitted with an antique stove and I could see wood-plank ceilings and a traditional cottage-style finish on the walls. I took a photo of the house, made it the screen saver on my phone, and practiced the art of visualizing myself as already living in the house. Of course it was going to take a miracle to turn this dream into a reality. I was up to my eyes in debt, having used all but a small portion of my half of the money from the sale of the house in Drum to pay off just a few of the enormous bills that Jake and I had acquired. I had managed to sell one of the three gyms and every cent of that money had gone into the black hole of debt. Ireland was still booming under a false sense of prosperity, but my own personal recession was already well under way. By some incredible twist of fate, I managed to secure a loan for the house. It would be at least a month before we could get in, so on February 23, my thirty-eighth birthday, I headed to Tenerife, in the Canary Islands, with my friend Steve for one last hoorah, before making the move.

*

I had a revelation on that trip about myself and my love life, following a conversation with Steve about our relationship. Late one night, we joked about running away together "as friends." How we would spend the money if we won the lottery. What our house would be like, he with his wing, and me with mine. Suddenly it dawned on me. I had allowed myself to become attracted to Steve, my love from another life, in this lifetime. He had recognized this, and was doing everything within his power to stop me from "going there." He was quick to remind me that soul mates come in many forms. I think had I not been so connected to him, this revelation would not have had the same impact. He was stopping me from making the same mistakes I had made in the past, by not engaging in yet another soul-mate relationship. At first I was mad, then offended, calling him cynical and afraid to love again. I stood on my soapbox and preached that I was a loving, caring, and affectionate woman. I had the capacity to love in a most remarkable way. I began to cry as I told him that eventually there would be a time when someone would love me with the same, incredible passion that I had inside of me. I wouldn't beg or push and it would be natural. Fantasy? Well I would make this my reality. I refused to be a martyr—there's nothing worse than a human scorned! All that was missing was the violin in the background.

Steve began to laugh so hard that eventually I snapped out of my soliloquy, and started laughing, too. He had done it again. He had provided a beautiful mirror in which I could see straight into my soul. My heartaches, my disappointments, my battered self-esteem had all stared me right back in the face as I embraced the incredible gift that this man had just given to me. He wasn't so shallow as to cave at instant gratification in place of lifelong friendship. He loved me in a way that I probably had never loved myself. Something changed in me that night. I reconnected with my own soul plan. I had been so busy helping others to connect with their journeys that I had forgotten to embrace mine. The last two years had been a nightmare at times, but I was the dreamer who had created it. At thirty-eight, I was finally starting to wake up.

# Chapter 36

THE GIRLS and I moved to our new home in Brideswell in March of 2007. Hardwood floors, plank ceilings, thick cottage walls, and an open stone fireplace; sounds like the inner sanctum of my local pub. But no, this was home. Situated only a few miles outside of Athlone, the girls and I had relocated to the solitude of the Irish countryside, complete with a garden adorned by apple trees, the obligatory stone walls, and rolling green fields. I guess I had become quite fond of the sheep, as they were now my neighbors, along with the cows, horses, and occasional donkey.

The peace and tranquility of the landscape that surrounded us was a reflection of the changes taking place within all three of us. It had not been easy for the little girls to say good-bye to the home that they loved, move house, see their father relocate to the other side of the world, and then pick up and move again. They were incredibly strong and I was so proud of how both of them handled these enormous changes in their own unique ways. And while I mourned the loss of the palatial home the girls' father and I had designed and built a few years earlier, I now looked around and embraced the idea of "Home Is Where the Heart Is." Not only was I an American living out her childhood fantasies of rainbows and fairy forts, I was living in a quaint Irish cottage that came with a little something extra. *Mr. Burke . . .*

From the first day we shifted our belongings, we had been

greeted by the smell of turf fires when no fire was lit, moving furniture when no one was moving it, and footsteps up and down the hallway on any given night. Music would often play quietly out of nowhere and on numerous occasions, the girls would see Mr. B. standing at the foot of their bed. They saw him, could describe his kind eyes and weathered face down to the last whisker, and they simply adored him. He was the new man in their lives, *body or not*, and quite frankly, this was my dream relationship. A male presence with no commitment required!

And thus began our relationship with George Burke. Mr. Burke had lived in the house until late in his life. I found this out from our next-door neighbors, the couple who had bought, meticulously renovated, and eventually sold the house to me. Anne Marie, Dermot, and their son, Shane, were the best neighbors that anyone could ask for. They were always around to lend a helping hand when we needed it and it didn't take long for the girls to start wearing a path to their back door. Dermot had told me that I would find out everything I wanted to know about our resident spirit from Brid and Ted, of O'Connell's pub, where I played music in the village.

A virtual cornucopia of local knowledge, both Brid and Ted told me wonderful tales of our house and of our new friend, Mr. B. The house had been built around 1912 by the Congested Districts Board under the British Land Act. People were relocated and given forty acres. George Burke's parents were the first to occupy the new house. George remained in the house, marrying later in life. He was known around these parts as a very witty character. I heard a story recounted where Mr. Burke had been in the pub, when his friends noticed that the cigarette he was holding was starting to burn his fingers. Appearing to have taken a "turn," the priest and George's son were both immediately called in to give him his last rites before carting him two doors down to the undertakers. He came around shortly after they arrived, everyone genuinely thinking he was on his way out of this world. He later told the O'Connells, "I'm telling ya now, the one thing you don't want to do in this place is fall asleep!"

I loved him already and was so delighted to hear that we were now living in the former home of such a live wire. A day didn't go by that the girls wouldn't open the back door as soon as we got home and yell:

"We're home, Mr. Burke, did you miss us?"

It was interesting that with the loss of one important male fig ure in their lives they seemed perfectly content with the new man on the scene . . . regardless of the fact that he wasn't in a body! I know, we're talking major therapy down the road, but hey, far be it from me to discourage something that was making the children feel safe and secure.

Jada would walk around the house, holding Mr. B. by the invisible hand, chatting away as if he was right there beside her. A departed spirit can leave an energetic impression of itself in a space that it has previously occupied. Those who are sensitive to these energies can easily pick up on them. How do they do things like move rocking chairs, create music out of thin air, or appear in front of sleeping children? It's all about the vibration. The innate ability that we all have upon our return to Spirit, to raise, lower, and manipulate energies. Some choose to lower their vibrations back to Earth's frequencies in order to say, "Hey, I'm still here!"

Everyone who came to the house remarked on the lovely en- ergy. Not just the general niceties, but specifically the lovely, warm energy in the place.

Jada had been showing many signs of her own unique gifts. Not only was she adept at conversing with Mr. Burke, she had also developed an uncanny ability to communicate with animals. I'm not talking about a child's normal attraction to playful puppies or furry little kittens, but she was drawn to these creatures and they to her. She would speak to them, listen, and then respond as if answering a question.

She would place her hands over the animals and tell me that she was healing them, something she continues to do to this day. She was also beginning to talk about not just one but numerous past lives. If I would do something she didn't like, Jada would say, "Dat's not how my udder mudder did it!" And then she would proceed to tell me how her other mother would do things differently. Most often it was a woman in India that she would describe in great detail, along with her other father, as well as her siblings.

One night, as I snuggled in bed next to the girls, Jemma and I were chatting away as Jada, who, just about to turn four, was starting to move into that space between barely awake and dream land. She looked at me with sleepy eyes and said, "Mommy, I bemember when I was Gracie." (I loved how she pronounced her words back then.) "Who was Gracie?" Jemma asked, knowing that her sister was recalling another lifetime.

"Gracie was big. I was big, Mommy. Being big made me have to go to the 'hosrible' (Jada's version of hospital). Gracie was on the table in a gown and a doctor had to put a big needle *tru deese bones.*"

Jada was pointing to her heart, describing what sounded like some sort of adrenaline shot into the heart. She continued with the story, periodically switching from referring to herself as Gracie, to "me" or "I."

"Ah, Mom, listen to our baby, she's remembering." Jemma was enjoying the story as I listened on with fascination.

"What happened to Gracie, honey?" I could not wait to hear what was coming next.

"Oh . . . she dived."

"Dived? What do you mean dived, Jada?"

"Died, Mom, come on!" Jemma looked at me, shaking her head in disgust as I struggled to follow Jada's lingo.

"She dived, Mommy, but den she came back."

"And what happened when she came back?"

"I gotted to see my family one last time."

"Oh, that's wonderful, sweetheart. Can you remember who any of them were?"

"I can't bemember the childrens, but the daddy, who is my daddy, Jake, was Gracie's husband."

*

From the time that Jake had put his life in Ireland behind him for good, Jemma had developed a cough that bordered on asthmatic. When dealing with anything that upset her, if she got nervous about something, or if we spoke about her dad, she would cough violently until she threw up. Together, her sister and I would wrap her in love and light at night, while she would ask her angels to help her to sleep. We would clear out her chakras in an exercise of spoken meditation, but nothing seemed to work. The doctor prescribed steroid inhalers, and as a holistic practitioner who would rather stab out her own eyeballs than give her five-year-old medication for a psychosomatic illness, I knew there had to be another way. Don't get me wrong, I'm not anti-anything under the appropriate circumstances, but I knew that this ran deeper than a coincidental diagnosis of asthma.

Afflictions of the chest and lungs are very often the result of grief. During her very short life, Jemma had seen her fair share of heartache. A new baby cramped her style at the age of two, she had seen her parents unable to resolve their conflicts, she had lost most of her hair due to stress as a toddler, she had been moved from the only home she knew, her father had left the country, and her "mile a minute" mother seemed to be at work all of the time. Jemma was also developing into an empathic psychic. Not only had she inherited the family gift, she felt her own and other people's emotions on a level I have never seen. She is truly sensitive. *So she coughed. . . .*

During this time, I was still working at my practice in Longford two days of the week. Chiropractic in the morning and evening, while facilitating healing sessions during my two-hour lunch breaks. I had always greatly appreciated the respite that Longford provided and I simply adored my new secretary.

Geri was an absolute tonic. In her mid-sixties, slight of build, she was a two-pack-a-day kind of gal, and her wit was as dry as her wheezy cough. One morning, out of the blue, Geri sat back in her chair, lacing her fingers behind her cynical little head with a sigh.

"If I had ever gotten married, I would have done it at the six a.m. mass at Mount Argus."

"Excuse me?" I jested, shocked at the mere mention that she would have even considered marriage in the first place.

Geri rarely had a promising word for those she referred to as "men of the other species."

"Yep, Mount Argus, at six in the morning, right after an all-night session on the town. Can't you just see it? Everyone rolling up to the doors, full of drink, high on life as I swished my way down the aisle!"

She was now up from her chair, gliding across the waiting room with an exaggerated swagger.

"Where the heck is Mount Argus? I've never even heard of it!"

"Near Harold's Cross in Dublin," she replied, with her raspy Dublin accent. "There's an old monastery there."

At that same moment, a patient came through the door and the conversation ended as abruptly as it had begun.

That evening, I drove back to Athlone on the twists and turns of the old Ballymahon Road. Radio reception wasn't great in that area and the only station I could pick up was a local Midlands chat show, with a few Irish tunes thrown in for good measure. "What did he just say?" I thought out loud while turning up the volume.

The radio presenter was talking away about none other than Mount Argus, a place that, until that very morning, I had never heard tell of. Now, for the second time in the same day, I was hearing it again. *Interesting . . .*

I arrived home to the warm hugs and beautiful faces of my two little girls. After catching me up on all of the news from Jemma's day in school and Jada's day with Lily, the girls got in bed and waited for a story. This would sound magical if I told you that the two little dears then drifted off into a peaceful slumber, giving me the rest of the night to myself. Yeah, right . . . these are my kids we're talking about here! The very moment I would step outside of the door . . .

"Mommy! Mommy! Are you there?! Whatchya doin'? I need water. Jemma has to go to the toilet. I'm not tired; can you come in the bed for a while?"

Usually, I did, only to awaken, arms and legs hanging off the bed about an hour later, in a total grump. I'd done it again. . . .

Following my introduction to Mount Argus the previous day, I looked through sleepy eyes the next morning to see Jemma tugging at my T-shirt. Not quite in focus, I could sense that she was excited and smiling, begging me to get out of bed. Had I overslept? Shoot! I hadn't even heard the alarm go off. That's because it hadn't. It was still dark out and my clock that runs twenty minutes fast hadn't yet hit six a.m. Uuuugghh . . . I am so not a morning person!

"Is everything all right, sweetie? Is Jada okay? What's going on?"

"Jada is still asleep, Mommy. I have something to show you!"

The hall light was on and Jemma's pudgy little hand squeezed mine as she tried to get the words out in her excitement.

"Mr. Burke woke me up, Mommy," she said, with as much ease as if she had been awakened by someone of *this* world.

Well, when your psychic child pulls you out of bed before six in the morning to show you something that a dead guy has shown her, you should probably have a look. I laughed at the idea that time really doesn't exist outside of our realm. Either that or Mr. Burke had no manners at all!

"My goodness," I huffed while sitting down on the windowsill, pulling her onto my lap.

"Wasn't he bold for waking up my girl and . . . ?"

"No, Mommy!" She retorted as if I had insulted them both. "He woke me up to give me a clue!"

"A clue? What kind of a clue?"

"You know, a clue like on *Scooby-Doo*! A clue that helps you!"

Now, completely intrigued, as any great fan of *Scoob* would be at the crack of dawn, I waited for the punch line. But this was no joke, she was dead serious, and what came next caught me completely off guard.

"You know my bad cough?"

"Of course, I do honey, it's tough ol' going sometimes, isn't it?"

My heart still ached at the thought that this gorgeous little being had to endure that dreadful hardship, seldom having a decent night's sleep since her father and I had parted ways.

"Well, Mommy, Mr. Burke said he knew what could fix it! He even showed me a clue to show you!"

"I'm all ears, darlin'."

But it was *all eyes* I needed for what came next. Jemma got off my lap, leading me by the hand to the steep cottage stairs.

"It's over here, Mommy!"

The wall that is next to our staircase is the original gray brick from 1912, when the house was first built and owned by Mr. Burke's parents. It had been covered over by thick plaster at some stage during Mr. Burke's occupancy. When my neighbors were renovating the house, Anne Marie attests to a battle of the wits between herself and her husband. Dermot wanted to leave the plaster intact, on account of the extra work involved and the unknown condition of the wall beneath. Despite his protest, she strategically began chipping away, *as any woman would have*, eventually revealing the beautiful old bricks. I'm ever so grateful in more ways than one!

Having walked up and down those stairs every day for months, I suppose I never really bothered to take a good, hard look at the bricks. At least, not the *right* ones.

"There, Mommy! There's one! Mr. Burke said those words were a clue to fix my cough. And look up there, it's upside down, but there's another one!"

It's a good thing I had now adjusted to being awake. If not, I would have probably keeled right over in disbelief. Halfway up my staircase, embedded in several of the old bricks, were two worn yet legible words . . . *Mount Argus*. That's right, folks. Mount *freakin'* Argus!

With my mouth hanging open, I turned to Jemma and nervously laughed, as I asked her to tell me *exactly* what Mr. Burke had said to her.

"He didn't say it out loud, Mommy, not like we talk. He talked in my head. Do you know what I mean?"

Did I what! She had been communicating telepathically with our ghost the very same way that I had been speaking to those in Spirit for the entirety of my life. I was so proud, so wigged out, and so curious about the place that had been revealed to me on *three* separate occasions in the last twenty-four hours. What in the world could this mean for Jemma and her cough?

When the hour was decent enough to make a phone call, I rang my secretary, Geri, in Longford.

"Okay," I demanded. "What's the story with Mount Argus?"

"Are you stone mad, ringing me at this hour? What's going on over there?" Geri replied, less than enthusiastic that I had awakened her for a chat about the old monastery. She hadn't even gotten a cup of coffee and cigarette into her, for God's sake!

I explained that after our unusual conversation about her wish for early morning nuptials at Mount Argus, I had again heard this mysterious monastic moniker on my drive home from work. Now I was sitting at the kitchen table with my five-year-old, as she recounted her midnight rendezvous with our resident spirit.

"For feck's sake!" Geri exclaimed, wheezing and laughing with a sound most suitable for the eerie conversation.

"Geri," I said with a more serious tone. "What in the world is going on?"

"Well, from what little history I do know of the place, it was put on the map by a particular priest in the nineteenth century. Charles was his name. He was originally from the Netherlands but was sent to Mount Argus early on in his priesthood, where he became renowned as a healer."

"A healer? I replied. Now she really had my attention.

"That's right. He was beatified in the late 1980s and . . .

"Beawhatified?"

"Beatified, you big dummy. Oh yeah, you're not Catholic. Sorry. The Catholic church was in the process of making him a saint. He was canonized by the pope just a few months ago."

Admittedly, I was certainly not up to date on the comings and goings of the pope or his church. It seems that this man had performed numerous healings during his ministry at Mount Argus that the church had deemed "not scientifically explicable."

"Geri, have you got any idea what people went to him for?"

"Yes, as a matter of fact I do. Among other things, he was very well known for healing afflictions of the chest."

"Oh, my God!" I yelled, as she hacked through her laughter. "Jemma's cough!"

I hung up the phone and looked at Jemma, who was now grinning from ear to ear, as she had been listening in on enough of the conversation to make sense of it.

"You see, Mommy! Just like *Scooby Doo!* Mr. Burke left us a clue!"

Now I had to go into the office that day like any other person doing a normal day's work. Those are the kind of days when this stuff cracks me up. A bit of sleep, wake up, chat to your child about the clue a dead guy left, a bit of breakfast, then out the door to the office. Welcome to my life.

During a break between patients, I went online and looked up the Blessed Charles of Mount Argus and found all that Geri had said to be true. Interesting, I thought. But what did a healer who had been dead over a hundred years, now sainted, have to do with Jemma, Mr. Burke, and her own affliction of the chest? *Tomorrow always comes. . . .*

The following morning I drove to Longford, pulled into the car park, and saw Geri sitting in her car, surrounded by a cloud of smoke. She rolled down the window, allowing the cloud to drift out and a bit of oxygen to creep in. She was dying to hear if I had any updates on the story. I was still in the dark, but not for long. Later that day, Saint Charles, or rather *a little piece of him*, would make a surprise appearance.

At lunch, I was in chatting with Mary, my friend and neighbor in the business. She was a bundle of energy and a pure delight. The door to her room opened and in walked her brother, Joe. We had only met at a few times at this point, but he was about to become one of those brief yet momentous messengers who have followed me throughout my spiritual journey.

"I brought you a gift. Something told me you could use this."

He produced a small card with a photograph of an elderly priest. In the bottom right hand corner was a tiny speck of something firmly secured under a piece of plastic.

"It's a relic," he informed me. "A relic of a man now known as Saint Charles of Mount Argus. He was a healer and because you are in the business as well, I had a feeling you might like to have it. Have you ever heard of him before?"

"Geeeeerrrrriiiiii!!!" I bellowed through the door and down the hallway, in a most professional manner. I then shared the events of the last forty-eight hours with Mary and her brother, Joe, and amid the colorful expressions of "Jaysus! Wha'?" and other choice colloquialisms, we marveled at the sheer madness of it all.

Ever mindful of such a tender moment, Geri gave me a pat on the back, almost giving us a rare smile at the same time.

"Too bad you're not a Catholic, hon. I don't think relics works on *your kind*!"

She laughed that kind of laugh where the facial expression never changes and hardly any sound comes out; laughing on the inside, Geri described it. The rest of us belly-laughed out loud until our sides nearly split.

That night, curiosity, faith, or maybe a bit of both saw me place this card under Jemma's pillow. Owing to the placebo effect, Mr. Burke's assistance, or the relic itself, Jemma slept the entire night through without as much as a tickle in her throat.

I won't say she never coughed again, but the dreadful, chronic bark that had plagued her for so long ceased for good. Was it the man or the religion, the faith or our own "holy spirit" that healed my daughter?

Nobody really knows why or how, and the reality is that it just doesn't matter. This was to become a most fortunate realization in my life as a healer, that the synchronistic nature of a group of Beings (in the case of Jemma's cough *two of the Beings were dead, even*), each with his and her own system of belief, could all work harmoniously. I realized, too, that we needed to allow possibilities to unfold, with no one claiming "the rights" to the miracle. We all walked away, each to our own doctrines of faith, with absolute gratitude and joy in the participation. From that day forward, I referred to myself as a *facilitator* of healing.

My mission was to connect the body to the mind and ultimately the soul's plan. I recognized that the only way to attempt to cure any illness was to determine its underlying cause. For some, the emotional experiences of the past would create physical ailments. For others, abuse of the physical body was responsible for emotional turmoil. For all, an imbalance in either of these areas could result in spiritual crisis. I now understood that crisis or massive change could occur if life became a monotonous cycle. Crisis could interrupt these patterns, offering the opportunity to change and grow. Metaphysical healing was allowing me to use my own unique gifts to help clear the physical, emotional, and spiritual imbalances in a person who was willing to change—willingness to change being the vital component, in that it would place the responsibility to heal not on the healer, but on the one seeking the healing. This would allow me to be free to act as a guide, a facilitator, unblocking the self or the circumstantially inflicted barriers to the endless potential that is innate in us all—the possibility to heal ourselves if it serves our higher purpose.

With a new understanding of the ongoing development of my soul, the piece of me that had mistaken myself as an individual with a gift for healing had just been healed. I now recognized that I was a member of an Omniversal team of facilitators, removing obstacles, creating new possibilities, and changing perspectives, to enrich people's experiences of this adventure we call life.

As the spring of 2007 came to a close, Jemma was finishing her last days in Junior Infants at St. Joseph's Primary School. While she was looking forward to her summer holidays, Jada couldn't wait for the summer to come and go because she would be starting preschool in the autumn with Trish, a dear friend of Maureen's for many years, who had become a very good friend of ours. Trish knew all about the difficult times we had been through, and provided a safe and nurturing environment for Jemma when she had been four and full of beans. We'd been so fortunate to have so many wonderful people in our lives, and as the summer approached, I finally had the feeling that things were starting to settle down.

There were still many challenges ahead. There were two gyms, both in serious financial difficulty, to close down and while the practice had remained intact, it had definitely suffered from all of the other distractions I had going on. Still, I felt the worst was over and the fact that I was able to come home at night and hang out with my girls without the constant strain of dealing with their father created a peaceful space that allowed me to begin my own healing process.

I worked on my first book during any free time I had in the day, and continued to write after putting the girls to bed at night. My mind-set had changed and I was embracing the idea of forgiveness, not of Jake but of myself. Everywhere I turned, there were signs telling me that a new phase had begun.

On a beautiful summer evening in July, I stood at the kitchen sink, washing up after our dinner. Jemma had gone upstairs to brush her teeth and Jada was in the back garden playing with our dog, Tinkerbell. Suddenly she burst through the back door shouting, "Mommy! Jemma! Come quickly! Quickly, they're here! The fairies are here!"

Jemma came flying down the stairs, toothbrush in hand, and ran out the back door. "Look Mommy, look! Can you see them?"

I stood frozen, like a statue. I simply could not believe what was in front of me. Coming across the field were these iridescent circles of light. Not one, but a multitude of them! They danced and weaved in playful patterns across the evening sky. I dashed back into the house and grabbed my camera. When I got back outside, the girls had gone running after these luminous orbs, right along with the dog. Tinkerbell was going crazy, barking and leaping up into the air, trying to catch the bouncing balls of light as they came closer to the house. I began snapping pictures and as Jada ran after one of the lights, Jemma jumped up on the wall and shouted, "Get my photo with the fairies, Mommy!"

They say that timing is everything. At this moment, we were in exactly the right place at the right time. With toothbrush still in hand, Jemma smiled her biggest smile and not only did I capture four of the circles with her but an enormous rainbow in the distance, right behind her head. To this day, we have no idea exactly what they were. They certainly were not the figment of *three* imaginations, and the way that they interacted with the children and the dog was incredible! For me, these beautiful circles of light marked a new direction in our lives. We had been given a playful reminder that something greater than us is always present. I felt grounded, reconnected, and ready to move forward with my work as a healer.

The healing sessions had become an integral part of my life. I began to see undeniable parallels between the people who would end up on my table and my own life story. As each session unfolded, I listened carefully to the information coming through me because I now understood that as much as it was for them, it was also for me. The cases were varied and ranged from the tenderest moments to the downright bizarre. Yet each and every healing brought me closer to my own truth and I made peace with all of the decisions I had made since moving to Ireland.

# PART III

---

# *The Land Beyond the River*

"When e'er the thoughts of death creep in
Coursing down your spine and shiver
Know, dear one, that we shall meet again
In the land beyond the river."
—*MHH*

# Chapter 37

EARLY IN December, the news was full of scary stories about the global virus of choice for 2008. The dreaded swine flu was front and center, the subject of most tabloid headlines, as the toll began to climb for those who had succumbed to its evil clutches. Drug companies were churning out experimental vaccines, while terrified punters were literally frightened into getting the jab.

Because I am in daily contact with numerous people, many who have traveled abroad, coming home with more than just souvenirs from their holidays and work trips, I tend to always pick up a virus or two early in the season. When I began to get the chills and the sudden urge to vomit, it was time to take myself home, take a day or two to recover, and then get back to work. Things didn't quite work out that way.

My hair began to hurt and I couldn't bear for the clothes on my back to touch my skin. After stopping to get sick several times during the fifteen-minute drive home, I rang my friend Irene and told her I needed help. I never asked for help, so she knew it was serious. She flew over to the house, and by the time she made it up the stairs, I was in a complete state of delirium. Our friend, Suzie, minded the children at her house, because at that point, I don't even think I knew that I had children. I rolled around the bed in agony, and Irene stayed close by.

It was a brave move for her, because only a week or two earlier,

she had stayed over with us for a girlie night of manicures and movies. The girls had given up the bed in Jemma's room and moved
into Jada's bunk beds, allowing "Aunty Irene" her own space for the
night. At some time in the wee hours, after hearing a year's worth of
stories about Mr. Burke, but never seeing him herself, Mr. B. paid
her a little visit. Standing at the end of her bed, simply watching,
she saw him as clear as day in his overcoat and cap. Afraid to move
a muscle, more so out of fear that he would leave, Irene was finally
introduced to the man of the house. She joked that she would
never sleep over again, but all jokes aside, she moved in for a few
days the following week to nurse me back to health.

At one point during my sickness, Irene could hear talking, a
full-blown conversation taking place in my bedroom. She crept up
to the door, knowing that I was too ill to be talking on the phone,
only to find me babbling away to thin air, *or so she thought*. As she
listened in at the door, she soon began to realize that these weren't
simply the ravings of a high fever, but that I was indeed speaking
to someone. I cried, protested, and then ultimately agreed with
whomever I was conversing with. To this day, she recounts it as one
of the most bizarre things she has ever witnessed.

As it happened, I wasn't babbling away to thin air. The room
filled with the familiar smell of Camel cigarettes and standing
before me, like so many times throughout my life, was Judge—
my grandfather, my guide, and personal physician in Spirit. The
conversation was not a product of my fever, but a very real, very
frightening wake-up call by a man who had no intention of seeing
me go out the same way that he had. Judge was no ordinary doctor.
Also a gifted healer, he worked tirelessly for his patients, day and
night, often to the neglect of time with his own family and most
certainly to the detriment of his own health.

He now stood before me, showing me firsthand a day long ago,
when he had been making rounds with his patients. He had arrived
home, crossed the threshold of his back door, and dropped with

a massive heart attack. I cried, protesting the comparison to my own life, but when he uttered the words that *I would not live past forty-two* if I did not change my ways, I was listening.

Irene heard the entire conversation. Too flabbergasted to interfere, she stood in the hallway, waited until she felt it was appropriate to enter, and then sat on the bed as I sobbed. I think Irene secretly enjoys the rare moments when my vulnerability shines through. I was human after all, she would say, and it reassured her that while so many wild and wonderful events take place in my life, I was still, deep down, the same as everyone else.

Eventually, I recovered. I had heard Judge's message loud and clear. The only problem was, I was at a complete loss as to how to make the changes. I had to work. Writing was my emotional outlet, so the only place I could really make room for change was the way I spent time with my children. My schedule remained full, but I made a concerted effort to create more quality and quantity with the girls. Only time would tell if this would be enough.

## Chapter 38

THE UNIVERSE does have a good sense of timing, and quite often I have found myself at the receiving end of some pretty big jokes and even bigger lessons. Christmas 2008 would be a big one and Judge's prophetic words of "change or die" were about to make complete sense. Jake had pleaded with me to let him take the girls for Christmas. Not only did he want them for the holidays, he wanted to take them to Disney World: *The Magic Kingdom.* The healer in me wanted to let them go. They had a short visit once or twice a year with their dad and now had the opportunity to go somewhere very special with him. I thought the chance to create some happy memories would be good for them all. The bitter and betrayed shadow side of me wanted nothing more than to tell Jake where he could go . . . and it "'tweren't" Florida!

"You're going to Disney, girls!" I announced, amid squeals of delight.

Right decision? Is there such a thing? I chose what I thought was the path of least resistance: a trip to Disney for the girls while I stayed with my auntie Joyce, nearby in DeLand. I would get to see my oldest brother and his family, now next-door neighbors with my aunt and uncle. I had agreed to meet Jake and the girls for one of the days that they were staying at a Disney resort. One day . . . The deal also included a trip home to see my parents, a win-win situation all the way around. What I didn't realize at the time was that the tiny raw spot in my heart that I had long since plastered over with positive affirmations, laughter, and numerous healing sessions was still, in fact, just a little too raw.

Disney at Christmas is simply spectacular. I recommend the experience to children of all ages. Trees full of sparkling baubles, princesses in red velvet gowns, snow on Main Street America after a day in the blazing sun, it's every kid's dream. The Enchanted Kingdom left my daughters full of wonder and delight, something I felt they deserved after a very tough couple of years.

Me? I was strong, and I knew I could handle whatever came my way. Reality? I watched my children bask in the love of both of their parents, simultaneously. Something they were too young to remember when it happened last. I was treading on very dangerous ground. Suddenly, all of my strength, my resolve to live my life in my own best interest, was beginning to succumb to the magic of Disney—a fantasy world of happy endings, where adversity was always overcome by true love. For a brief moment, I allowed myself to consider the possibility, despite all that had gone down between us in the past: a family unit, a loving mother and father putting their own differences aside to create a stable home for their children. I felt the love . . . that is, until the rage set in. *What a difference a day can make. . . .*

*Who did he think he was? What was I thinking?* I had raised those girls, I had been there for every cough and cold, every scraped knee, every dance recital, every visit from the tooth fairy, *Every Everything*! He had run to a kingdom, far, far away. I have yet to see that Disney movie hit the big screen. I had supported those children on my own. How could I have agreed to let him swan in and take the girls to the most fantastic place on Earth? *It should have been me! It should have been me.* That tiny little raw spot had festered into a putrefied, open wound. *I had so thought I was past this.*

When we said our good-byes to Jake, I ran for my life, all the while wiping the girls' tears as they left their dad behind, not knowing when they might see him again. Mom and Dad were delighted to see their Irish grandbabies and I had never been so relieved to see my parents. I needed my own mommy. I was safe for the time being . . . from me, and from my foolish heart.

✳

The girls and I returned to Ireland, ready to start 2009 with a bang. It was not just any bang. It was a Big Bang. I found myself in a parallel existence. Was it 2009 or 1993? Standing in the shower, a routine wash, not an exam, inadvertently revealed a familiar feeling. This time, I wasn't twenty-two, in a marriage to my best friend that was destined not to last. I was a month shy of forty, and had just returned from a blast to the past with Jake that was so fraught with emotion, I had, for the second time in my life, developed a breast tumor.

A trip to the hospital in Galway disclosed what I already knew. The response from this surgeon was also the same as it had been from the surgeon in Charleston nearly twenty years earlier.

"Give me three weeks," I insisted.

"That's not a good idea," she emphatically responded.

"I just needed confirmation that my disgust with my recent choices had now manifested physically."

*I was certain that a smattering of victim mentality had slipped under the radar.*

"That's very forward thinking, but I don't think you should neglect proper medical attention just to prove a point," she offered. "We may be able to get it all without having to use . . ."

"Ah, ah ah . . . Don't even say it! I did this to myself, I will fix this myself."

"I'm scheduling you for . . ."

"I'll see you for a checkup before a month is up, then we'll talk." I spoke defiantly, cutting her off midsentence.

She nodded, knowing there was no use trying to change my mind.

I left the clinic, drove to a beach on the coast road, sat by the water, and cried. I didn't cry in fear of her diagnosis, I had already known what that would be. I didn't cry because I was unsure of my future. That, too, I knew was secured. I cried to allow myself to be angry. Like any other human being was capable of, I had missed the mark. I had stepped out of character, away from all that I had learned from facilitating healings, and had created the perfect circumstances for my emotions to make me sick.

Only a few weeks earlier, I had allowed the girls to go to Disney with Jake, but I had made one deadly error. It wasn't with unconditional love that I sent them on their way. I thought that it was best for them to develop happy memories, with their long-distance daddy, *regardless of my feelings*. Had I done this with no attachments, the outcome most likely would have been different. It certainly was no coincidence. I had just become a very common statistic, and I knew better. I've never yet met a breast cancer patient that didn't involve overnurturing on some level, regardless of whether physical, chemical, or emotional influences had been the initial catalyst.

The healer began to heal that afternoon on the shores of the Atlantic. I reflected on the recent events, shook hands with the anger, and the betrayal of my feelings, not by Jake but by me. No one had forced me to do anything. I had made the ultimate decision to allow the girls time with their father. Under an overcast Irish sky, the islands in the distance seemed so mysterious and wise, the perfect backdrop for self-discovery. I expressed my thanks for the experience of being human and mapped out a plan. As with all things that I chalk up to experience, I knew that this, too, would find a perfect place in my story and that I would use it someday to help anyone with ears to hear it.

A diet of raw foods and two and a half bottles of Essiac cancer tea, the very same concoction I had used to assist myself the first time I had a breast tumor, would complete the task at hand. The tea had been lovingly prepared by my dear friend Maria, a card-carrying member of the "former overnurturers club," and self-healed through self-discovery. With each day that passed, my confidence grew, my lump shrank, and the time returned that I would see the surgeon for my follow-up appointment in Galway.

"Remarkable." All she could do was shake her head.

"I thought you'd say that. Will I tell how I did it?"

She smiled as I shared my insights, and I knew that our worlds were so close, yet so far away. I also knew this would never happen to me again.

"Will I see you in six months for a checkup?"

"Thanks for the offer, but it's not necessary. I promise I'll always keep tabs on the situation, but I've checked this box off for the last time."

*

School was winding down for the year just following the girls' seventh and ninth birthdays at the beginning of June. During the last few weeks of school, things were a little hectic in the intuitive children's department. Jemma was having trouble sleeping. Her dreams had become a bit too vivid for her liking and this was upsetting her. I could totally relate, doing my best to talk her through, mother to child, resisting the temptation to speak to her clairvoyant to clairvoyant. I constantly had to remind myself that no matter how much I wanted to help integrate the girls into the parallel reality of the paths they had chosen, they were still very young. I wanted them to feel secure in the knowledge that I understood and was there to guide them, but I did not want to overprotect them from learning to deal with their own abilities, absorbing the light through their own "indi-visual" lenses.

Jemma awakened one morning in complete distress. She is a

fantastically dramatic child on any day, but on this day, she was truly disturbed.

"*Mommy!*" Jemma screamed from her bedroom.

I ran in to find Jada with her arms wrapped around her big sister. Jemma looked as if she had been terribly frightened by a very scary dream.

"It wasn't a dream, Mommy, it was a vision!" she sobbed.

I sat on the bed beside her as she told me of the "movie" in her head that was as clear as the ones on TV. There were two boys in blue school uniforms. One was lying in the middle of the road.

"He looked dead, Mommy!" Tears poured down her little cheeks.

Jemma wiped her eyes and then sniffed.

"I would know him anywhere if I saw him. He had the strangest shape, like lightning, in his haircut."

I nearly felt cruel sending her off to school that day. I had to pull her teacher out into the hallway and explain why Jemma was so upset. I got the "Okay, crazy lady" nod, a smile, and the assurance that she would be well looked after. I drove in to work and, as always, Maureen knew something was up. I told her the story, which she followed with, "Ahh, no, the poor little pet." We then got busy for the morning.

After returning from lunch, I was standing at the reception desk chatting to Maureen while we waited for the next patient to arrive. I was looking out the front window, where directly across the road two boys, about eleven or twelve, were walking up the footpath. Wearing dark blue uniforms and carrying schoolbags, they were messing around, laughing and pushing one another along. They dropped their bags, still laughing, when suddenly one of the boys lay down in the road, playing "chicken" with the oncoming traffic. I ran out the door screaming wildly, giving him such a fright that he jumped out of the way, just as the car that nearly hit him screeched to a halt, furiously honking the horn. His friend was in hysterics, and as the boy grabbed his bag and started running, I noticed the *lightning bolt* that was shaved into the back of his neatly cut hair. My heart was in my throat as the two boys were now halfway down the block. I went back into the office and looked at Maureen, white as a ghost. All she said was,"Jemma!"

That evening, I sat Jemma down and told her that her vision and the fact that she had shared it with me set things in motion that had me in the right place at just the right time. Stunned by her accuracy, she was equally as relieved that I had been able to scream in time to stop the boy from being run over.

The following morning, I filled the teacher in on the drama. She looked at the child who spent a good portion of her time in the naughty corner and shook her head in disbelief.

During the summer of 2009, Jemma and Jada went to New Zealand for a few weeks to spend time with their dad and his family. This precious time alone was desperately needed and consequently created just the right atmosphere for a new romance to blossom.

Barry was a Dubliner, through and through. Also a single parent of two, he was a brilliant conversationalist and we shared a lot of common interests. While he was open to all of the unusual carry-on in my life, he remained quite pragmatic when it came to all things metaphysical, forever looking for reasonable explanations for the sublime. With a thick head of short, salt-and-pepper curls, Barry had a jovial smile, a bubbly personality, and was just plain fun to be around. Without having the children at home for the summer, we actually got the opportunity to really get to know each other.

We had been dating for a few months when after a night out in town with some friends, Barry got his first personal experience of "metaphysical me." I could hear myself talking but simply wasn't able to wake up, intervene, or change my state. According to Barry, the conversation took place for quite some time. When I finally opened my eyes, I was aware of what had seemed like a rolling documentary of the lives of two vaguely familiar people. Things had become so interesting during the night that Barry had gotten up and started to take notes.

It seems that we had been introduced to *ourselves* . . . two thousand years earlier, give or take a few decades.

Jean and Francine Taber (*Tay-bear*) lived in Gaul, ancient France. There were detailed descriptions of the portly husband and wife and the contributions they had made to their adopted community. Their homeland remained a secret, as did the real reason behind their relocation to the South of France.

Barry's notes related that Francine was a hands-on healer and herbalist, gifted at healing with natural remedies and energy. Jean was known for his knowledge and wisdom on spiritual matters, as well as for his skill at producing some type of beverage that resembled mead. I had spoken at length in my sleeping trance about the finer details involved in the brewing process of this drink.

I also described their home place, how it was constructed, and where it was located in relation to the rest of the village. Hanging on a wall in the home, I could see an intricate mandala painted on some sort of linen cloth. There was something extremely important about the pattern. Concealed within its delicate design was a mysterious secret regarding mankind's true power to harness our Divine resources. This enigma was something that the Tabers had vowed to protect. With that, I woke up.

Very excited by what he had just witnessed, I, too, was delighted that Barry finally had the opportunity to experience a little piece of the "real" me. My delight quickly turned to apprehension, however, as this had been just the first innuendo of a past life together. I really liked Barry and things were going so well, but I was wary that the soul-mate scenario might throw us (me, really) offtrack. Barry wasn't the slightest bit concerned, but why should he be? He had no personal investment in the past-life possibilities between us in the here and now. The difference, I told myself, was that in this past life, Jean/Barry and I appeared to be working on the continuation of a long-standing undertaking that I continue to be deeply entrenched in to this day. That *must* count for something.

Whenever doubts crept in of being steered off course by a romance with someone not currently working directly with "the cause," I kept reminding myself of the Tabers. I turned a blind eye to the fact that Barry's soul might have incarnated having chosen to take a breather when it came to the "work," *the apotheosis*—the exaltation of humankind rediscovering its true Divine nature. This was not a part-time job for me, and just because Barry's interests and talents were in a different field didn't make us unsuitable; this just had the potential to completely distract me. I know myself. If I'm not careful, I can easily lose focus if my heart is involved. Yes, I came here to experience the many forms of love, but not in place of my mission—in addition to it. The human side of Mary Helen can become as lackadaisical as enlightened, in the blink of an eye. It was for this very reason, that Barry and I would not last. . . .

*

As the summer of 2011 came to a close, my attention was directed across the Atlantic to my home in Virginia. My father had become increasingly unstable, sleeping little to none during the night, with erratic catnaps during the day. His memory was failing him and this once incredibly articulate public speaker was now having difficulty stringing a complete sentence together. I spoke to my mother on a daily basis. She was concerned for his safety and equally concerned that she might not be able to adequately provide care for him, on her own. Enter serendipity.

One of my dearest friends from my days at Coker College was a gorgeous, sun-kissed babe from Myrtle Beach, South Carolina. All of these years later, Shannon had reconnected with Roger, another close friend of ours from college, who happened to be from my hometown and now lived just five doors down from my parents.

Reconnection turned to romance and Shannon moved to Martinsville after marrying Roger in September of 2011. She was in need
of a good challenge in her new surroundings and I was desperately
in need of a trustworthy set of eyes and pair of hands across the
ocean. Shannon immediately stepped in and became a companion
to my mother and invaluable helper in caring for my dad. The circle
of life never ceases to amaze.

Dad was having tremendous difficulty with lymphedema. The
congestive heart failure was causing his body to literally drown
in its own secretions. His innate intelligence had opened up the
pores of his arm to relieve the internal pressure that was building
and he was now weeping, actually, pouring fluid at a rate that Mom
could hardly keep up with. He was soaking his clothing, the bed
constantly had to be changed, and Dad had to attend therapy for
lymphatic massage to drain the excess fluid. Shannon was a god-
send. She graciously did everything from DIY around the house
to taking Dad to therapy so Mom could get some rest. She was
exhausted. Not from the extra care that Dad now required, but
from the strange episodes occurring at night.

On one Sunday morning, early in October, Mom and I discovered that something very peculiar had taken place in her home
and mine, at exactly the same time. Dad had been experiencing
something akin to night terrors, only he wasn't sleeping when it
would happen.

On that same Sunday morning in Ireland, Jada was getting out
of the tub when she called me into the bathroom.

"Mom, do you remember the fire festival?"

She was referring to the festival of fires on the Hill of Uisneach
that we had attended to celebrate what was known as Bealtaine, or
May Day, in ancient Ireland.

"Of course I do, honey. Why do you ask?"

"Well, do you remember when I was screaming when they
'turned on the fires'?"

Did I remember? When the massive bonfire had been lit, Jada went into a complete panic. This was no ordinary crying. She dropped to the ground, covered her head, and wailed inconsolably, until I finally had to carry her away, back down the hill, to the car.

"Well, I want to tell you why that made me so upset."

I couldn't wait to hear this one. Here she stood, wrapped in a towel, sixth months later, ready to recount her night of terror on the mountain.

"I remembered something when they made the fire, Mommy. In my head, I could see lots of people in old clothes and there were men with swords and other men holding big, shiny gold crosses on tall sticks. They made me walk into the fire, Mommy. They made me burn 'til I died. And, Mommy . . . Coach [my dad] was there."

Hand over mouth, I leaned against the wall. I nearly got weak as my seven-year-old recounted a vision that suddenly sounded very familiar. I immediately thought back to a trip I had taken to France earlier in the year, standing amid the ruins of Montségur, some 3,000 feet high, adjacent to the Pyrenees, the site where the heretical sect known as the Cathars had been besieged by the royal Catholic French troops. The last hundred-plus Cathars standing were walked into a bonfire and burned alive for their beliefs.

Later that day, while still morning in Virginia, I placed a call to my mother, to catch up on the news, and to find out how Dad was doing.

"We had a really rough night. Dad was in bed, and at first, it sounded like he was praying out loud. I'm telling you, it sounded like he was speaking in some really strange foreign language. All of a sudden, his vocabulary just changed to perfect, old-style English with some kind of bizarre accent. He was calling himself unworthy, begging, 'Do not forsake me.' He was obviously anguished, and I didn't know what to do. He cried out, almost like he was being tortured or burned alive. "

When I told Mom what Jada had said when getting out of the

bath, only a few hours earlier, the phone went silent. We simply could not believe the synchronicity between the two stories.

Two weeks later, after suddenly turning blue and collapsing at the house, Dad was rushed to the hospital. Mom went straight to the ER, where she was told that things were not looking good. Dad would never make it home again.

# Chapter 39

I TOOK the earliest flight I could get from Dublin to Charlotte, North Carolina, hired a car, and then drove the two hours north to Martinsville, heading straight to the hospital. There, both of my brothers, my sister, and my sister-in-law, Susan, were sitting with my mom, as my dad sat propped up in the bed. Much to my relief, he recognized me immediately and the family filled me in on the day's events. They had all been there for the day, so Mom and I spent the night so that the others could go back to the house and get some sleep. For the next few days, the jet lag worked to my advantage, and I was able to pull the night shifts because my internal clock was five hours ahead. Rather than attempt to reset it, my brothers and sisters sat with Dad all day, and I spent the nights, so that he was never without one of us there at any time.

Physically, although Dad would never recover from the congestive heart failure, he seemed to be rallying somewhat. Mentally, something had changed. We were never sure if it was the medication, but Dad became extremely agitated, pulling out tubes from his hands, confused and unable to remember why he was in the hospital at all. For someone in his condition, his strength was hulkish and there were times when he was bordering on violent.

One night, as I lay on the couch next to Dad, I must have dozed off. I suddenly got the overpowering smell of cigarettes. This had accompanied the appearance of my grandfather Judge on many occasions, as he had always smoked Camel cigarettes in his younger days. I woke with a start, to find Dad choking violently. He had a look of terror in his eyes as I said to myself, *Not like this, Dad!* I pulled him up, banging him on the back, pressed the call button for help, and the nurses came running in. He was drowning in his own fluid. The fact that Judge had awakened me meant that it wasn't time, and that there apparently was no need for Dad to die choking to death and terrified. Besides, this was not "how or when" he had told me that Dad would die so many years ago, when I was a child.

As the days progressed and Dad's mental state seemed to deteriorate, he physically was no longer a candidate to stay any longer in the hospital. After a lot of red tape, Dad was moved to a facility that in my youth had been a nursing home but was now a short-term "rehab" facility, where patients would work their way through a program with the intention of being sent home in the end. This was not really a viable option as our house was completely unequipped to support Dad's needs, and the reality was that without twenty-four-hour help, my mother would not be able to cope.

We took things one day at a time. When Dad's own doctor came in to see him, it was quite obvious that he was most concerned that Dad's dignity remained intact and that he was kept as comfortable as possible. He wanted to be sure that we all understood that Dad would not be getting better, and our main goal was to keep him safe and at ease. He wasn't only Dad's doctor, he had been a very dear friend over the years, and it absolutely tore Mom up to see his distress. Mom and I both agreed that this was the most difficult part. There had been more than one occasion when Dad's friends had come to visit him in the hospital and had broken down in tears when they walked out the door.

They were calling it dementia. I had heard one doctor in the hospital use Alzheimer's, but all we knew was that Dad was completely confused. He could be present one minute, then not know who in the world we were, the next. Whenever he got really irritated with me, I would tell him that I was my sister, Beth. (You have to keep a sense of humor!)

Speaking of a sense of humor, two of Dad's buddies had come to visit. Both were wonderful men and they had also been known to have a good time socially. Dad never drank, smoked, said a swear word, and he lived an extremely disciplined lifestyle. As they were leaving, one turned to the other, shrugged his shoulders, and sighed, "So much for clean living." Mom totally cracked up.

It was this statement that prompted me to see Dad's illness from an entirely different perspective. So many people had passed comment that it was heart-breaking to see a man who had dedicated his life to motivating, coaching, teaching God's word, a true pillar of the community, reduced to losing his dignity. I did not see it that way at all. I looked at a man who had chosen a life path of service requiring sheer discipline; an immaculate lifestyle in order to teach by example; a set of life rules that would not see him express on the outside anything but the positive; the possibilities available to those who were willing to take ownership of their lives. Now, as he approached the end of his life, an illness would allow his soul to express rage, disappointment, tears, even violence, all emotions of the human condition, and none the less valuable in his experience as an inhabitant of Earth. Nobody would judge because he was "sick," and his soul could continue to fill up its toolbox with as many emotional interactions as possible, before he took his last breath.

Dad was experiencing something referred to as Sundowner's Syndrome. When nighttime rolled around, his levels of irritation rose dramatically. It was nearly impossible to get him to settle. The medication seemed to make it worse and it was a real struggle as he would sit down, stand up, and attempt to walk into the hall, becoming enraged if anyone tried to stop him.

One night, after everyone but Mom and I had gone home, Dad had a particularly tough time with the agitation. He refused to lie down in the bed, because he feared that he would die if he did. He was restless, sitting on the edge of the bed, shuffling to the bathroom, to the hallway, to his chair, back to the bed. Confused and very upset, he went to the bathroom and washed his hands ... again. It was late. Mom and I were both tired, but her sweet little face never lost its look of compassion. Without warning, Dad made his way over to the bed. He crawled in under the blankets and was starting to giggle, nearly giddy with delight. Mom and I looked at each other, as Dad lay down and lifted his arm toward the ceiling. He was beaming as he looked up in disbelief, at something that neither Mom nor I could see.

"Oh, it's beautiful. I can see it. I can see it."

*Uh oh*, I thought. But at the same time, his auric field did not appear like any I had ever seen around someone preparing to cross over.

"What is it, Dad? What can you see?"

He laughed, and all of a sudden, he sounded like my dad again.

"It's more beautiful than anything you've ever written about." He patted me on the hand and smiled lovingly.

"Tell me about it, what are you seeing?"

"The land beyond the river, darlin'. Oh, it's so beautiful."

Mom looked at me as if to say, "Is this it?" I shook my head no.

"Do you see anybody you know?"

He chuckled again.

"Momma. I see Momma and she looks so young."

With that, Dad's eyes became as big as saucers. He gasped out loud.

"Daddy. Oh my gosh, Daddy is there!"

✳

Now, for my dad, this was a very big deal. I never knew his father, and I'm sure that he was a decent man. According to my dad's sisters, he was a most wonderful person. But for Dick Hensley, his father had not "cut the mustard" when it came to exemplary living. Let's just put it this way, the *last* person that my dad, a die-hard, disciplined Christian man, expected to see in "the land beyond the river" was my grandfather.

Dad's eyes began to tear up and he was overwhelmed with emotion. After eighty-four years of believing with all of his heart that heaven was a place reserved for those who had met with a certain criteria, Dad ecstatically proclaimed:

"I've had it wrong! I've had it wrong all along! Everybody is welcome here!" He couldn't contain his enthusiasm.

*"You can't mess this thing up!"*

My mom looked over at me, in the throes of a most sanctified, precious moment, her pale-green eyes, aged with worry and brimming with tears, and whispered, *"Write that down!"*

Dad was eventually moved from the rehab facility to a nursing home in town. I stayed long enough to get him settled in before heading back to my eagerly awaiting children in Ireland. Although I implicitly trusted my Source regarding Dad's final departure date, I clocked up a serious amount of frequent flyer miles from November to July, just to check in on Mom and to sit with Dad.

He didn't want to speak. Even in his altered state of awareness, he seemed to know that when he would try to talk, the gibberish that would come out of his mouth resembled nothing that he wanted to say.

When Jemma and Jada finished school at the end of June, we packed our bags and headed back to Virginia for the summer. I spent many late nights sitting with Dad, watching his favorite movie, *The Quiet Man*, over and over again. He had full-time sitters in his room, as he was now a danger to himself if left alone. We had initially decorated his space, trying to give it a more personal feel, but the photographs of his children and grandchildren upset him and had to be removed. Next to the hospital bed, there was a simple wooden nightstand, with a small lamp and a single framed picture of my mother, her auburn hair flowing gently over her shoulders, in her early twenties. Mom's college photo and his tattered blue prayer book were the only items he allowed.

On August 21, I climbed into bed in my old room at home. Although the room had changed somewhat over the years, there were still a few of my childhood belongings, trophies for acting and good sportsmanship, dolls from Scotland, and my favorite Nancy Drew books resting on an overstuffed bookshelf. I was absolutely weary. The energy in Dad's auric field had changed, weeks earlier, from the pulsating glow of a once-vibrant human being to the sparks and flashes I had seen so many times before, as one prepared to cross over. I finally drifted off to sleep only to be awakened at about 3:30 a.m. by the sound of my own screams. When my mother rounded the corner from her bedroom and turned on my light, I was sitting up in bed, breathless, in a cold sweat. "Are you okay?" she asked with great concern. "What is it? What happened?" I simply could not answer. I got out of bed and walked past her to the bathroom and splashed cold water on my face. She was waiting for me when I returned.

"I just can't talk about it right now, Mom." Tears were streaming down my cheeks. "I'll tell you in the morning."

Instinctively knowing that she shouldn't pry, Mom accepted my reply and went back to bed. Safely back under the covers, I tossed and turned until, for the second time that night, I drifted into a troubled sleep. Within minutes, I sat back up, panting and perspiring, this time catching myself before screaming aloud. It was a vision.

I could see a tattered tartan, wrapped around dirty yet feminine legs, some sort of animal skin shoes bound with leather straps, and a pair of slender yet strong hands . . . my hands. On the ground before me was a giant of a man, no less than six and a half feet, with jet-black hair, laced with straw and muck. His face was filthy, his yellowed teeth clenched as he writhed around in agony. His chest was bare, bar the markings of some sort of ancient symbols that had been painted or dyed across his massive upper torso. On one of his legs, just below the knee, was a gaping wound, festering and septic in appearance, the obvious source of his pain and imminent demise. I heard the woman, *myself*, as I was now certain, pleading with the warrior in old Gaelic, telling him to rest, to go. She begged this man, her Beloved, to allow himself to go into the Light. I could feel her pounding heart breaking as she pleaded with the man to let go of life, end his suffering, and return home. At that moment, he rolled on to his side, sweat and filth matting his once impressive mane of hair to his face. He lifted an arm in her direction and gave one final command in his native tongue. "Leave me, woman, this death is mine alone." I realized at that moment that I was looking into the eyes of the soul who had become my father.

The following morning, as my mother was getting dressed to go to the nursing home, I told her about the vision. With mouth agape, she shook her head in disbelief as I recounted every detail of this former incarnation with my father . . . as my Beloved. Both of us stunned, we agreed to meet later that day at the nursing home after I had run a few errands and taken the girls to the pool.

Dad's love for Scotland and the ancient Celts had come from his pride in his lineage as a direct descendent of Rob Roy Mac-Gregor, Scotland's answer to Robin Hood. Although folklore had greatly added to his fame over the years, Rob Roy had indeed been a most colorful and real character in eighteenth-century Scottish history. "Robert the Red" was not only known by his trademark mane of red hair, but for his distinctive birthmark, referred to as the "black knee." Dad had always been very proud of his own unmistakable birthmark under his knee, reputed to be found on any number of the male descendants of Rob Roy. I had even photographed it months earlier, as Mom and I thought it would be an interesting keepsake for posterity.

That afternoon, I opened the door to Dad's room only to be

stopped by my mother, who had obviously been anxiously waiting. "You're not going to believe this!" she whispered in a mixture of awe and fright. She then giggled nervously as she realized that the words she spoke had so often been my opening line. She told me to pull off the blanket covering Dad's legs. Puzzled, I walked over to the bed where Dad was in a restless sleep. "Go ahead," she urged. When I pulled the blanket down I nearly got weak. The dark brown birthmark and distinctive mole that for eighty-five years had held a place of honor on Dad's leg was gone. I did a double take, looked at Mom, and back again at the spot on his leg to make sure my own eyes weren't deceiving me. *Gone.* She motioned for me to step away and come back to the door. "Your dream last night, the vision, whatever it was . . . you've got to get out of here!" Knowing what she implied before she even spoke the words, I agreed. Although the vision had taken place at a time that appeared to have been many years earlier than the great Rob Roy had been married to *Mary Helen* MacGregor, the message was clear. It was as if the prophetic communication had come from the earliest ancestors of the bloodline.

It was me—my presence was holding Dad back from making his transition home. So many times I had been in this same situation with members of a family who were holding vigil by the bedside of a loved one preparing to die. And so many times I had encouraged them to give space to the individual to cross on their own if they wished, in the peace of their own thoughts, as every dying soul doesn't necessarily want to be surrounded by the good intentions of those grieving their loss. It seems I had carelessly ignored my own advice.

I spent my last moments with Dad, thanking him and whispering vivid details of what awaited him on the other side of death, just as I had each day for the last six weeks. I kissed his forehead, his third eye, one last time, went home, and changed my tickets for departure to Ireland the following day.

I spent the flight home explaining to the girls that they had been so blessed to have had wonderful quality time with Coach that summer and that Mommy needed to return to America to be Coach's little girl. Surprisingly, they completely understood. We arrived in an uncharacteristically sunny Ireland on the morning of the twenty-third; I left them with some good friends, repacked my bag, and waited for the phone call. The following morning, August 24, 2012, Mom phoned to say that Dad had passed peacefully before dawn. I had been sitting outside on a stone fence, thousands of miles away, watching the sun dance across the rolling green fields when I felt him go. I drove straight back to Dublin and boarded the next flight home.

I was strangely relaxed as I reflected on the last few days and how it all had unfolded. I thought about Judge and how he had told me, so many years ago, the precise time and way that Dad would pass. I actually chuckled at my own "human-ness" as I had lingered about, hoping to outwit destiny's plan, to be present when the soft glow of death lifted Dad from his slumber. That, in fact, had been left for a complete stranger. One of the sitters had been forever transformed having witnessed the angelic presence and beautiful glow that emanated from Dad's face as his Spirit left his body.

For hours, I relaxed, legs outstretched as I had a bulk head seat with only empty space in front of me. A movie was on the screen, and I could hear the occasional laughter of those watching, but mostly there was just the hum of the engines, lulling me into a meditative state.

I thought about my decision to leave the children behind, my desire to give myself the time and the space to be a daughter burying her father, rather than a mother tending to her children. My girls were such wonderfully enlightened souls and I knew that our adventures of psychic discovery, unlocking our collective past and future work, were only in the early stages. I recounted the hundreds of healing sessions over the years, smiling as I acknowledged that in the end, it was my own growth and healing that were taking place with every life I had been privileged to touch. I even thought about how I would eventually put this story into words. I was writing chapters in my mind as the smell of instant coffee in Styrofoam cups wafted through the air, marking less than an hour until we touched down in the oppressive heat of summer in the South.

Although I wanted to bypass the plan and stay by his side, ultimately I understood that this would be making it all about me. The experience of death and the kaleidoscope of unfathomable wonders that await, once the soul has departed the physical form, belongs to the individual. It may have taken a while to grasp, but in the end I got it.

As the plane was ready to land, I prepared myself as best I could for the unfamiliar feeling of opening the squeaky back door of my childhood home for the first time in forty-three years without my father's loving embrace to greet me. The wheels unlocked and the plane touched down as my mind took one final glance back at my travels . . . my life's journey. From my highly unusual experiences as a child, the monumental car crash that had completely altered my course, lost loves along the way, to becoming an ancient symbol-chasing spine doc on the Emerald Isle, with two girls, mini metaphysicians in their own right, now under my care and tutelage . . . indeed, what a long, strange trip, it had been.

It all began with a promise made to my father by an otherworldly Being at the start of my life. Now it was I, at the end of his life, who was making promises to care for my mother and carry on with my work as a steward of humanity . . . promises I intend to keep. In the dynamically understated words of Michelangelo . . . "I'm still learning."

# Epilogue

HEREIN LIES the moment when I must put my own neck on the line. I have always attempted to share any information I have in a way that is honoring, respectful of an individual's right to believe whatever he or she chooses, being open to all possibilities, while remaining true to my own values. Personally, I have a NO DOGMAS ALLOWED policy!

I realize how much of what I have to say is uncomfortably out of the spectrum for some, yet I have also found just as many people who deeply resonate with my stories. For those of you experiencing life from inside any given box, this next bit might be difficult to digest. However, I have been asked so often, I think it's time that I take the risk, like it or not, because this is how it really happens for me.

I am asked time and time again as to the source of the information I receive. *"Who tells you the intimate details that you use to facilitate a healing? The voices, the visions, are they from God? Is Jesus your Lord and Savior? Are you sure forces of darkness aren't working through you?"* Well, unless the forces of darkness are into healing physical, emotional and spiritual maladies, bringing people closer to their own divinity, removing fear, restoring faith . . . then the answer is yes, I'm sure it's not "the dark side." Then who?

For many years now, I have worked with a council. *Counsel,* I think is more appropriate, due to the role that they play in my life. In the beginning, there were nine. Then there were twelve.

So yes, to those of you who have wondered if the members of this "Circle of Twelve" that I refer to are of this world or not, *they are not*. I have circles of light here, as do we all—those who are currently incarnate, working right along beside us on similar life paths; learning, growing, teaching; helping us to enhance our human experience.

Then there is *The Counsel*.

They have been with me so long, I can't really remember when it all started. At first, they were Voices. I had been told at the time of my accident, by my two Guardian Beings, that if I chose to walk this new path, I would be guided in a most tangible way. These were different, however, from the voices I hear belonging to the spirits of people who once walked the Earth in human form, now physically deceased. Those voices are more like impressions, giving factual information of things that *have been*, things pertaining to their experiences and interactions while on Earth, in addition to insights as to what they are encountering beyond the veil. The other Voices, The Counsel, give me information relative to me, to my teachings and healings, to world events, past, present, and future. Somewhere in my late twenties, I consciously made the request that the Voices show themselves. That day is branded on my mind for all eternity.

In the most sensational experience of astral travel or being out of body I have ever experienced, I found myself, my *true self*, in what appeared to be a large room. The truly curious thing was that the room seemed to breathe, giving the feeling of enclosure, but there were no walls. There before me were nine of the most unusual and incredible Beings I could have ever imagined. In the visits to follow, there were twelve.

They certainly don't look like us. I liken my first meeting with The Counsel to a blond-haired, blue-eyed European seeing the tanned, reddish hue and dark silky hair of a Native American for the first time, or an African, who has only ever known her own kind, with ebony skin and ivory white teeth, first encountering the pale, yellowish skin and slender eyes of someone from the Orient. There was recognition of similarity, yet we were different. Each being was contrasting in color, skin tone, features, and manner of attire. Whether this was for my benefit or not, I'm still not sure. Somehow clothing seemed unnecessary, yet most of them wore some sort of covering.

The one who struck me the most was a female, her skin the most beautiful shade of pale blue, a periwinkle of sorts, with unusual markings that looked like intricate tattoo art. Think *Avatar*, only far more petite. It was with this being that I felt a kinship, as if I "knew" her, "knew" her homeland, and " 'knew" that we shared something that I didn't necessarily remember when looking at the other members of The Counsel.

Each of the nine was obviously from a different locale, but all were easy to distinguish as male and female. It wasn't until I later met the final three, that I grasped the true meaning of androgynous. These beautiful entities simply "were." There was a vibration and a sense of wisdom about them that made it impossible for me to label them as either male or female.

In my mind, I was aware that each representative had their own indigenous forms of communication. Some spoke to my mind, others through a mouth. Again, I think this was for my benefit, and not out of necessity. They were loving in nature, yet serious in their thoughts and words, much like parents giving firm guidance to a child. They clarified that they had been providing information outside of the "normal" five human senses since my birth. They also expressed that they had watched me grow, having to accept on more than one occasion that I might not find my way back to my chosen path in this lifetime. If I hadn't, there would have been others to fill the space until I remembered, in this life or perhaps the next. I was by no means the only one they watched.

"Did you cause my accident?" My first question was greeted with warm understanding.

"No, *you did*. You reached deep into your core and rediscovered your purpose. We only obliged your request for immediate change."

*Whoa!* It took a moment for me to get my head around the idea that I had requested such a bold intervention. The plan had been that if I had not managed to decipher my path and utilize the gifts with which I had incarnated (using my own free will), this accident would provide an opportunity for me to remember, once I had reached adulthood. I was speechless.

The first meeting seemed, in itself, to last a lifetime. In truth, it was only one night. From that day forward, the Voices now had faces.

So, am I telling you that I believe that there are Beings out there who are wiser, more experienced, more focused, more loving, striving to guide us through our personal and planetary evolution? You bet I am! With all of my heart, with every crazy bone in my body, I live in gratitude that we aren't doing this thing alone.

So where is God in all of this? God, my friends, is one of many names given to the Divine loving force behind all of our lives. Does *The Counsel* work for God? Well, I highly doubt they are on a weekly wage of sunshine and rainbows, working for a bearded monarch in a white gown, perched high atop a golden throne. They are, however, representatives of the Love, the Light, the Creative Force behind *All That Is*. You may call that God, Allah, the Great I AM, or whatever name we human beings have coined since the dawn of time, to encapsulate that which cannot be described. All I know is that it is Divine, and of the Greatest Good.

In all of the years that I have been facilitating healings, no one who has been on the receiving end of an immediate change in their cancer, AIDS, infertility, emotional trauma, or spiritual void has ever cared who sent it or how it got there. Funnily enough, the only ones who have ever questioned the Source are those who were actually afraid of what the answer might be. From those of every color, race, or religious creed who have ever experienced this interaction, I have never heard anything expressed but pure, unadulterated gratitude.

People seem to have no problem with angels, equally as mystical and out of this world, as a collective group of unearthly Protectors concentrating their efforts on service to humanity. Mine just don't have wings. Is it so hard to believe that there may just be other Beings of Light?

In whom do I believe? My faith, my trust, my heartfelt gratitude belongs to every Divine Being who has ever graced this planet or lovingly watched over our growth and evolution from another realm. *I believe in those who have lived and died in the name of Love. And let me fill you in on a little something . . . there have been many.*

So there, the cat is out of the bag! I work hand in hand with a counsel of Universal Stewards, a mere smattering of what and *who* is really out there. They guide me in my work, *and we all work for the Light.*

Why me? Well, friends, after a lifetime of asking myself that very question, the best I can come up with is . . . I am a willing conduit of the One Love. Why not me?

# Acknowledgments

Throughout the creation of *Promised by Heaven*, there have been numerous wonderful people who have contributed to my success, not only as an author, but as an individual. So many have mirrored some aspect of the glorious human experience for me, I dare not attempt to call all by name. However, I can definitively say, if you have brushed past me in a fleeting moment, sat holding my hand, laughed or cried with me, or simply glanced a "knowing" look my way, I have felt you and you matter to me. There are no exes or former friends, and certainly no negative experiences, only reflections of the human nature in us all. I treasure the time I have had with all who have touched my life, no matter how brief or in what manner the role was played. I thank you all.

Niall, at Book Hub Publishing, the journey all began with you and your vision and I am forever grateful that it was you who provided the foundation for my growth as a writer.

Maureen, my rock of ages, you are irreplaceable, invaluable, and so close to my heart.

Mairead, my heartfelt thanks for your role in creating an opportunity for my words to reach an audience through Spirit One Seminars. Your angelic support has always been constant and unconditional.

Vaishali and Elliott, my deepest appreciation to you both for creating the space on the airwaves for us all to spread the love.

Your friendship, your circles of light, and the chance to banter on all things metaphysical are truly a highlight in my life.

Steven, for your eagle eyes, divine insights, and helpful suggestions, I am ever so grateful for your love and understanding of my reason for being here this time around. LA crew, I love you all and am so grateful to have your laughter, love, and support. From the mountains to the sea, my Virginia friends are dear to my heart and so important to my story.

Gary and Janice, I have been blessed by your well-timed reappearance in my life and your unwavering belief in the work we are here to do together.

Lew, the time has finally returned. Many lifetimes, many more adventures to come.

Kate, your kindness knows no limits and your influence in my life and the lives of my girls is so deeply appreciated. Your honesty, insights, and open heart are truly inspiring.

Aidan and Murtagh, I am blessed to call you my friends and I love your love.

Patricia, my soul sister, how does one thank another for making their dreams come true? Your gentle guidance, the laughter and belief in the "knowing" of what we came here to do . . . Priceless. You are living proof that family is not solely of blood, but a matter of the heart.

Great thanks to you, Wendy, for your honesty, expertise, and editing insights.

Judith, Johanna, and the Simon & Schuster family, what more can I say but thanks for taking a chance on me. You are so much more than a publishing company, you are a catalyst for monumental change, and your willingness to share the real stories of those living "outside of the box" speaks volumes about your integrity and commitment to the personal growth of your readers.

Jase, we cast ourselves in the most difficult roles for one another, but we played a blinder, birthed two inspiring souls, and emerged victorious. I have to reinvent myself every day because of your influence. What greater gift can one soul give to another?

My brothers, Randy and Jonathan, and my sister, Beth, little do you know just how important and influential you have been along the way.

My darling daughters, Jemma Skye and Jada Pacifica, my greatest gifts, mirrors of my own soul's journey and the very reason I am doing any of this. I know that you came back to this world for a purpose, and that's enough for me to dedicate my life to ensuring its future. I love you with all that I am.

To my father, returned, for now, to Spirit, you live within me through your legacy of strength, wisdom, and accountability. Your willingness to mess up and keep on trying is the most valuable gift you have given to me. I love you, my daddy.

And the very best for last . . . My dear, sweet mother, Helen. I always knew you were something mighty special, but how blessed am I to have grown wise enough to genuinely appreciate you for who and what you really are. None of this would be as much fun without you. I love you so.

## About the Author

Dr. Mary Helen Hensley is a chiropractor, metaphysical healer, and international motivational speaker. She has authored numerous books, including *The Pocket Coach* and *The Chakra Fairies*. She lives and creates in Ireland with her two daughters, Jemma Skye and Jada, also gifted outside of the five senses.

You can find more about Mary Helen at maryhelenhensley.com.